FARM

Farm Sermons

—messages preached to country congregations

C. H. Spurgeon

Gwasg **Bryntirion** Press

First published by Passmore and Alabaster, London,
1882
This edition published by Gwasg **Bryntirion** Press,
1997 (formerly the Evangelical Press of Wales)

ISBN 1 85049 137 2

Cover design:
burgum boorman ltd.

Published by Gwasg **Bryntirion** Press,
Bryntirion, Bridgend, CF31 4DX, Wales, UK
Printed by WBC Book Manufacturers, Bridgend, Wales

PREFACE

WHILE the earth abideth, with her seed-time and harvest, some men will be tillers of the soil. The day may come when there will be no more squires, but there will be sure to be farmers. Whether there be lords, they shall cease; or lawyers, they shall vanish away; but farmers shall remain. Both good and evil husbandmen, Cains and Noahs, will plough furrows and reap harvests until the end come. Hence there will always be need of

FARM SERMONS

Sermons to slingers and archers, to falconers and troubadours would now find scarce a reader; but farmers are as plentiful as ever, and discourses designed for them will find hearers if they deserve them.

It is fit that farmers should have sermons gathered out of their own occupation, for it is one which, above all others, abounds in holy teaching; and, as it would be ill for dwellers in the Indies to go from home for gold and spices, so would it be unwise to leave the field and the plough in search of instruction. He who dwells at Newcastle wastes time when he goes far for coals; he who lives by the labour of the field will be foolish if he neglects the teaching of nature for the most glittering philosophy. Some of the mightiest of prophets and preachers came from the plough, and surely that must be a good college which has furnished such able divines. As all the world is fed by the produce

5

of the farm, so may all men's minds find food in meditating upon the ways of God in nature and providence, as seen by the husbandman. Hence we have sought

LESSONS FROM THE ACRES

He who despises truth because it wears in this case no other adornment than a garland of the flowers of the field about its neck, or a wreath of barley around its brows, has no eye wherewith to discern beauty, which is as fascinating in rural dress as in classic attire. So long as the soul is fed it is small matter whether the subjects were suggested by the palace or the barn. Reader, if you are a farmer, it will be for your eternal pleasure and profit if the Great Husbandman should meet you by his Holy Spirit in the pages of this book, and exercise his skill upon you, that you may become in his hand as a land which is both tilled and sown. Paul says of believers, "Ye are God's husbandry": may this be true of both reader and author.

Farmers should make brave Christians when grace renews them, for God is everywhere about them, and in his presence gracious souls are sure to thrive. Of old the Lord met men by the bush, the brook, and the well, and spake with them in the field, the threshing-floor, and the sheep-fold; and he still seems nearer in the country than in the grimy town. Never can the tiller of the ground open his eyes without learning something if he is willing to be taught. Weeds and plants, frost and sunshine, green shoots and yellow ears, drills and reapers, hedges and ditches, foxes and sheep, drought into flood, waggons and horses, harrows and ploughs—all reveal some spiritual mystery concerning God and our own souls. Surely those men should learn much who find a schoolmaster and a lesson-book in every acre which they cultivate.

Moreover, the farmer is in a very special sense made to see his dependence upon God from season to season. He has never done; his labour is never ending, still beginning; and his hopes are never all fulfilled. From the time he sows the seed to the day when he sees the corn in the ear he is every hour dependent upon the Lord for sunshine and shower; and even when the grain is ready for the garner a stretch of rainy weather will take his harvest from him and leave him mourning at the last. He can never count his profits till he has them in his pocket, and hardly then. This manifest absolute, and daily, dependence should help the good farmer to learn the lesson of faith right thoroughly. He *must* look up, for where else can he look? He must leave his business in the Lord's hands, for who else can be his helper? Faith which is daily tried, and tried all the day long, has a fair opportunity of becoming unusually strong, and hence our agricultural Christians ought to be the strongest believers in the land. They have not of late been indulged with much temporal prosperity, but our hope is that a succession of adversities may have driven them to set less store by the world, to look more eagerly for the better portion, and to leave all things more believingly in the Lord's hands. This will be good out of evil beyond all question, and such good we ought to look for. Sharp discipline should by this time have made good soldiers of our yeomanry. If it be so, the failing purse is more than recompensed by the enlarged heart: if our farmers are wiser men through their bad seasons, that will be better than being richer men.

For farmers these sermons were prepared, and to them I dedicate them, with fervent prayers that when

I am dead and gone some living seed may spring up from these pages, and bring forth fruit to God's glory and the benefit of immortal souls. True religion in former generations found many of her sturdiest defenders among the farmers of England and Scotland. It is to be feared that things have sadly changed in many a homestead, and the world has the mastery where once there was a church in the house. Oh that the good old times might be repeated in grange, and farm, and lodge, till every village shall have in it a sanctified people who shall glorify the Lord.

Reader, yours truly,

C. H. SPURGEON.

CONTENTS

The Sluggard's Farm

"I went by the field of the slothful, and by the vineyard of the man void of understanding; And, lo, it was all grown over with thorns, and nettles had covered the face thereof, and the stone wall thereof was broken down. Then I saw, and considered it well: I looked upon it, and received instruction."—Proverbs xxiv. 30-32.

NO doubt Solomon was sometimes glad to lay aside the robes of state, escape from the forms of court, and go through the country unknown. On one occasion, when he was doing so, he looked over the broken wall of a little estate which belonged to a farmer of his country. This estate consisted of a piece of ploughed land and a vineyard. One glance showed him that it was owned by a sluggard, who neglected it for the weeds had grown right plentifully and covered all the face of the ground. From this Solomon gathered instruction. Men generally learn wisdom if they have wisdom. The artist's eye sees the

11

beauty of the landscape because he has beauty in his mind. "To him that hath shall be given," and he shall have abundance, for he shall reap a harvest even from a field that is covered with thorns and nettles. There is a great difference between one man and another in the use of the mind's eye. I have a book entitled, "The Harvest of a Quiet Eye," and a good book it is: the harvest of a quiet eye can be gathered from a sluggard's land as well as from a well-managed farm. When we were boys we were taught a little poem, called, "Eyes and no Eyes," and there was much of truth in it, for some people have eyes and see not, which is much the same as having no eyes; while others have quick eyes for spying out instruction. Some look only at the surface, while others see not only the outside shell but the living kernel of truth which is hidden in all outward things.

We *may find instruction everywhere.* To a spiritual mind nettles have their use, and weeds have their doctrine. Are not all thorns and thistles meant to be teachers to sinful men? Are they not brought forth of the earth on purpose that they may show us what sin has done, and the kind of produce that will come when we sow the seed of rebellion against God? "I went by the field of the slothful, and by the vineyard of the man void of understanding," says Solomon; "I saw, and considered it well: I looked upon it, and received instruction." Whatever you see, take care to consider it well, and you will not see it in vain. You shall find books and sermons everywhere, in the land and in the sea, in the earth and in the skies, and you shall learn from every living beast, and bird, and fish, and insect, and from every useful or useless plant that springs out of the ground.

We *may also gather rare lessons from things that*

we do not like. I am sure that Solomon did not in the least degree admire the thorns and the nettles that covered the face of the vineyard, but he nevertheless found instruction in them. Many are stung by nettles, but few are taught by them. Some men are hurt by briars but here is one who was improved by them. Wisdom hath a way of gathering grapes of thorns and figs of nettles and she distils good from herbs which in themselves are noisome and evil. Do not fret, therefore, over thorns but get good out of them. Do not begin stinging yourself with nettles, grip them firmly, and then use them for your soul's health. Trials and troubles, worries and turmoils, little frets and little disappointments, may all help you if you will. Like Solomon, see and consider them well—look upon them, and receive instruction.

As for us, we will now, first, consider *Solomon's description of a sluggard:* he is "a man void of understanding"; secondly, we shall notice *his description of the sluggard's land:* "it was all grown over with thorns, and nettles had covered the face thereof." When we have attended to these two matters we will close by *endeavouring to gather the instruction which this piece of waste ground may yield us.*

First, think of SOLOMON'S DESCRIPTION OF A SLOTHFUL MAN. Solomon was a man whom none of us would contradict, for he knew as much as all of us put together; and besides that, he was under divine inspiration when he wrote this Book of Proverbs. Solomon says, a sluggard is "a man void of understanding." The slothful does not think so; he puts his hands in his pockets, and you would think from his important air that he had all the Bank of England at his disposal. You can see that he is a very wise man in his own esteem, for he gives himself airs which are meant to impress you with a sense of his superior abilities. How he has come by his wisdom it would be hard to say. He has never taken the trouble to think, and yet I dare not say that he jumps at his conclusions, because he never does such a thing as jump, he lies down and rolls into a conclusion. Yet he knows everything, and has settled all points: meditation is too hard work for him, and learning he never could endure; but to be clever by nature is his delight. He does not want to know more than he knows, for he knows enough already, and yet he knows nothing. The proverb is not complimentary to him, but I am certain that Solomon was right when he called him "a man void of understanding." Solomon was rather rude according to the dainty manners of the present times, because this gentleman had a field and a vineyard, and as Poor Richard saith, "When I have a horse and a cow every man biddeth me good morrow." How can a man be void of understanding who has a field and a vineyard! Is it not generally understood that you must measure a man's understanding by the amount of his ready cash? At all events you shall soon be flattered for your attainments if you have attained unto wealth. Such is the way of the world, but such is not the way of Scripture. Whether he has a field and a vineyard or not, says Solomon, if he is a sluggard he is a fool, or if you would like to see his name written out a little larger, he is a man empty of understanding. Not only does he not understand anything, but he has no understanding to understand with. He is empty-headed if he is a sluggard. He may be called a gentleman, he may be a landed proprietor, he may have a vineyard and a field; but he is none the better for what he has: nay, he is so much the worse, because he is a man void of understanding, and is therefore unable to make use of his property.

I am glad to be told by Solomon so plainly that a slothful man is void of understanding, for it is useful information. I have met with persons who thought they perfectly understood the doctrines of grace, who could accurately set forth the election of the saints, the predestination of God, the firmness of the divine decree, the necessity of the Spirit's work, and all the glorious doctrines of grace which build up the fabric of our faith; but these gentlemen have inferred from these doctrines that they have to do nothing, and thus they have become sluggards. Do-nothingism is their creed. They will not even urge other people to labour for the Lord, because, say they, "God will do his own work. Salvation is all of grace!" The notion of these sluggards is that a man is to wait, and do nothing; he is to sit still, and let the grass grow up to his ankles in the hope of heavenly help. To arouse himself would be an interference with the eternal purpose, which he regards as altogether unwarrantable. I have known him look sour, shake his aged head, and say hard things against earnest people who were trying to win souls. I have known him run down young people, and like a great steam ram, sink them to the bottom, by calling them unsound and ignorant. How shall we survive the censures of this dogmatic person? How shall we escape from this very knowing and very captious sluggard! Solomon hastens to the rescue and extinguishes this gentleman by informing us that he is void of understanding. Why, he is the standard of orthodoxy, and he judges everybody! Yet Solomon applies another standard to him, and says he is void of understanding. He may know the doctrine, but he does not understand it; or else he would know that the doctrines of grace lead us to seek the grace of the doctrines; and that when we see God at work we learn that he worketh in us, not to make us go to sleep, but to will and to do of his own good pleasure. God's predestination of a people is his ordaining them unto good works that they may show forth his praise. So, if you or I shall from any doctrines, however true, draw the inference that we are warranted in being idle and indifferent about the things of God, we are void of understanding; we are acting like fools; we are misusing the gospel; we are taking what was meant for meat and turning it into poison. The sluggard, whether he is sluggish about his business or about his soul, is a man void of understanding.

As a rule we may measure a man's understanding by his useful activities; this is what the wise man very plainly tells us. Certain persons call themselves "cultured," and yet they cultivate nothing. Modern thought, as far as I have seen anything of its actual working, is a bottle of smoke, out of which comes nothing solid; yet we know men who can distinguish and divide, debate and discuss, refine and refute, and all the while the hemlock is growing in the furrow, and the plough is rusting. Friend, if your knowledge, if your culture, if your education does not lead you practically to serve God in your day and generation, you have not learned what Solomon calls wisdom, and you are not like the Blessed One, who was incarnate wisdom, of whom we read that "he went about doing good." A lazy man is not like our Saviour, who said, "My Father worketh hitherto, and I work." True wisdom is practical: boastful culture vapours and theorizes. Wisdom ploughs its field, wisdom hoes its vineyard, wisdom looks to its crops, wisdom tries to make the best of everything; and he who does not do so, whatever may be his knowledge of this, of that, or of the other, is a man void of understanding.

Why is he void of understanding? Is it not because *he has opportunities which he does not use?* His day has come, his day is going, and he lets the hours glide by to no purpose. Let me not press too hardly upon anyone, but let me ask you all to press as hardly as you can upon yourselves while you enquire each one of himself—Am I employing the minutes as they fly? This man had a vineyard, but he did not cultivate it; he had a field, but he did not till it. Do you, brethren, use all your opportunities? I know we each one have some power to serve God; do we use it? If we are his children he has not put one of us where we are of necessity useless. Somewhere we may shine by the light which he has given us, though that light be only a farthing candle. Are we thus shining? Do we sow beside all waters! Do we in the morning sow our seed, and in the evening still stretch out our hand; for if not, we are rebuked by the sweeping censure of Solomon, who saith that the slothful is a "man void of understanding."

Having opportunities he did not use them, and next, *being bound to the performance of certain duties he did not fulfil them.* When God appointed that every Israelite should have a piece of land, under that admirable system which made every Israelite a landowner, he meant that each man should possess his plot, not to let it lie waste, but to cultivate it. When God put Adam in the garden of Eden it was not that he should walk through the glades and watch the spontaneous luxuriance of the unfallen earth, but that he might dress it and keep it, and he had the same end in view when he allotted each Jew his piece of land; he meant that the holy soil should reach the utmost point of fertility through the labour of those who owned it. Thus the possession of a field and a vineyard involved responsibilities upon the sluggard which he never fulfilled, and therefore he was void of understanding. What is your position, dear friend? A father? A master? A servant? A minister? A teacher? Well, you have your farms and your vineyards in those particular spheres; but if you do not use those positions aright you will be void of understanding, because you neglect the end of your existence. You miss the high calling which your Maker has set before you.

The slothful farmer was unwise in these two respects, and in another also; for *he had capacities which he did not employ.* He could have tilled the field and cultivated the vineyard if he had chosen to do so. He was not a sickly man, who was forced to keep his bed, but he was a lazybones who was there of choice.

You are not asked to do in the service of God that which is utterly beyond you, for it is expected of us according to what we have and not according to what we have not. The man of two talents is not required to bring in the interest of five, but he is expected to bring in the interest of two. Solomon's slothful was too idle to attempt tasks which were quite within his power. Many have a number of dormant faculties of which they are scarcely aware, and many more have abilities which they are using for themselves, and not for him who created them. Dear friends, if God has given us any power to do good, pray let us do it, for this is a wicked, weary world. We should not even cover a glow-worm's light in such a darkness as this. We should not keep back a syllable of divine truth in a world that is so full of falsehood and error. However feeble our voices, let us lift them up for the cause of truth and righteousness. Do not let us be void of understanding, because we have opportunities that we do not use, obligations that we do not fulfil, and capacities which we do not exercise.

As for a sluggard in soul matters, he is indeed void of understanding, for *he trifles with matters which demand his most earnest heed.* Man, hast thou never cultivated thy heart? Has the ploughshare never broken up the clods of thy soul! Has the seed of the Word never been sown in thee! or has it taken no root? Hast thou never watered the young plants of desire? Hast thou never sought to pull up the weeds of sin that grow in thy heart? Art thou still a piece of the bare common or wild heath! Poor soul! Thou canst trim thy body, and spend many a minute at the glass; dost thou not care for thy soul? How long thou takest to decorate thy poor flesh, which is but worm's meat, or would be in a minute if God took away thy breath! And yet all the while thy soul is uncombed, unwashed, unclad, a poor neglected thing! Oh it should not be so. You take care of the worse part and leave the better to perish through neglect. This is the height of folly! He that is a sluggard as to the vineyard of his heart is a man void of understanding. If I must be idle, let it be seen in my field and my garden, but not in my soul.

Or are you a Christian? Are you really saved, and are you negligent in the Lord's work? Then, indeed, whatever you may be, I cannot help saying you have too little understanding; for surely, when a man is saved himself, and understands the danger of other men's souls, he must be in earnest in trying to pluck the firebrands from the flame. A Christian sluggard! Is there such a being? A *Christian* man on half time! A Christian man working not at all for his Lord; how shall I speak of him? *Time* does not tarry, DEATH does not tarry, HELL does not tarry; Satan is not lazy, all the powers of darkness are busy: how is it that you and I can be sluggish, if the Master has put us into his vineyard? Surely we must be void of understanding if, after being saved by the infinite love of God, we do not spend and be spent in his service. The eternal fitness of things demands that a saved man should be an earnest man.

The Christian who is slothful in his Master's service *has no idea what he is losing;* for the very cream of religion lies in holy consecration to God. Some people have just enough religion to make it questionable whether they have any or no. They have enough godliness to make them uneasy in their ungodliness. They have washed enough of their face to show the dirt upon the rest of it. "I am glad," said a servant, "that my mistress takes the sacrament, for otherwise I should not know she had any religion at all." You smile, and well you may. It is ridiculous that some people should have no goods in their shop, and yet advertise their business in all the papers; should make a show of religion, and yet have none of the Spirit of God. I wish some professors would do Christ the justice to say, "No, I am *not* one of his disciples; do not think so badly of him as to imagine that I can be one of them." We ought to be reflections *of* Christ; but I fear many are reflections *upon* Christ. When we see a lot of lazy servants, we are apt to think that their master must be a very idle person himself, or he would never put up with them. He who employs sluggards, and is satisfied with their snail-like pace, cannot be a very active man himself. O, let not the world think that Christ is indifferent to human woe, that Christ has lost his zeal, that Christ has lost his energy: yet I fear they will say it or think it if they see those who profess to be labourers in the vineyard of Christ nothing better than mere sluggards. The slothful, then, is a man void of understanding; he loses the honour and pleasure which he would find in serving his Master; he is a dishonour to the cause which he professes to venerate, and he is storing up thorns for his dying pillow. Let that stand as settled—the slothful, whether he be a minister, deacon, or private Christian, is a man void of understanding.

Now, secondly, LET US LOOK AT THE SLUGGARD'S LAND: "I went by the field of the slothful, and by the vineyard of the man void of understanding; And, lo, it was all grown over with thorns, and nettles had covered the face thereof." Note, first, that *land will produce something.* Soil which is good enough to be made into a field and a vineyard must and will yield some fruit or other; and so you and I, in our hearts and in the sphere God gives us to occupy, will be sure to produce something. We cannot live in this world as entire blanks; we shall either do good or do evil, as sure as we are alive. If you are idle in Christ's work, you are active in the devil's work. The sluggard by sleeping was doing more for the cultivation of thorns and nettles than he could have done by any other means. As a garden will either yield flowers or weeds, fruits or thistles, so something either good or evil will come out of our household, our class, or our congregation. If we do not produce a harvest of good wheat by labouring for Christ, we shall grow tares to be bound up in bundles for the last dread burning.

Note again that, if it be not farmed for God, *the soul will yield its natural produce;* and what is the natural produce of land if left to itself? What but thorns and nettles, or some other useless weeds? What is the natural produce of your heart and mine? What but sin and misery? What is the natural produce of your children if you leave them untrained for God? What but unholiness and vice? What is the natural produce of this great city if we leave its streets, and lanes, and alleys without the gospel? What but crime and infamy? Some harvest there will be, and the sheaves will be the natural produce of the soil, which is sin, death, and corruption.

If we are slothful, *the natural produce of our heart and of our sphere will be most inconvenient and unpleasant to ourselves.* Nobody can sleep on thorns, or make a pillow of nettles. No rest can come out of an idleness which lets ill alone, and does not by God's Spirit strive to uproot evil. While you are sleeping, Satan will be sowing. If you withhold the seed of good, Satan will be lavish with the seed of evil, and from that evil will come anguish and regret for time, and it may be for eternity. O man, the garden put into thy charge, if thou waste thy time in slumber, will reward thee with all that is noisome and painful. "Thorns also and thistles shall it bring forth to thee."

In many instances there will be a great deal of this evil produce; for a field and a vineyard will yield more thistles and nettles than a piece of ground that has never been reclaimed. If the land is good enough for a garden, it will present its owner with a fine crop of weeds if he only stays his hand. A choice bit of land fit for a vineyard of red wine will render such a profusion of nettles to the slothful that he shall rub his eyes with surprise. The man who might do most for God, if he were renewed, will bring forth most for Satan if he be let alone. The very region which would have glorified God most if the grace of God were there to convert its inhabitants, will be that out of which the vilest enemies of the gospel will arise. Rest assured of that; the best will become the worst if we neglect it. Neglect is all that is needed to produce evil. If you want to know the way of salvation I must take some pains to tell you; but if you want to know the way to be lost, my reply is easy; for it is only a matter of negligence;— "How shall we escape if we neglect so great salvation!" If you desire to bring forth a harvest unto God, I may need long to instruct you in ploughing, sowing, and watering; but if you wish your mind to be covered with Satan's hemlock, you have only to leave the furrows of your nature to themselves. The slothful asks for "A little sleep, a little slumber, a little folding of the hands to sleep," and the thorns and thistles multiply beyond all numbering, and prepare for him many a sting.

While we look upon the lazy man's vineyard let us also peep into the ungodly sluggard's heart. He does not care about repentance and faith. To think about his soul, to be in earnest about eternity, is too much for him. He wants to take things easy, and have a little more folding of the arms to sleep. What is growing in his mind and character? In some of these spiritual sluggards you can see drunkenness, uncleanness, covetousness, anger, and pride, and all sorts of thistles and nettles; or where these ranker weeds do not appear, by reason of the restraint of pious connections, you find other sorts of sin. The heart cannot be altogether empty, either Christ or the devil will possess it. My dear friend, if you are not decided for God, you cannot be a neutral. In this war every man is for God or for his enemy. You cannot remain like a sheet of blank paper. The legible handwriting of Satan is upon you—can you not see the blots? Unless Christ has written across the page his own sweet name, the autograph of Satan is visible. You may say, "I do not go into open sin; I am moral," and so forth. Ah, if you would but look, and consider, and search into your heart, you would see that enmity to God and to his ways, and hatred of purity, are there. You do not love God's law, nor love his Son, nor love his gospel, you are alienated in your heart, and there is in you all manner of evil desires and vain thoughts, and these will flourish and increase so long as you are a spiritual sluggard, and leave your heart uncultivated. O, may the Spirit of God arouse you; may you be stirred to anxious, earnest thought, and then you will see that these rank growths must be uprooted, and that your heart must be turned up by the plough of conviction, and sown with the good seed of the gospel, till a harvest rewards the great Husbandman.

Friend, if you believe in Christ, I want to peep over the hedge into *your heart* also, if you are a sluggish Christian; for I fear that nettles and thistles are threatening you also! Did I not hear you sing the other day—

"'Tis a point I long to know"?

That point will often be raised, for doubt is a seed which is sure to grow in lazy men's minds. I do not remember reading in Mr. Wesley's diary a question about his own salvation. He was so busy in the harvest of the Master that it did not occur to him to distrust his God. Some Christians have little faith in consequence of their having never sown the grain of mustard seed which they have received. If you do not sow your faith by using it how can it grow! When a man lives by faith in Christ Jesus, and his faith exercises itself actively in the service of his Lord, it takes root, grows upward, and becomes strong, till it chokes his doubts. Some have sadly morbid forebodings; they are discontented, fretful, selfish, murmuring, and all because they are idle. These are the weeds that grow in sluggards' gardens. I have known the slothful become so peevish that nothing could please them; the most earnest Christian could not do right for them; the most loving Christians could not be affectionate enough; the most active church could not be energetic enough; they detected all sorts of wrong where God himself saw much of the fruit of his Spirit. This censoriousness, this contention, this perpetual complaining is one of the nettles that are quite sure to grow in men's gardens when they fold their arms in sinful ease. If your heart does not yield fruit to God it will certainly bring forth that which is mischievous in itself, painful to you, and injurious to your fellow-men. Often the thorns choke the good seed; but it is a very blessed thing when the good seed comes up so thick and fast that it chokes the thorns. God enables certain Christians to become so fruitful in Christ that their graces and works stand thick together, and when Satan throws in the tares they cannot grow because there is no room for them. The Holy Spirit by his power makes evil to become weak in the heart, so that it no longer keeps the upper hand. If you are slothful, friend, look over the field of your heart, and weep at the sight.

May I next ask you to look into *your own house* and home? It is a dreadful thing when a man does not cultivate the field of his own family. I recollect in my early days a man who used to walk out with me into the villages when I was preaching, I was glad of his company till I found out certain facts, and then I shook him off, and I believe he hooked on to somebody else, for he must needs be gadding abroad every evening of the week. He had many children, and these grew up to be wicked young men and women, and the reason was that the father, while he would be at this meeting and that, never tried to bring his own children to the Saviour. What is the use of zeal abroad if there is neglect at home? How sad to say, "My own vineyard have I not kept." Have you never heard of one who said he did not teach his children the ways of God because he thought they were so young that it was very wrong to prejudice them, and he had rather leave them to choose their own religion when they grew older? One of his boys broke his arm, and while the surgeon was setting it the boy was swearing all the time. "Ah," said the good doctor, "I told you what would happen. You were afraid to prejudice your boy in the right way, but the devil had no such qualms; he has prejudiced him the other way, and pretty strongly too." It is our duty to prejudice our field in favour of corn, or it will soon be covered with thistles. Cultivate a child's heart for good, or it will go wrong of itself, for it is already depraved by nature. O that we were wise enough to think of this, and leave no little one to become a prey to the destroyer.

As it is with homes, so is it with *schools*. A gentleman who joined this church some time ago had been an atheist for years, and in conversing with him I found that be had been educated at one of our great public schools, and to that fact he traced his infidelity. He said that the boys were stowed away on Sunday in a lofty gallery at the far end of a church, where they could scarcely hear a word that the clergyman said, but simply sat imprisoned in a place where it was dreadfully hot in summer and cold in winter. On Sundays there were prayers, and prayers, and prayers, but nothing that ever touched his heart; until he was so sick of prayers that he vowed if he once got out of the school he would have done with religion. This is a sad result, but a frequent one. You Sunday-school teachers can make your classes so tiresome to the children that they will hate Sunday. You can fritter away the time in school without bringing the lads and lasses to Christ, and so you may do more hurt than good. I have known Christian fathers who by their severity and want of tenderness have sown their family field with the thorns and thistles of hatred to religion instead of scattering the good seed of love to it. O that we may so live among our children that they may not only love us, but love our Father who is in heaven. May fathers and mothers set such an example of cheerful piety that sons and daughters shall say, "Let us tread in our father's footsteps, for he was a happy and a holy man. Let us follow our mother's ways, for she was sweetness itself." If piety does not rule in your house, when we pass by your home we shall see disorder, disobedience, pride of dress, folly, and the beginnings of vice. Let not your home be a sluggard's field, or you will have to rue it in years to come.

Let every deacon, every class-leader, and also every minister enquire diligently into the state of the field he has to cultivate. You see, brothers and sisters, if you and I are set over any department of our Lord's work, and we are not diligent in it, we shall be like barren trees planted in an orchard, which are a loss altogether, because they occupy the places of other trees which might have brought forth fruit unto their owners. We shall cumber the ground, and do damage to our Lord, unless we render him actual service. Will you think of this? If you could be put down as a mere cipher in the accounts of Christ, that would be very sad; but, brother, it cannot be so. You will cause a deficit unless you create a gain. Oh that through the grace of God we may be profitable to our Lord and Master. Who among us can look upon his life's work without some sorrow? If anything has been done aright we ascribe it all to the grace of God; but how much there is to weep over! How much that we would wish to amend! Let us not spend time in idle regrets, but pray for the Spirit of God, that in the future we may not be void of understanding, but may know what we ought to do, and where the strength must come from with which to do it and then give ourselves up to the doing of it.

I beg you once more to look at the great field of *the world.* Do you see how it is overgrown with thorns and nettles? If an angel could take a survey of the whole race, what tears he would shed, if angels could weep! What a tangled mass of weeds the whole earth is! Yonder the field is scarlet with the poppy of popery, and over the hedge it is yellow with the wild mustard of Mahometanism. Vast regions are smothered with the thistles of infidelity and idolatry. The world is full of cruelty, oppression, drunkenness, rebellion, uncleanness, misery. What the moon sees! What God's sun sees! What scenes of horror! How far is all this to be attributed to a neglectful church! Nearly nineteen hundred years are gone, and the sluggard's vineyard is but little improved! England has been touched with the spade, but I cannot say that it has been thoroughly weeded or ploughed yet. Across the ocean another field equally favoured knows well the ploughman, and yet the weeds are rank. Here and there a little good work has been done, but the vast mass of the world still lies a moorland never broken up, a waste, a howling wilderness. What has the church been doing all these years? She ceased after a few centuries to be a missionary church, and from that hour she almost ceased to be a living church. Whenever a church does not labour for the reclaiming of the desert it becomes itself a waste. You shall not find on the roll of history that for a length of time any Christian community has flourished after it has become negligent of the outside world. I believe that if we are put into the Master's vineyard, and will not take away the weeds, neither shall the vine flourish, nor shall the corn yield its increase. However, instead of asking what the church has been doing for this nineteen hundred years, let us ask ourselves, What are we going to do now? Are the missions of the churches of Great Britain always to be such poor, feeble things as they are? Are the best of our Christian young men always going to stay at home? We go on ploughing the home field a hundred times over, while millions of acres abroad are left to the thorn and nettle. Shall it always be so? God send us more spiritual life, and wake us up from our sluggishness, or else when the holy watcher gives in his report, be will say, "I went by the field of the sluggish church, and it was all grown over with thorns and nettles, and the stone wall was broken down, so that one could scarcely tell which was the church and which was the world, yet still she slept, and slept, and slept, and nothing could waken her."

I conclude by remarking that THERE MUST BE SOME LESSON IN ALL THIS. I cannot teach it as I would, but I want to learn it myself. I will speak it as though I were talking to myself.

The first lesson is, that *unaided nature always will produce thorns and nettles, and nothing else.* My soul, if it were not for grace, this is all thou wouldst have produced. Beloved, are you producing anything else? Then it is not nature, but the grace of God that makes you produce it. Those lips that now most charmingly sing the praises of God would have been delighted with an idle ballad if the grace of God had not sanctified them. Your heart, that now cleaves to Christ, would have continued to cling to your idols—you know what they were—if it had not been for grace divine. And why should grace have visited you or me—why? Echo answers, Why? What answer can we give? "'Tis even so, Father, for so it seemed good in thy sight." Let the recollection of what grace has done move us to manifest the result of that grace in our lives. Come, brothers and sisters, inasmuch as we were aforetime rich enough in the soil of our nature to produce so much of nettle and thistle—and God only knows how much we did produce—let us now pray that our lives may yield as much of good corn for the great Husbandman. Will you serve Christ less than you served your lusts? Will you make less sacrifice for Christ than you did for your sins? Some of you were whole-hearted enough when in the service of the evil one, will you be half-hearted in the service of God? Shall the Holy Spirit produce less fruit in you than that which you yielded under the spirit of evil?

God grant that we may not he left to prove what nature will produce if left to itself.

We see here, next, *the little value of natural good intentions;* for this man, who left his field and vineyard to be overgrown, always meant to work hard one of these fine days. To do him justice, we must admit that he did not mean to sleep much longer, for he said—"Yet a little sleep, a little slumber, a little folding of the hands to sleep." Only a little doze, and then he would tuck up his sleeves and show his muscle. Probably the worst people in the world are those who have the best intentions, but never carry them out. In that way Satan lulls many to sleep. They hear an earnest sermon; but they do not arise and go to their Father; they only get as far as saying, "Yes, yes, the far country is not a fit place for me; I will not stay here long. I mean to go home by-and-by." They said that forty years ago, but nothing came of it. When they were quite youths they had serious impressions, they were almost persuaded to be Christians, and yet they are not Christians even now. They have been slumbering forty years! Surely that is a liberal share of sleep! They never intended to dream so long, and now they do not mean to lie in bed much longer. They will not turn to Christ at once, but they are resolved to do so one day. When are you going to do it, friend? "Before I die." Going to put it off to the last hour or two, are you? And so, when unconscious, and drugged to relieve your pain, you will begin to think of your soul? Is this wise? Surely you are void of understanding. Perhaps you will die in an hour. Did you not hear the other day of the alderman who died in his carriage? Little must he have dreamed of that. How would it have fared with you had you also been smitten while riding at your ease? Have you not heard of persons who fall dead at their work? What is to hinder your dying with a spade in your hand? I am often startled when I am told in the week that one whom I saw on Sunday is dead—gone from the shop to the judgment-seat. It is not a very long time ago since one went out at the doorway of the Tabernacle, and fell dead on the threshold. We have had deaths in the house of God, unexpected deaths; and sometimes people are hurried away unprepared who never meant to have died unconverted, who always had from their youth up some kind of desire to be ready, only still they wanted a little more sleep. Oh, my hearers, take heed of little delays, and short puttings off. You have wasted time enough already, come to the point at once before the clock strikes again. May God the Holy Spirit bring you to decision.

"Surely you do not object to my having a little more sleep?" says the sluggard. "You have waked me so soon. I only ask another little nap." "My dear man, it is far into the morning." He answers, "It is rather late, I know; but it will not be much later if I take just another doze." You wake him again, and tell him it is noon. He says, "It is the hottest part of the day: I daresay if I had been up I should have gone to the sofa and taken a little rest from the hot sun." You knock at his door when it is almost evening, and then he cries, "It is of no use to get up now, for the day is almost over." You remind him of his overgrown field and weedy vineyard, and he answer; "Yes, I must get up, I know." He shakes himself and says, "I do not think it will matter much if I wait till the clock strikes. I will rest another minute or two." He is glued to his bed, dead while he liveth, buried in his laziness. If he could sleep for ever he would, but he cannot, for the judgment-day will rouse him. It is written, "And in hell he lift up his eyes, being in torment." God grant that you spiritual sluggards may wake before that; but you will not unless you bestir yourselves betimes, for "now is the accepted time"; and it may be now or never. Tomorrow is only to be found in the calendar of fools; today is the time of the wise man, the chosen season of our gracious God. Oh that the Holy Spirit may lead you to seize the present hour, that you may at once give yourselves to the Lord by faith in Christ Jesus, and then from his vineyard—

"Quick uproot
The noisome weeds, that without profit suck
The soil's fertility from wholesome plants;"

The Broken Fence

"I went by the field of the slothful, and by the vineyard of the man void of understanding; and lo, it was all grown over with thorns, and nettles had covered the face thereof, and *the stone wall thereof was broken down*. Then I saw, and considered it well: I looked upon it and received instruction."—Proverbs xxiv. 30-32.

THIS slothful man did no hurt to his fellow men: he was not a thief, nor a ruffian, nor a meddler in anybody else's business. He did not trouble himself about other men's concerns, for he did not even attend to his own, it required too much exertion. He was not grossly vicious, he had not energy enough to care for that. He was one who liked to take things easily. He always let well alone and for the matter of that he let ill alone, too, as the nettles and the thistles in his garden plainly proved. What was the use of disturbing himself? It would be all the same a hundred years hence; and so, he took things just as they came. He

33

was not a bad man, so some said of him; and yet, perhaps, it will be found at last that there is no worse man in the world than the man who is not good, for in some respects he is not good enough to be bad; he has not enough force of character about him to serve either God or Baal. He simply serves himself, worshipping his own case and adoring his own comfort. Yet he always meant to be right. Dear me! he was not going to sleep much longer. He would have forty winks more, and then he would be at his work, and show you what he could do. One of these days he meant to be thoroughly in earnest, and make up for lost time. The time never actually came for him to begin, but it was always coming. He always meant to repent, but he went on in his sin. He meant to believe, but he died an unbeliever. He meant to be a Christian, but he lived without Christ. He halted between two opinions because he could not trouble himself to make up his mind; and so he perished of delay.

This picture of the slothful man and its garden and field overgrown with nettles and weeds represents many a man who has professed to be a Christian, but who has become slothful in the things of God. Spiritual life has withered in him. He has backslidden; he has come down from the condition of healthy spiritual energy into one of listlessness, and indifference to the things of God; and while things have gone wrong within his heart, and all sorts of mischiefs have come into him and grown up and seeded themselves in him, mischief is also taking place externally in his daily conduct. The stone wall which guarded his character is broken down, and he lies open to all evil. Upon this point we will now meditate. "The stone wall thereof was broken down."

Come, then, let us take a walk with Solomon, and

stand with him and consider and learn instruction while we *look at this broken-down fence.* When we have examined it, let us *consider the consequences of broken-down walls;* and then, in the last place, let us try to *rouse up this sluggard that his wall may yet be repaired.* If this slothful person should be one of ourselves, may God's infinite mercy rouse us up before this ruined wall has let in a herd of prowling vices.

I. First let us take a LOOK AT THIS BROKEN FENCE.

You will see that in the beginning it was a very good fence, for it was a stone wall. Fields are often surrounded with wooden palings which soon decay, or with hedges which may very easily have gaps made in them; but this was a stone wall. Such walls are very usual in the East, and are also common in some of our own counties where stone is plentiful. It was a substantial protection to begin with, and well shut in the pretty little estate which had fallen into such bad hands. The man had a field for agricultural purposes, and another strip of land for a vineyard or a garden. It was fertile soil, for it produced thorns and nettles in abundance, and where these flourish better things can be produced; yet the idler took no care of his property, but allowed the wall to get into bad repair, and in many places to be quite broken down.

Let me mention some of the stone walls that men permit to be broken down when they backslide.

In many cases *sound principles were instilled in youth*, but these are forgotten. What a blessing is Christian education! Our parents, both by persuasion and example, taught many of us the things that are pure and honest and of good repute. We saw in their lives how to live. They also opened the word of God before us, and they taught us the ways of right both towards God and towards men. They prayed for us, and they prayed with us, till the things of God were placed round about us and shut us in as with a stone wall. We have never been able to get rid of our early impressions. Even in times of wandering, before we knew the Lord savingly, these things had a healthy power over us; we were checked when we would have done evil, we were assisted when we were struggling towards Christ. It is very sad when people permit these first principles to be shaken, and to be removed like stones which fall from a boundary wall. Young persons begin at first to talk lightly of the old-fashioned ways of their parents. By-and-by it is not merely the old-fashionedness of the ways, but the ways themselves that they despise. They seek other company, and from that other company they learn nothing but evil. They seek pleasure in places which it horrifies their parents to think of. This leads to worse, and if they do not bring their fathers' grey hairs with sorrow to the grave it is no virtue of theirs. I have known young men, who really were Christians, sadly backslide through being induced to modify, conceal, or alter those holy principles in which they were trained from their mother's knee. It is a great calamity when professedly converted men become unfixed, unstable, and carried about with every wind of doctrine. It shows great faultiness of mind, and unsoundness of heart when we can trifle with those grave and solemn truths which have been sanctified by a mother's tears, and by a father's earnest life. "I am thy servant," said David, "and the son of thy handmaid": he felt it to be a high honour, and, at the same time a sacred bond which bound him to God, that he was the son of one who could be called God's handmaid. Take care, you who have had Christian training, that you do not trifle with it. "My son, keep thy father's commandment, and forsake not the law of thy mother: bind them continually upon thine heart, and tie them about thy neck."

Protection to character is also found in the fact that *solid doctrines have been learned.* This is a fine stone wall. Many among us have been taught the gospel of the grace of God, and they have learned it well, so that they are able to contend earnestly for the faith once delivered to the saints. Happy are they who have a religion that is grounded upon a clear knowledge of eternal verities. A religion which is all excitement, and has little instruction in it, may serve for transient use; but for permanent life-purposes there must be a knowledge of those great doctrines which are fundamental to the gospel system. I tremble when I hear of a man's giving up, one by one, the vital principles of the gospel and boasting of his liberality. I hear him say, "These are my views, but others have a right to their views also." That is a very proper expression in reference to mere "views," but we may not thus speak of *truth* itself as revealed by God: that is one and unalterable, and all are bound to receive it. It is not your view of truth, for that is a dim thing; but the very truth itself which will save you if your faith embraces it. I will readily yield my way of stating a doctrine, but not the doctrine itself. One man may put it in this way, and one in another; but the truth itself must never be given up. The spirit of the Broad School robs us of everything like certainty. I should like to ask some great men of that order whether they believe that anything is taught in the Scriptures which it would be worth while for a person to die for, and whether the martyrs were not great fools for laying down their lives for mere opinions which might be right or might be wrong? This Broad-churchism is a breaking down of stone walls, and it will let in the devil and all his crew, and do infinite harm to the church of God, if it be not stopped. A loose state of belief does great damage to any man's mind.

We are not bigots, but we should be none the worse if we so lived that men called us so. I met a man the other day who was accused of bigotry and I said, "Give me your hand, old fellow. I like to meet with bigots now and then, for the fine old creatures are getting scarce, and the stuff they are made of is so good that if there were more of it we might see a few men among us again and fewer molluscs." Lately we have seen few men with backbone; the most have been of the jelly-fish order. I have lived in times in which I should have said, "Be liberal, and shake off all narrowness": but now I am obliged to alter my tone and cry, "Be steadfast in the truth." The faith once delivered to the saints is now all the more attractive to me because it is called narrow, for I am weary of that breadth which comes of broken hedges. There are fixed points of truth, and definite certainties of creed, and woe to you if you allow these stone walls to crumble down. I fear me that the slothful are a numerous band, and that ages to come may have to deplore the laxity which has been applauded by this negligent generation.

Another fence which is too often neglected is that of *godly habits which had been formed:* the sluggard allows this wall to be broken down. I will mention some valuable guards of life and character. One is the habit of *secret prayer*. Private prayer should be regularly offered, at least in the morning and in the evening. We cannot do without set seasons for drawing near to God. To look into the face of man without having first seen the face of God is very dangerous: to go out into the world without locking up the heart and giving God the key is to leave it open to all sorts of spiritual vagrants. At night, again, to go to your rest as the swine roll into their sty, without thanking God for the mercies of the day, is shameful. The evening sacrifice should be devoutly offered as surely as we have enjoyed the evening fireside: we should thus put ourselves under the wings of the Preserver of men. It may be said, "We can pray at all times." I know we can: but I fear that those who do not pray at stated hours seldom pray at all. Those who pray in season are the most likely persons to pray at all seasons. Spiritual life does not care for a cast-iron regulation, but since life casts itself into some mould or other, I would have you careful of its external habit as well as its internal power. Never allow great gaps in the wall of your habitual private prayer.

I go a step farther, I believe that there is a great guardian power about *family prayer,* and I feel greatly distressed because I know that very many Christian families neglect it. Romanism, at one time, could do nothing in England, because it could offer nothing but the shadow of what Christian men had already in substance. "Do you hear that bell tinkling in the morning?" "What is that for?" "To go to church to pray." "Indeed," said the Puritan, "I have no need to go there to pray. I have had my children together, and we have read a passage of Scripture, and prayed, and sang the praises of God, and we have a church in our house." Ah, there goes that bell again in the evening. What is that for? Why, it is the vesper bell. The good man answered that he had no need to trudge a mile or two for that, for his holy vespers had been said and sung around his own table, of which the big Bible was the chief ornament. They told him that there could be no service without a priest, but he replied that every godly man should be a priest in his own house. Thus have the saints defied the overtures of priestcraft, and kept the faith from generation to generation. Household devotion and the pulpit are, under God, the stone walls of Protestantism, and my prayer is that these may not be broken down.

Another fence to protect piety is found in *weeknight services.* I notice that when people forsake week-night meetings the power of their religion evaporates. I do not speak of those lawfully detained to watch the sick, and attend to farm-work and other business, or as domestic servants and the like; there are exceptions to all rules: but I mean those who could attend if they had a mind to do so. When people say, "It is quite enough for me to be wearied with the sermons of the Sunday; I do not want to go out to prayer-meetings, and lectures, and so forth,"—then it is clear that they have no appetite for the word; and surely this is a bad sign. If you have a bit of wall built to protect the Sunday and then six times the distance left without a fence, I believe that Satan's cattle will get in and do no end of mischief.

Take care, also, of the stone wall of *Bible reading,* and of speaking often one to another concerning the things of God. Associate with the godly, and commune with God, and you will thus, by the blessing of God's Spirit, keep up a good fence against temptations, which otherwise will get into the fields of your soul, and devour all goodly fruits.

Many have found much protection for the field of daily life in the stone wall of a *public profession of faith.* I am speaking to you who are real believers, and I know that you have often found it a great safe-guard to be known and recognised as a follower of Jesus. I have never regretted—and I never shall regret—the day on which I walked to the little river Lark, in Cambridgeshire, and was there buried with Christ in baptism. In this I acted contrary to the opinions of all my friends whom I respected and esteemed, but as I had read the Greek Testament for myself, I felt bound to be immersed upon the profession of my faith, and I was so. By that act I said to the world, "I am dead to you, and buried to you in Christ, and I hope henceforth to live in newness of life." That day, by God's grace, I imitated the tactics of the general who meant to fight the enemy till he conquered, and therefore he burned his boats that there might be no way of retreat. I believe that a solemn confession of Christ before men is as a thorn hedge to keep one within bounds, and to keep off those who hope to draw you aside. Of course it is nothing but a hedge, and it is of no use to fence in a field of weeds, but when wheat is growing a hedge is of great consequence. You who imagine that you can be the Lord's, and yet lie open like a common, are under a great error; you ought to be distinguished from the world, and obey the voice which saith, "Come ye out from among them, be ye separate." The promise of salvation is to the man who with his heart believeth and with his mouth confesseth. Say right boldly, "Let others do as they will; as for me and my house, we will serve the Lord." By this act you come out into the king's highway, and put yourself under the protection of the Lord of pilgrims, and he will take care of you. Oftentimes, when otherwise you might have hesitated, you will say, "The vows of the Lord are upon me: how can I draw back?" I pray you, then, set up the stone wall, and keep it up, and if it has at any corner been tumbled over, set it up again, and let it be seen by your conduct and conversation that you are a follower of Jesus, and are not ashamed to have it known.

Keep to your religious principles like men, and do not turn aside for the sake of gain, or respectability. Do not let wealth break down your wall, for I have known some make a great gap to let their carriage go through, and to let in wealthy worldlings for the sake of their society. Those who forsake their principles to please men will in the end be lightly esteemed, but he who is faithful shall have the honour which cometh from God. Look well to this hedge of steadfast adherence to the faith, and you shall find a great blessing in it.

There is yet another stone wall which I will mention, namely, *firmness of character*. Our holy faith teaches a man to be decided in the cause of Christ, and to be resolute in getting rid of evil habits. "If thine eye offend thee"—wear a shade? No; "pluck it out." "If thine arm offend thee"—hang it in a sling? No; "cut it off and cast it from thee." True religion is very thorough in what it recommends. It says to us, "touch not the unclean thing." But many persons are so idle in the ways of God that they have no mind of their own: evil companions tempt them, and they cannot say, "No." They need a stone wall made up of noes. Here are the stones "no, *no,* NO." Dare to be singular. Resolve to keep close to Christ. Make a stern determination to permit nothing in your life, however gainful or pleasurable, if it would dishonour the name of Jesus. Be dogmatically true, obstinately holy, immovably honest, desperately kind, fixedly upright. If God's grace sets up this hedge around you, even Satan will feel that he cannot get in, and will complain to God "hast thou not set a hedge about him?"

I have kept you long enough looking over the wall,

let me invite you in, and for a few minutes let us CONSIDER THE CONSEQUENCES OF A BROKEN-DOWN FENCE.

To make short work of it, first, *the boundary has gone.* Those lines of separation which were kept up by the good principles which were instilled in him by religious habits, by a bold profession and by a firm resolve, have vanished, and now the question is, "Is he a Christian, or is he not!" The fence is so far gone that he does not know which is his Lord's property and which remains an open common: in fact, he does not know whether he himself is included in the Royal domain or left to be mere waste of the world's manor. This is for want of keeping up the fences. If that man had lived near to God, if he had walked in his integrity, if the Spirit of God had richly rested on him in all holy living and waiting upon God, he would have known where the boundary was, and he would have seen whether his land lay in the parish of All-saints, or in the region called No-man's-land, or in the district where Satan is the lord of the manor. I heard of a dear old saint the other day who, when she was near to death, was attacked by Satan, and, waving her finger at the enemy, in her gentle way, she routed him by saying, "Chosen! chosen! chosen!" She knew that she was chosen, and she remembered the text, "The Lord that hath chosen Jerusalem rebuke thee." When the wall stands in its integrity all round the field, we can resist the devil by bidding him leave the Lord's property alone. "Begone! Look somewhere else. I belong to Christ, not to you." To do this you must mend the hedges well so that there shall be a clear boundary line, and you can say, "Trespassers, beware!" Do not yield an inch to the enemy, but make the wall all the higher, the more he seeks to enter. O that this adversary may never find a gap to enter by.

Next, when the wall has fallen, *the protection is gone.*
When a man's heart has its wall broken, all his
thoughts will go astray, and wander upon the
mountains of vanity. Like sheep, thoughts need careful
folding, or they will be off in no time. "I hate vain
thoughts," said David, but slothful men are sure to
have plenty of them, for there is no keeping your
thoughts out of vanity unless you stop every gap and
shut every gate. Holy thoughts, comfortable
meditations, devout longings, and gracious
communings will be off and gone if we sluggishly allow
the stone wall to get out of repair.

Nor is this all, for as good things go out so bad
things come in. When the wall is gone every passer-
by sees, as it were, an invitation to enter. You have
set before him an open door, and in he comes. Are
there fruits? He plucks them; of course. He walks
about as if it were a public place, and he pries everywhere. Is there any secret corner of your heart which
you would keep for Jesus? Satan or the world will walk
in; and do you wonder? Every passing goat, or roaming
ox, or stray ass visits the growing crops and spoils
more than he eats, and who can blame the creature
when the gaps are so wide? All manner of evil lusts
and desires, and imaginations prey upon an unfenced
soul. It is of no use for you to say, "Lead us not into
temptation." God will hear your prayer; and he will
not lead you there; but you are leading yourself into
it, you are tempting the devil to tempt you. If you leave
yourself open to evil influences the Spirit of God will
be grieved, and he may leave you to reap the result of
your folly. What think you, friend? Had you not better
attend to your fences at once?

And then there is another evil, for *the land itself
will go away.* "No," say you; "how can that be?" If a

stone wall is broken down round a farm in England a man does not thereby lose his land, but in many parts of Palestine the land is all ups and downs on the sides of the hills, and every bit of ground is terraced and kept up by walls. When the walls fall the soil slips over, terrace upon terrace, and the vines and trees go down with it; then the rain comes and washes the soil away, and nothing is left but barren crags which would starve a lark. In the same manner a man may so neglect himself, and so neglect the things of God, and become so careless and indifferent about doctrine, and about holy living, that his power to do good ceases, and his mind, his heart, and his energy seem to be gone. The prophet said, "Ephraim is a silly dove, without heart": there are flocks of such silly doves. The man who trifles with religion sports with his own soul, and will soon degenerate into so much of a trifler that he will be averse to solemn thought, and incapable of real usefulness. I charge you, dear friends, to be sternly true to yourselves and to your God. Stand to your principles in this evil and wicked day. Now, when everything seems to be turned into marsh and mire and mud, and religious thought appears to be silently sliding and slipping along, descending like a stream of slime into the Dead Sea of Unbelief,—get solid walls built around your life, around your faith, and around your character. Stand fast, and having done all, still stand. May God the holy Ghost cause you to be rooted and grounded, built up and established, fixed and confirmed, never "casting away your confidence, which hath great recompense of reward."

Lastly, I want, if I can, TO WAKE UP THE SLUGGARD. I would like to throw a handful of gravel up to his window. It is time to get up, for the sun has drunk up all the dew. He craves "a little more sleep." My dear fellow, if you take a little more sleep, you will never wake at all till you lift up your eyes in another world. Wake at once. Leap from your bed before you are smothered in it. Wake up! Do you not see where you are? You have let things alone till your heart is covered with sins like weeds. You have neglected God and Christ till you have grown worldly, sinful, careless, indifferent, ungodly. I mean some of you who were once named with the sacred name. You have become like worldlings, and are almost as far from being what you ought to be as others who make no profession at all. Look at yourselves, and see what has come of your neglected walls. Then look at some of your fellow-Christians, and mark how diligent they are. Look at many among them who are poor and illiterate, and yet they are doing far more than you for the Lord Jesus. In spite of your talents and opportunities, you are an unprofitable servant, letting all things run to waste. Is it not time that you bestirred yourself? Look, again, at others who, like yourself, went to sleep, meaning to wake in a little while. What has become of them? Alas, for those who have fallen into gross sin, and dishonoured their character, and who have been put away from the church of God; yet they only went a little further than you have done. Your state of heart is much the same as theirs, and if you should be tempted as they have been, you will probably make shipwreck as they have done. Oh, see to it, you that slumber, for an idle professor is ready for anything. A slothful professor's heart is tinder for the devil's tinder-box: does your heart thus invite the sparks of temptation?

Remember, lastly, the coming of the Lord Jesus Christ. Shall he come and find you sleeping?

Remember the judgment. What will you say to excuse yourself, for opportunities lost, time wasted, and talents wrapped up in a napkin, when the Lord shall come?

As for you, my unconverted friend, if you go dreaming through this world, without any sort of trouble, and never look to the state of your heart at all, you will be a lost man beyond all question. The slothful can have no hope, for "if the righteous scarcely are saved," who strive to serve their Lord, where will those appear who sleep on in defiance of the calls of God? Salvation is wholly and alone of grace, as you well know; but grace never works in men's minds towards slumbering and indifference; it tends towards energy, activity, fervour, importunity, self-sacrifice. God grant us the indwelling of his Holy Spirit that all things may be set in order, sins cut up by the roots within the heart, and the whole man protected by sanctifying grace from the wasters which lurk around, hoping to enter where the wall is low. O Lord, remember us in mercy, fence us about by thy power, and keep us from the sloth which would expose us to evil, for Jesus' sake. Amen.

Frost and Thaw

"He giveth snow like wool: he scattereth the hoarfrost like ashes. He casteth forth his ice like morsels: who can stand before his cold? He sendeth out his word, and melteth them: he causeth his wind to blow, and the waters flow."—Psalm cxlvii 16-18.

LOOKING out of our window one morning we saw the earth robed in a white mantle; for in a few short hours the earth had been covered to a considerable depth with snow. We looked out again in a few hours and saw the fields as green as ever, and the ploughed fields as bare as if no single flake had fallen. It is no uncommon thing for a heavy fall of snow to be followed by a rapid thaw.

These interesting changes are wrought by God, not only with a purpose toward the outward world, but with some design toward the spiritual realm. God is always a teacher. In every action that he performs he is instructing his own children, and opening up to them the road to inner mysteries. Happy are those who find food for their heaven-born spirits, as well as for their mental powers, in the works of the Lord's hand.

I shall ask your attention, first, *to the operations of nature spoken of in the text;* and secondly, *to those operations of grace of which they are the most fitting symbols.*

I. Consider first THE OPERATIONS OF NATURE. We shall not think a few minutes wasted if we call your attention to the hand of God in frost and thaw, even upon natural grounds.

1. Observe the *directness* of the Lord's work. I rejoice, as I read these words, to find how present our God is in the world. It is not written, "the laws of nature produce snow," but "HE *giveth snow,*" as if every flake came directly from the palm of his hand. We are not told that certain natural regulations form moisture into hoarfrost; no, but as Moses took ashes of the furnace and scattered them upon Egypt, so it is said of the Lord " HE *scattereth the hoarfrost like ashes.*" It is not said that the Eternal has set the world going, and by the operation of its machinery ice is produced. Oh no, but every single granule of ice descending in the hail is from God; "HE *casteth forth his ice like morsels.*" Even as the slinger distinctly sends the stone out of his sling, so the path of every hailstone is marked by the Divine power. The ice is called, you observe, *his* ice; and in the next sentence we read of *his* cold. These words make nature strangely magnificent. When we look upon every hailstone as God's hail, and upon every fragment of ice as his ice, how precious the watery diamonds become! When we feel the cold nipping our limbs and penetrating through every garment, it consoles us to remember that it is *his* cold.

When the thaw comes, see how the text speaks of it;— *"he sendeth out his word."* He does not leave it to certain forces of nature, but like a king, *"he sendeth out his word and melteth them: he causeth* HIS *wind to blow."* He has a special property in every wind: whether it comes from the north to freeze, or from the south to melt, it is *his* wind. Behold how in God's temple everything speaketh of his glory. Learn to see the Lord in all scenes of the visible universe, for truly he worketh all things.

This thought of the directness of the Divine operations must be carried into providence. It will greatly comfort you if you can see God's hand in your losses and crosses; surely you will not murmur against the direct agency of your God. This will put an extraordinary sweetness into daily mercies, and make the comforts of life more comfortable still, because they are from a Father's hand. If your table be scantily furnished it shall suffice for your contented heart, when you know that your Father spread it for you in wisdom and love. This shall bless your bread and your water; this shall make the bare walls of an ill-furnished room as resplendent as a palace, and turn a hard bed into a couch of down;—my Father doth it all. We see his smile of love even when others see nothing but the black hand of Death smiting our best beloved. We see a Father's hand when the pestilence lays our cattle dead upon the plain. We see God at work in mercy when we ourselves are stretched upon the bed of languishing. It is ever our Father's act and deed. Do not let us get beyond this; but rather let us enlarge our view of this truth, and remember that this is true of the little as well as of the great. Let the lines of a true poet strike you:—

> "If pestilence stalk through the land, ye say the Lord
>   hath done it—
> Hath he not done it when an aphis creepeth upon the
>   rosebud?
> If an avalanche tumbles from its Alp, ye tremble at
>   the will of Providence—
> Is not that will as much concerned when the sere
>   leaves fall from the poplar?"

Let your hearts sing of everything, Jehovah-Shammah,
the Lord is there.

2. Next, I beg you to observe, with thanksgiving,
the *ease* of Divine working. These verses read as if
the making of frost and snow were the simplest matter
in all the world. A man puts his hand into a wool-
pack and throws out the wool; God giveth snow as
easily as that: "He giveth snow like wool." A man takes
up a handful of ashes, and throws them into the air,
so that they fall around: "He scattereth the hoarfrost
like ashes." Rime and snow are marvels of nature:
those who have observed the extraordinary beauty of
the ice-crystals have been enraptured, and yet they
are easily formed by the Lord. "He casteth forth his
ice like morsels"—just as easily as we cast crumbs of
bread outside the window to the robins during wintry
days. When the rivers are hard frozen, and the earth
is held in iron chains, then the melting of the whole—
how is that done? Not by kindling innumerable fires,
nor by sending electric shocks from huge batteries
through the interior of the earth—no; "He sendeth forth
his word, and melteth them; he causeth his wind to
blow, and the waters flow." The whole matter is
accomplished with a word and a breath. If you and I
had any great thing to do, what puffing and panting,
what straining and tugging there would be: even the
great engineers, who perform marvels by machinery,

make much noise and stir about it. It is not so with
the Almighty One. Our globe spins round in four-and-
twenty hours, and yet it does not make so much noise
as a humming-top; and yonder ponderous worlds
rolling in space track their way in silence. If I enter a
factory I hear a deafening din, or if I stand near the
village mill, turned by water dropping over a wheel,
there is a never-ceasing click-clack, or an undying
hum; but God's great wheels revolve without noise or
friction: divine machinery works smoothly. This ease
is seen in providence as well as in nature. Your
heavenly Father is as able to deliver you as he is to
melt the snow, and he will deliver you in as simple a
manner if you rest upon him. He openeth his hand,
and supplies the want of every living thing as readily
as he works in nature. Mark the ease of God's
working,—he does but open his hand.

3. Notice in the next place the *variety* of the Divine
operations in nature. When the Lord is at work with
frost as his tool he creates snow, a wonderful
production, every crystal being a marvel of art; but
then he is not content with snow—from the same water
he makes another form of beauty which we call
hoarfrost, and yet a third lustrous sparkling
substance, namely glittering ice; and all these by the
one agency of cold. What a marvellous variety the
educated eye can detect in the several forms of frozen
water! The same God who solidified the flood with cold
soon melts it with warmth; but even in thaw there is
no monotony of manner: at one time the joyous
streams rush with such impetuosity from their
imprisonment that rivers are swollen and floods cover
the plain; at another time by slow degrees, in scanty
driblets, the drops regain their freedom. The same
variety is seen in every department of nature. So in

providence the Lord has a thousand forms of frosty trials with which to try his people, and he has ten thousand beams of mercy with which to cheer and comfort them. He can afflict you with the snow trial, or with the hoarfrost trial, or with the ice-trial if he will; and anon he can with his word relax the bonds of adversity, and that in countless ways. Whereas men are tied to two or three methods in accomplishing their will, God is infinite in understanding, and worketh as he wills by ways unguessed of mortal mind.

4. I shall ask you also to consider the works of God in nature in their *swiftness.* It was thought a wonderful thing in the days of Ahasuerus that letters were sent by post upon swift dromedaries. In our country we thought we had arrived at the age of miracles when the axles of our cars glowed with speed, and now that the telegraph is at work we stretch out our hands into infinity: but what is our rapidity compared with that of God's operations? Well does the text say, "He sendeth forth his commandment upon earth: his word runneth very swiftly." Forth went the word, "Open the treasures of snow," and the flakes descended in innumerable multitudes; and then it was said, "Let them be closed," and not another snow-feather was seen. Then spake the Master, "Let the south wind blow and the snow be melted": lo, it disappeared at the voice of his word. Believer, you cannot tell how soon God may come to your help. "He rode upon a cherub and did fly," says David; "yea, he did fly upon the wings of the wind." He will come from above to rescue his beloved. He will rend the heavens and come down; with such speed will he descend, that he will not stay to draw the curtains of heaven, but he will rend them in his haste, and make the mountains to flow down at his feet, that he may deliver those who cry unto him

in the hour of trouble. That mighty God who can melt the ice so speedily can take to himself the same eagle wings, and haste to your deliverance. Arise, O God! and let thy children be helped, and that right early.

5. One other thought: consider the *goodness* of God in all the operations of nature and providence. Think of that goodness negatively. "Who can stand before his cold?" You cannot help thinking of the poor in a hard winter—only a hard heart can forget them when you see the snow lying deep. But suppose that snow continued to fall! What is there to hinder it? The same God who sends us snow for one day could do the like for fifty days if he pleased. Why not? And when the frost pinches us so severely, why should it not be continued month after month? We can only thank the goodness which does not send "His cold" to such an extent that our spirits expire. Travellers towards the North Pole tremble as they think of this question, "Who can stand before his cold?" For cold has a degree of omnipotence in it when God is pleased to let it loose. Let us thank God for the restraining mercy by which he holds the cold in check.

Not only negatively, but positively there is mercy in the snow. Is not that a suggestive metaphor! "He giveth snow *like wool.*" The snow is said to warm the earth; it protects those little plants which have just begun to peep above ground, and might otherwise be frost-bitten: as with a garment of down the snow protects them from the extreme severity of cold. Hence Watts sings, in his version of the hundred-and-forty-seventh Psalm,—

> "His flakes of snow like wool he sends,
> And thus the springing corn defends."

It was an idea of the ancients that snow warmed the heart of the soil, and gave it fertility, and therefore they praised God for it. Certainly there is much mercy in the frost, for pestilence might run a far longer race if it were not that the frost cries to it, "Hitherto shalt thou come, but no farther." Noxious insects would multiply until they devoured the precious fruits of the earth, if sharp nights did not destroy millions of them, so that these pests are swept from off the earth. Though man may think himself a loser by the cold, he is a great ultimate gainer by the decree of Providence which ordains winter. The quaint saying of one of the old writers that "snow is wool, and frost is fire, and ice is bread, and rain is drink," is true, though it sounds like a paradox. There is no doubt that frost in breaking up the soil promotes fruitfulness, and so the ice becomes bread. Thus those agencies, which for the moment deprive our workers of their means of sustenance, are the means by which God supplies every living thing. Mark, then, God's goodness as clearly in the snow and frost as in the thaw which clears the winter's work away.

Christian, remember the goodness of God in the frost of adversity. Rest assured that when God is pleased to send out the biting winds of affliction he is in them, and he is always love, as much love in sorrow as when he breathes upon you the soft south wind of joy. See the loving-kindness of God in every work of his hand! Praise him—he maketh summer and winter—let your song go round the year! Praise him— he giveth day and sendeth night—thank him at all hours! Cast not away your confidence, it hath great recompense of reward. As David wove the snow, and rain, and stormy wind into a song, even so combine your trials, your tribulations, your difficulties and adversities into a sweet psalm of praise, and say perpetually—

"Let us, with a gladsome mind,
   Praise the Lord, for he is kind."

Thus much upon the operations of nature. It is a very tempting theme, but other fields invite me.

II. I would address you very earnestly and solemnly upon THOSE OPERATIONS OF GRACE, OF WHICH FROST AND THAW ARE THE OUTWARD SYMBOLS.

There is a period with God's own people when he comes to deal with them by *the frost of the law*. The law is to the soul as the cutting north wind. Faith can see love in it, but the carnal eye of sense cannot. It is a cold, terrible, comfortless blast. To be exposed to the full force of the law of God would be to be frost-bitten with everlasting destruction; and even to feel it for a season would congeal the marrow of one's bones, and make one's whole being stiff with affright. "Who can stand before his cold?" When the law comes forth thundering from its treasuries, who can stand before it? The effect of law-work upon the soul is to bind up the rivers of human delight. No man can rejoice when the terrors of conscience are upon him. When the law of God is sweeping through the soul, music and dancing lose their joy, the bowl forgets its power to cheer, and the enchantments of earth are broken. The rivers of pleasure freeze to icy despondency. The buds of hope are suddenly nipped, and the soul finds no comfort. It was satisfied once to grow rich, but rust and canker are now upon all gold and silver. Every promising hope is frost-bitten, and the spirit is winter-bound in despair. This cold makes the sinner feel how ragged his garments are. He could strut about, when it was summer weather, and think his rags right royal robes, but now the cold frost finds out every rent in his garment, and in the hands of the terrible law he shivers like the leaves upon the aspen. The north wind of judgment searches the man through and through. He did not know what was in him, but now he sees his inward parts to be filled with corruption and rottenness. These are some of the terrors of the wintry breath of the law.

This frost of law and terrors only tends to harden. Nothing splits the rock or makes the cliff tumble like frost when succeeded by thaw, but frost alone makes the earth like a mass of iron, breaking the ploughshare which would seek to pierce it. A sinner under the influence of the law of God, apart from the gospel, is hardened by despair, and cries, "There is no hope, and therefore after my lusts will I go. Whereas there is no heaven for me after this life, I will make a heaven out of this earth; and since hell awaits me, I will at least enjoy such sweets as sin may afford me here." This is not the fault of the law; the blame lies with the corrupt heart which is hardened by it; yet, nevertheless, such is its effect.

When the Lord has wrought by the frost of the law, he sends *the thaw of the gospel*. When the south wind blows from the land of promise, bringing precious remembrances of God's fatherly pity and tender loving-kindness, then straightway the heart begins to soften, and a sense of blood-bought pardon speedily dissolves it. The eyes fill with tears, the heart melts in tenderness, rivers of pleasure flow freely, and buds of hope open in the cheerful air. A heavenly spring whispers to the flowers that were sleeping in the cold earth; they hear its voice, and lift up their heads, for "the rain is over and gone; the flowers appear on the earth, the time of the singing of birds is come, and the voice of the turtle is heard in our land." God sendeth his Word, saying, "Thy warfare is accomplished, and thy sin is pardoned;"

and when that blessedly cheering word comes with power to the soul, and the sweet breath of the Holy Spirit acts like the warm south wind upon the heart, then the waters flow, and the mind is filled with holy joy, and light, and liberty.

> "The legal wintry state is gone,
> The frosts are fled, the spring comes on,
> The sacred turtle-dove we hear
> Proclaim the new, the joyful year."

Having shown you that there is a parallel between frost and thaw in nature and law and gospel in grace, I would utter the same thoughts concerning grace which I gave you concerning nature.

1. We began with the directness of God's works in nature. Now, beloved friends, remark the *directness of God's works in grace*. When the heart is truly affected by the law of God, when sin is made to appear exceeding sinful, when carnal hopes are frozen to death by the law, when the soul is made to feel its barrenness and utter death and ruin—this is the finger of God. Do not speak of the minister. It was well that he preached earnestly: God has used him as an instrument, but God worketh all. When the thaw of grace comes, I pray you discern the distinct hand of God in every beam of comfort which gladdens the troubled conscience, for it is the Lord alone who bindeth up the broken in heart and healeth all their wounds. We are far too apt to stop in instrumentalities. Folly makes men look to sacraments for heart-breaking or heart-healing, but sacraments all say, "It is not in us." Some of you look to the preaching of the Word, and look no higher; but all true preachers will tell you, "It is not in us." Eloquence and earnestness at their highest pitch can neither break nor heal a heart. This is God's work. Ay, and not God's secondary work in

the sense in which the philosopher admits that God is in the laws of nature, but God's personal and immediate work. He putteth forth his own hand when the conscience is humbled, and it is by his own right hand that the conscience is eased and cleansed.

I desire that this thought may abide upon your minds, for you will not praise God else, nor will you be sound in doctrine. All departures from sound doctrine on the point of conversion arise from forgetfulness that it is a divine work from first to last; that the faintest desire after Christ is as much the work of God as the gift of his dear Son; and that our whole spiritual history through, from the Alpha to the Omega, the Holy Spirit works in us to will and to do of his own good pleasure. As you have evidently seen the finger of God in casting forth his ice and in sending thaw, so I pray you recognise the handiwork of God in giving you a sense of sin, and in bringing you to the Saviour's feet. Join together in heartily praising the wonder-working God, who doeth all things according to the counsel of his will.

> "Our seeking thy face
> Was all of thy grace,
> Thy mercy demands, and shall have all the praise:
> No sinner can be
> Beforehand with thee,
> Thy grace is preventing, almighty and free."

2. The second thought upon nature was *the ease with which the Lord worked.* There was no effort or disturbance. Transfer that to the work of grace. How easy it is for God to send law-work into the soul. Yon stubborn sinner, *you* cannot touch him, and even providence has failed to awaken him. He is dead—altogether dead in trespasses and sins. But if the

glorious Lord will graciously send forth the wind of his Spirit, that will melt him. The swearing reprobate, whose mouth is blackened with profanity, if the Lord doth but look upon him and make bare his arm of irresistible grace, shall yet praise God, and bless his name, and live to his honour. Do not limit the Holy One of Israel. Persecuting Saul became loving Paul, and why should not that person be saved of whose case you almost despair? Your husband may have many points which make his case difficult, but no case is desperate with God. Your son may have offended both against heaven and against you, but God can save the most hardened. The sharpest frost of obstinate sin must yield to the thaw of grace. Even huge icebergs of crime must melt in the Gulf-stream of infinite love.

Poor sinner, I cannot leave this point without a word to you. Perhaps the Master has sent the frost to you, and you think it will never end. Let me encourage you to hope, and yet more, to pray for gracious visitations. Miss Steele's verses will just suit your mournful yet hopeful state.

> "Stern winter throws his icy chains,
>   Encircling nature round:
> How bleak, how comfortless the plains,
>   Late with gay verdure crown'd!
>
> The sun withdraws his vital beams,
>   And light and warmth depart:
> And, drooping lifeless, nature seems
>   An emblem of my heart—
>
> My heart, where mental writer reigns
>   In night's dark mantle clad,
> Confined in cold, inactive chains;
>   How desolate and sad!

> Return, O blissful sun, and bring
>   Thy soul-reviving ray;
> This mental winter shall be spring,
>   This darkness cheerful day."

It is easy for God to deliver you. He says, "I have blotted out like a thick cloud thy transgressions." I stood the other evening looking up at a black cloud which was covering all the heavens, and I thought it would surely rain; I entered the house, and when I came out again the sky was all blue—the wind had driven the cloud away. So may it be with your soul. It is an easy thing for the Lord to put away sin from repenting sinners. All obstacles which hindered our pardon were removed by Jesus when he died upon the tree, and if you believe in him you will find that he has cast your sins into the depths of the sea. If thou canst believe, all things are possible to him that believeth.

3. The next thought concerning the Lord's work in nature was the *variety* of it. Frost produces a sort of trinity in unity—snow, hoarfrost, ice; and when the thaw comes its ways are many. So is it with the work of God in the heart. Conviction comes not alike to all. Some convictions fall as the snow from heaven: you never hear the flakes descend, they alight so gently one upon the other. There are soft-coming convictions: they are felt, but we can scarcely tell when we began to feel them. A true work of repentance may be of the gentlest kind. On the other hand, the Lord casteth forth his ice like morsels, the hailstones rattle against the window, and you think they will surely force their way into the room, and so to many persons convictions come beating down till they remind you of hailstones. There is variety. It is as true a frost which produces the noiseless snow as that which brings forth the

terrible hail. Why should you want hailstones of terror? Be thankful that God has visited you, but do not dictate to him the way of his working.

With regard to the gospel thaw. If you may but be pardoned by Jesus, do not stipulate as to the manner of his grace. Thaw is universal and gradual, but its commencement is not always discernible. The chains of winter are unloosed by degrees: the surface ice and snow melt and by-and-by the warmth permeates the entire mass till every rock of ice gives way. But while thaw is universal and visible in its effects you cannot see the mighty power which is doing all this. Even so you must not expect to discern the Spirit of God. You will find him gradually operating upon the entire man, enlightening the understanding, freeing the will, delivering the heart from fear, inspiring hope, waking up the whole spirit, gradually and universally working upon the mind and producing the manifest effects of comfort, and hope, and peace; but you can no more see the Spirit of God than you can see the south wind. The effect of his power is to be felt, and when you feel it, do not marvel if it be somewhat different from what others have experienced. After all, there is a singular likeness in snow and hoarfrost and ice, and so there is a remarkable sameness in the experience of all God's children; but still there is a great variety in the inward operations of divine grace.

4. We must next notice the *rapidity* of God's works. "His word runneth very swiftly." It did not take many days to get rid of the last snow. A contractor would take many a day to cart it away, but God sendeth forth his word, and the snow and ice disappear at once. So is it with the soul: the Lord often works rapidly when he cheers the heart. You may have been a long time under the operation of his frosty law, but there is no

reason why you should be another hour under it. If the Spirit enables you to trust in the finished work of Christ, you may go out of this house rejoicing that every sin is forgiven. Poor soul, do not think that the way from the horrible pit is to climb, step by step, to the top. Oh no; Jesus can set your feet upon a rock ere the clock shall have gone round the dial. He can in an instant bring you from death to life, from condemnation to justification. "To-day shalt thou be with me in Paradise," was spoken to a dying thief, black and defiled with sin. Only believe in the atoning sacrifice of Jesus Christ, and thou shalt be saved.

5. Our last thought upon the operation of God was *his goodness* in it all. What a blessing that God did not send us more law-work than he did! "Who can stand before his cold?" Oh! beloved, when God has taken away from man natural comfort, and made him feel divine wrath in his soul, it is an awful thing. Speak of a haunted man; no man need be haunted with a worse ghost than the remembrance of his old sins. The childish tale of the sailor with the old man of the mountain on his back, who pressed him more and more heavily, is more than realised in the history of the troubled conscience. If one sin do but leap on a man's back, it will sink the sinner through every standing-place that he can possibly mount upon; he will go down, down, under its weight till he sinks to the lowest depths of hell. There is no place where sin can be borne till you get upon the Rock of Ages, and even there the joy is not that you bear it, but that Jesus has borne it all for you. The spirit would utterly fail before the law, if it had full sway. Thank God, "he stayeth his rough wind in the day of his east wind." At the same time, how thankful we may be, that we ever felt the law-frost in our soul. The folly of self-

righteousness is killed by the winter of conviction. We should have been a thousand times more proud, and foolish, and worldly, than we are, if it had not been for the sharp frost with which the Lord nipped the growths of the flesh.

But how shall we thank him sufficiently for the thaw of his loving-kindness? How great the change which his mercy made in us as soon as its beams had reached our soul! Hardness vanished, cold departed, warmth and love abounded, and the life-floods leaped in their channels. The Lord visited us, and we rose from our grave of despair, even as the seeds arise from the earth. As the bulb of the crocus holds up its golden cup to be filled with sunshine, so did our new-born faith open itself to the glory of the Lord. As the primrose peeps up from the sod to gaze upon the sun, so did our hope look forth for the promise, and delight itself in the Lord. Thank God that spring-tide has with many of us matured into summer, and winter has gone never to return. We praise the Lord for this every day of our lives, and we will praise him when time shall be no more in that sunny land—

> "Where everlasting spring abides,
> And never withering flowers.
> A thread-like stream alone divides
> That heavenly land from ours."

Believe in the Lord, ye who shiver in the frost of the law, and the thaw of love shall soon bring you warm days of joy and peace. So be it. Amen.

The Corn of Wheat dying to bring forth Fruit

"And Jesus answered them, saying, The hour is come, that the Son of man should be glorified. Verily, verily, I say unto you, Except a corn of wheat fall into the ground and die, it abideth alone: but if it die, it bringeth forth much fruit. He that loveth his life shall lose it; and he that hateth his life in this world shall keep it unto life eternal."—John xii. 23-25.

CERTAIN Greeks desired to see Jesus. These were Gentiles, and it was remarkable that they should, just at this time, have sought an interview with our Lord. I suppose that the words "We would see Jesus" did not merely mean that they would like to look at him, for that they could have done in the public streets; but they would "see" him as we speak of seeing a person with whom we wish to hold a conversation. They desired to be introduced to him, and to have a few words of instruction from him.

These Greeks were the advanced guard of that great multitude that no man can number, of all nations, and people, and tongues, who are yet to come to Christ. The Saviour would naturally feel a measure of joy at the sight of them, but he did not say much about it, for his mind was absorbed just then with thoughts of his great sacrifice and its results; yet he took so much notice of the coming of these Gentiles to him that it gave a colour to the words which are here recorded by his servant John.

I notice that the Saviour here *displays his broad humanity,* and announces himself as the "Son of man." He had done so before, but here with new intent. He says, "The hour is come, that the Son of man should be glorified." Not as "the Son of David" does he here speak of himself, but as "the Son of man." No longer does he make prominent the Jewish side of his mission, though as a preacher he was not sent save to the lost sheep of the house of Israel; but as the dying Saviour he speaks of himself as one of the race, not the Son of Abraham, or of David, but "the Son of man": as much brother to the Gentile as to the Jew. Let us never forget the broad humanity of the Lord Jesus. In him all kindreds of the earth are joined in one, for he is not ashamed to bear the nature of our universal manhood; black and white, prince and pauper, sage and savage, all see in his veins the one blood by which all men are constituted one family. As the Son of man Jesus is near akin to every man that lives.

Now, too, that the Greeks were come, our Lord *speaks somewhat of his glory* as approaching. "The hour is come," saith he, "that the Son of man should be glorified." He does not say "that the Son of man should be crucified," though that was true, and the crucifixion must come before the glorification; but the sight of those first-fruits from among the Gentiles makes him dwell upon his glory. Though he remembers his death, he speaks rather of the glory which would grow out of his great sacrifice. Remember, brethren, that Christ is glorified in the souls that he saves. As a physician wins honour by those he heals, so the Physician of souls gets glory out of those who come to him. When these devout Greeks came, saying, "Sirs, we would see Jesus," though a mere desire to see him is only as the green blade, yet he rejoiced in it as the pledge of the harvest, and he saw in it the dawn of the glory of his cross.

I think, too, that the coming of these Greeks somewhat *led the Saviour to use the metaphor of the buried corn.* We are informed that wheat was largely mixed up with Grecian mysteries, but that is of small importance. It is more to the point that our Saviour was then undergoing the process which would burst the Jewish husk in which, if I may use such terms, his human life had been enveloped. I mean this: aforetime our Lord said that he was not sent save to the lost sheep of the house of Israel, and when the Syrophenician woman pleaded for her daughter he reminded her of the restricted character of his commission as a prophet among men. When he sent out the seventy, he bade them not to go into the cities of the Samaritans, but to seek after the house of Israel only. Now, however, that blessed corn of wheat is breaking through its outer integument. Even before it is put into the ground to die the divine corn of wheat begins to show its living power, and the true Christ is being manifested. The Christ of God, though assuredly the Son of David, was, on the Father's side, neither Jew nor Gentile, but simply man; and the great sympathies of his heart were with all mankind. He regarded all whom he had chosen as his own brethren without distinction of sex, or nation, or the period of the world's history in which they should live; and, at the sight of these Greeks, the true Christ came forth and manifested himself to the world as he had not done before. Hence, perhaps, the peculiar metaphor which we have now to explain.

In our text, dear friends, we have two things upon which I will speak briefly, as I am helped of the Spirit. First, we have *profound doctrinal teaching,* and, secondly, we have *practical moral principle.*

First, we have PROFOUND DOCTRINAL TEACHING.

Our Saviour suggested to his thoughtful disciples a number of what might be called doctrinal paradoxes.

First, that, *glorious as he was, he was yet to be*

glorified. "The hour is come, that the Son of man should be glorified." Jesus was always glorious. It was a glorious thing for the human person of the Son of man to be personally one with the Godhead. Our Lord Jesus had also great glory all the while he was on earth in the perfection of his moral character. The gracious end for which he came here was real glory to him: his condescending to be the Saviour of men was a great glorification of his loving character. His way of going about his work—the way in which he consecrated himself to his Father and was always about his Father's business, the way in which he put aside Satan with his blandishments, and would not be bribed by all the kingdoms of the world—all this was his glory. I should not speak incorrectly if I were to say that Christ was really as to his moral nature never more glorious than when throughout his life on earth he was obscure, despised, rejected, and yet the faithful servant of God, and the ardent lover of the sons of men. The apostle says, "The Word was made flesh, and dwelt among us, and we beheld his glory, the glory as of the only begotten of the Father, full of grace and truth," in which he refers not only to the transfiguration, in which there were special glimpses of the divine glory, but to our Lord's tabernacling among men in the common walks of life. Saintly, spiritual minds beheld the glory of his life, the glory of grace and truth such as never before had been seen in any of the sons of men. But though he was thus, to all intents and purposes, already glorious, Jesus had yet to be glorified. Something more was to be added to his personal honour. Remember, then, that when you have the clearest conceptions of your Lord, there is still a glory to be added to all that you can see even with the word of God in your hands. Glorious as the living Son of man had been, there was a further glory to come upon him through his death, his resurrection, and his entrance within the veil. He was a glorious Christ, and yet he had to be glorified.

A second paradox is this,—that *his glory was to come to him through shame.* He says, "The hour is come, that the Son of man should be glorified," and then he speaks of his death. The greatest fulness of our Lord's glory arises out of his emptying himself, and becoming obedient to death, even the death of the cross. It is his highest reputation that he made himself of no reputation. His crown derives new lustre from his cross; his ever living is rendered more honourable by the fact of his dying unto sin once. Those blessed cheeks would never have been so fair as they are in the eyes of his chosen if they had not once been spat upon. Those dear eyes had never had so overpowering a glance if they had not once been dimmed in agonies of death for sinners. His hands are as gold rings set with the beryl, but their brightest adornments are the prints of the cruel nails. As the Son of God his glory was all his own by nature, but as Son of man his present splendour is due to the cross, and to the ignominy which surrounded it when he bore our sins in his own body. We must never forget this, and if ever we are tempted to merge the crucified Saviour in the coming King we should feel rebuked by the fact that thus we should rob our Lord of his highest honour. Whenever you hear men speak lightly of the atonement stand up for it at once, for out of this comes the main glory of your Lord and Master. They say, "Let him come down from the cross, and we will believe on him." If he did so what would remain to be believed? It is on the cross, it is from the cross, it is through the cross that Jesus mounts to his throne, and the Son of man has a special honour in heaven to-day because he was slain and has redeemed us to God by his blood.

The next paradox is this,—*Jesus must be alone or abide alone*. Notice the text as I read it: "Except a corn of wheat fall into the ground and die," and so gets alone, "it abideth alone." The Son of man must be alone in the grave, or he will be alone in heaven, He must fall into the ground like the corn of wheat and be there in the loneliness of death, or else he will abide alone. This is a paradox readily enough explained; our Lord Jesus Christ as the Son of man, unless he had trodden the winepress alone, unless beneath the olives of Gethsemane he had wrestled on the ground, and as it were sunk into the ground until he died, if he had not been there alone, and if on the cross he had not cried, "My God, my God, why hast thou forsaken me?" so that he felt quite deserted and alone, like the buried corn of wheat,—could not have saved us. If he had not actually died he would as man have been alone for ever: not without the eternal Father and the divine Spirit, not without the company of angels; but there had not been another man to keep him company. Our Lord Jesus cannot bear to be alone. A head without its members is a ghastly sight, crown it as you may. Know ye not that the church is his body, the fulness of him that filleth all in all. Without his people Jesus would have been a shepherd without sheep; surely it is not a very honourable office to be a shepherd without a flock. He would have been a husband without his spouse; but he loves his bride so well that for this purpose did he leave his Father and become one flesh with her whom he had chosen. He clave to her, and died for her; and had he not done so he would have been a bridegroom without a bride. This could never be. His heart is not of the kind that can enjoy a selfish happiness which is shared by none. If you have read Solomon's Song, where the heart of the Bridegroom is revealed, you will have seen that he desires the company of his love, his dove, his undefiled. His delights were with the sons of men. Simon Stylites on the top of a pillar is not Jesus Christ; the hermit in his cave may mean well, but he finds no warrant for his solitude in him whose cross he professes to venerate. Jesus was the friend of men, not avoiding them, but seeking the lost. It was truly said of him, "This man receiveth sinners, and eateth with them." He draws all men unto him, and for this cause he was lifted up from the earth. Yet must this great attractive man have been alone in heaven if he had not been alone in Gethsemane, alone before Pilate, alone when mocked by soldiers, and alone upon the cross. If this precious grain of wheat had not descended into the dread loneliness of death it had remained alone, but since he died he "bringeth forth much fruit."

This brings us to the fourth paradox,—*Christ must die to give life.* "Except a corn of wheat fall into the ground and die, it abideth alone: but if it die, it bringeth forth much fruit": Jesus must die to give life to others. Persons who do not think confuse dying with non-existence, and living with existence—very, very different things. "The soul that sinneth it shall die:" it shall never go out of existence, but it shall die by being severed from God who is its life. There are many men who exist, and yet have not true life, and shall not see life, but "the wrath of God abideth on them." The grain of wheat when it is put into the ground dies; do we mean that it ceases to be? Not at all. What is death? It is the resolution of anything possessing life into its primary elements. With us it is the body parting from the soul; with a grain of wheat it is the dissolving of the elements which made up the corn. Our divine Lord when put into the earth did not see corruption, but his soul was parted from his body for a while, and thus he died; and unless he had literally and actually died he could not have given life to any of us.

Beloved friends, this teaches us where the vital point of Christianity lies, *Christ's death is the life of his teaching.* See here: if Christ's preaching had been the essential point, or if his example had been the vital point, he could have brought forth fruit and multiplied Christians by his preaching, and by his example. But he declares that, except he shall die, he shall not bring forth fruit. Am I told that this was because his death would be the completion of his example, and the seal of his preaching? I admit that it was so, but I can conceive that if our Lord had rather continued to live on,—if he had been here constantly going up and down the world preaching and living as he did, and if he had wrought miracles as he did, and put forth that mysterious, attracting power, which was always with him, he might have produced a marvellous number of disciples. If his teaching and living had been the way in which spiritual life could have been bestowed, without an atonement, why did not the Saviour prolong his life on earth? But the fact is that no man among us can know anything about spiritual life except through the atonement. There is no way by which we can come to a knowledge of God except through the precious blood of Jesus Christ by which we have access to the Father. If, as some tell us, the ethical part of Christianity is much more to be thought of than its peculiar doctrines, then, why did Jesus die at all? The ethical might have been brought out better by a long life of holiness. He might have lived on till now if he had chosen, and still have preached, and still have set an example among the sons of men; but he assures us that only by death could he have brought forth fruit. What, not with all that holy living? No. What, not by that matchless teaching? No. Not one among us could have been saved from eternal death except an expiation had been wrought by Jesus' sacrifice. Not one of us could have been quickened into spiritual life except Christ himself had died and risen from the dead.

Brethren, all the spiritual life that there is in the world is the result of Christ's death. We live under a dispensation which shadows forth this truth to us. Life first came into the world by a creation: that was lost in the garden. Since then, the father of our race is Noah, and life by Noah came to us by a typical death, burial, and resurrection. Noah went in unto the ark, and was shut in, and so buried. In that ark Noah went among the dead, himself enveloped in the rain and in the ark, and he came out into a new world, rising again, as it were, when the waters were assuaged. That is the way of life to-day. We are dead with Christ, we are buried with Christ, we are risen with Christ; and there is no real spiritual life in this world except that which has come to us by the process of death, burial, and resurrection with Christ. Do you know anything about this, dear friends?—for if you do not, you know not the life of God. You know the theory, but do you know the experimental power of this within your own spirit? Whenever we hear the doctrine of the atonement attacked, let us stand up for it. Let us tell the world that while we value the life of Christ even more than they do, we know that it is not the example of Christ that saves anybody, but his death for our sakes. If the blessed Christ had lived here all these nineteen hundred years, without sin, teaching all his marvellous precepts with his own sublime and simple eloquence, yet he had not produced one single atom of spiritual life among all the sons of men. Without dying he brings forth no fruit. If you want life, my dear hearer, you will not get it as an unregenerate man by attempting to imitate the example of Christ. You may get good of a certain sort that way, but you will never obtain spiritual life and eternal salvation by that method. You must believe on Jesus as dying for you. You have to understand that the blood of Jesus Christ, God's dear Son, cleanses us from all sin. When you have learned that truth, you shall study his life with advantage; but unless you recognise that the grain of wheat is cast into the ground, and made to die, you will never realise any fruit from it in your own soul, or see fruit in the souls of others.

One other blessed lesson of deep divinity is to be learnt from our text: it is this,—*since Jesus Christ did really fall into the ground and die, we may expect much as the result of it.* "If it die, it bringeth forth much fruit:" Some have a little Christ, and they expect to see little things come of him. I have met with good people who appear to think that Jesus Christ died for the sound people who worship at Zoar Chapel, and, perhaps, for a few more who go to Ebenezer in a neighbouring town, and they hope that one day a chosen few—a scanty company indeed they are, and they do their best by mutual quarrelling to make them fewer—will glorify God for the salvation of a very small remnant. I will not blame these dear brethren, but I do wish that their hearts were enlarged. We do not yet know all the fruit that is to come out of our Lord Jesus. May there not come a day when the millions of London shall worship God with one consent? I look for a day when the knowledge of the glory of God shall cover the earth as the waters cover the sea, when kings shall fall down before the Son of God, and all nations shall call him blessed. "It is too much to expect," says one; "missions make very slow progress." I know all that, but missions are not the seed: all that we look for is to come out of that corn of wheat which fell into the ground and died: this is to bring forth much fruit. When I think of my Master's blessed person as perfect Son of God and Son of man; when I think of the infinite glory which he laid aside, and of the unutterable pangs he bore, I ask whether angels can compute the value of the sacrifice he offered? God only knows the love of God that was manifested in the death of his Son, and do you think that there will be all this planning and working and sacrifice of infinite love, and then an insignificant result? It is not like God that it should be so. The travail of the Son of God shall not bring forth a scanty good. The result shall be commensurate with the means, and the effect shall be parallel with the cause. The Lord shall reign for ever and ever. Hallelujah! Ay, as the groanings of the cross must have astounded angels, so shall the results of the cross amaze the seraphim, and make them admire the excess of glory which has arisen from the shameful death of their Lord. O beloved, great things are to come out of our Jesus yet. Courage, you that are dispirited. Be brave, you soldiers of the cross. Victory awaits your banner. Wait patiently, work hopefully, suffer joyfully, for the kingdom is the Lord's, and he is the governor among the nations.

Thus have I spoken upon profound divinity.

I close with a few words upon PRACTICAL INSTRUCTION. Learn now that what is true of Christ is in measure true of every child of God: "Except a corn of wheat fall into the ground and die, it abideth alone: but if it die, it bringeth forth much fruit." This is so far applicable to us, as the next verse indicates,—"He that loveth his life shall lose it; and he that hateth his life in this world shall keep it unto life eternal."

First, *we must die if we are to live.* There is no spiritual life for you, for me, for any man, except by

dying into it. Have you a fine-spun righteousness of
your own? It must die. Have you any faith in yourself?
It must die. The sentence of death must be in yourself,
and then you shall enter into life. The withering power
of the Spirit of God must be experienced before his
quickening influence can be known: "The grass
withereth, the flower fadeth because the spirit of the
Lord bloweth upon it." You must be slain by the sword
of the Spirit before you can be made alive by the breath
of the Spirit.

Next, *we must surrender everything to keep it.* "He
that loveth his life shall lose it." Brother, you can never
have spiritual life, hope, joy, peace, heaven, except by
giving everything up into God's hands. You shall have
everything in Christ when you are willing to have
nothing of your own. You must ground your weapons
of rebellion, you must drop the plumes of your pride,
you must give up into God's hand all that you are and
all that you have; and if you do not thus lose everything
in will, you shall lose everything in fact; indeed, you
have lost it already. A full surrender of everything to
God is the only way to keep it. Some of God's people
find this literally true. I have known a mother keep
back her child from God, and the child has died.
Wealthy people have worshipped their wealth, and as
they were God's people, he has broken their idols into
shivers. You must lose your all if you would keep it,
and renounce your most precious thing if you would
have it preserved to you.

Next, *we must lose self in order to find self.* "He that
hateth his life shall keep it unto life eternal." You must
entirely give up living for yourself, and then you
yourself shall live. The man who lives for himself does
not live; he loses the essence, the pleasure, the crown
of existence; but if you live for others and for God you

will find the life of life. "Seek ye first the kingdom of God and his righteousness, and all these things shall be added unto you." There is no way of finding yourself in personal joy like losing yourself in the joy of others.

Once more: if you *wish to be the means of life to others, you must in your measure die yourself.* "Oh," say you, "will it actually come to death?" Well, it may not but you should be prepared for it if it should. Who have most largely blessed the present age? I will tell you I believe we owe our gospel liberties mainly to the poor men and women who died at the stake for the faith. Call them Lollards, Anabaptists, or what you will, the men who died for it gave life to the holy cause. Some of all ranks did this, from bishops downward to poor boys. Many of them could not preach from the pulpit, but they preached grander sermons from the faggots than all the reformers could thunder from their rostrums. They fell into the ground and died, and the "much fruit" abides to this day. The self-sacrificing death of her saints was the life and increase of the church. If we wish to achieve a great purpose, establish a great truth, and raise up a great agency for good, it must be by the surrender of ourselves, yea, of our very lives to the one all-absorbing purpose. Not else can we succeed. There is no giving it to others, without taking so much out of yourself. He who serves God and finds that it is easy work will find it hard work to give in his account at the last. A sermon that costs nothing is worth nothing; if it did not come from the heart it will not go to the heart. Take it as a rule that wear and tear must go on, even to exhaustion, if we are to be largely useful. Death precedes growth. The Saviour of others cannot save himself. We must not, therefore, grudge the lives of those who die under the evil climate of Africa, if they die for Christ; nor must we murmur if here and there God's best servants are cut down by brain exhaustion: it is the law of divine husbandry that by death cometh increase.

And you, dear friend, must not say, "Oh, I cannot longer teach in the Sunday-school: I work so hard all the week that I—I—I"—shall I finish the sentence for you? You work so hard for yourself all the week that you cannot work for God one day in the week. Is that it? "No, not quite so, but I am so fagged." Very true, but think of your Lord. He knew what weariness was for you, and yet he wearied not in well doing. You will never come to sweat of blood as he did. Come, dear friend, will you be a corn of wheat laid up on the shelf alone? Will you be like that wheat in the mummy's hand, unfruitful and forgotten or would you grow? I hear you say, "Sow me somewhere." I will try to do so. Let me drop you into the Sunday-school field, or into the Tract-lending acre, or into the Street-preaching parcel of land. "But if I make any great exertion it will half kill me." Yes; and if it shall quite kill, you will then prove the text, "If it die, it bringeth forth much fruit." Those who have killed themselves of late in our Lord's service are not so numerous that we need be distressed by the fear that an enormous sacrifice of life is likely to occur. Little cause is there just now to repress fanaticism, but far more reason to denounce to self-seeking. O, my brethren, let us rise to a condition of consecration more worthy of our Lord and of his glorious cause, and henceforth may we be eager to be as the buried, bidden, dying, yet fruit-bearing wheat for the glory of our Lord. Thus have I merely glanced at the text; another day may it be our privilege to dive into its depths.

The Ploughman

"Doth the plowman plow all day to sow?"—Isaiah xxviii. 24.

NLESS they are cultivated, fields yield us nothing but briars and thistles. In this we may see ourselves. Unless the great Husbandman shall till us by his grace, we shall produce nothing that is good, but everything that is evil. If one of these days I shall hear that a country has been discovered where wheat grows without the work of the farmer, I may then, perhaps, hope to find one of our race who will bring forth holiness without the grace of God. Hitherto all land on which the foot of man has trodden has needed labour and care; and even so among men the need of gracious tillage is universal. Jesus says to all of us, "Ye must be born again." Unless God the Holy Spirit breaks up the heart with the plough of the law, and sows it with the seed of the gospel, not a single ear of holiness will any of us produce, even though we may be children of godly parents, and may be regarded as excellent moral people by those with whom we live.

Yes, and the plough is needed not only to produce that which is good, but to destroy that which is evil. There are diseases which, in the course of ages, wear themselves out, and do not appear again among men; and there may be forms of vice which, under changed circumstances, do not so much abound as they used to do; but human nature will always remain the same, and therefore there will always be plentiful crops of the weeds of sin in man's fields, and nothing can keep these under but spiritual husbandry, carried on by the Spirit of God. You cannot destroy weeds by exhortations, nor can you tear out the roots of sin from the soul by moral suasion; something sharper and more effectual must be brought to bear upon them. God must put his own right hand to the plough, or the hemlock of sin will never give place to the corn of holiness. Good is never spontaneous in unrenewed humanity, and evil is never cut up till the ploughshare of almighty grace is driven through it.

The text leads our thoughts in this direction, and gives us practical guidance through asking the simple question, "Doth the ploughman plough all day to sow?" *This question may be answered in the affirmative,* "Yes, in the proper season he does plough all day to sow"; and, secondly, *this text may more properly be answered in the negative,* "No, the ploughman does not plough every day to sow; he has other work to do according to the season."

I. First, our text may be ANSWERED IN THE AFFIRMATIVE,—"Yes, the ploughman does plough all day to sow." When it is ploughing time he keeps on at it till his work is done; if it requires one day, or two days, or twenty days to finish his fields, he continues at his task while the weather permits. The perseverance of the ploughman is instructive, and it teaches us a double lesson. When the Lord comes to plough the heart of man he ploughs all day, and herein is his patience; and, secondly, so ought the Lord's servants to labour all day with men's hearts, and herein is our perseverance.

"Doth the ploughman plough all day?" *So doth God plough the heart of man, and herein is his patience.* The team was in the field in the case of some of us very early in the morning, for our first recollections have to do with conscience and the furrows of pain which it made in our youthful mind. When we were little children we woke in the night under a sense of sin; our father's teaching and our mother's prayers made deep and painful impressions upon us, and though we did not then yield our hearts to God, we were greatly stirred, and all indifference to religion was made impossible. When we were boys at school the reading of a chapter in the Word of God, or the death of a playmate, or an address at a Bible-class, or a solemn sermon, so affected us that we were uneasy for weeks. The strivings of the Spirit of God within urged us to think of higher and better things. Though we quenched the Spirit, though we stifled conviction, yet we bore the marks of the ploughshare; furrows were made in the soul, and certain foul weeds of evil were cut up by the roots although no seed of grace was as yet sown in our hearts. Some have continued in this state for many years, ploughed but not sown; but, blessed be God, it was not so with others of us; for we had not left boyhood before the good seed of the gospel fell upon our heart. Alas! there are many who do not thus yield to grace, and with them the ploughman ploughs all day to sow. I have seen the young man coming to London in his youth, yielding to its temptations, drinking in its poisoned sweets, violating his conscience, and yet continuing unhappy in it all, fearful, unrestful, stirred about even as the soil is agitated by the plough. In how many cases has this kind of work gone on for years, and all to no avail. Ah! and I have known the man come to middle life, and still he has not received the good seed, neither has the ground of his hard heart been thoroughly broken up. He has gone on in business without God: day after day he has risen and gone to bed again with no more religion than his horses, and yet all this while there have been ringing in his ears warnings of judgment to come, and chidings of conscience, so that he has not been at peace. After a powerful sermon he has not enjoyed his meals, or been able to sleep, for he has asked himself, "what shall I do in the end thereof?" The ploughman has ploughed all day, till the evening shadows have lengthened and the day has faded to a close. What a mercy it is when the furrows are at last made ready and the good seed is cast in, to be received, nurtured, and multiplied a hundredfold.

It is mournful to remember that we have seen this ploughing continue till the sun has touched the horizon and the night dews have begun to fall. Even then the long-suffering God has followed up his work—ploughing, ploughing, ploughing, ploughing, till darkness ended all. Do I address any aged ones whose lease must soon run out? I would affectionately beseech them to consider their position. What! Three score years old and yet unsaved? Forty years did God suffer the manners of Israel in the wilderness, but he has borne with you for sixty years. Seventy years old, and yet unregenerated! Ah, my friend, you will have but little time in which to serve your Saviour before

you go to heaven. But will you go there at all? Is it not
growing dreadfully likely that you will die in your sins
and perish for ever? How happy are those who are
brought to Christ in early life; but still remember—

> "While the lamp holds out to burn,
> The vilest sinner may return."

It is late, it is very late, but it is not too late. The
ploughman ploughs all day; and the Lord waits that
he may be gracious unto you. I have seen many aged
persons converted, and therefore I would encourage
other old folks to believe in Jesus. I once read a
sermon in which a minister asserted that he had
seldom known any converted who were over forty years
of age if they had been hearers of the gospel all their
lives. There is certainly much need to caution those
who are guilty of delay, but there must be no
manufacturing of facts. Whatever that minister might
think, or even observe, my own observation leads me
to believe that about as many people are converted to
God at one age as at another, taking into consideration
the fact that the young are much more numerous than
the old. It is a dreadful thing to have remained an
unbeliever all these years; but yet the grace of God
does not stop short at a certain age; those who enter
the vineyard at the eleventh hour shall have their
penny, and grace shall be glorified in the old as well
as in the young. Come along, old friend, Jesus Christ
invites you to come to him even now, though you have
stood out so long. You have been a sadly tough piece
of ground, and the ploughman has ploughed all day;
but if at last the sods are turned, and the heart is
lying in ridges, there is hope of you yet.

"Doth the ploughman plough all day?" I answer,—
Yes, however long the day may be, God in mercy

ploughs still, he is long-suffering, and full of tenderness and mercy and grace. Do not spurn such patience, but yield to the Lord who has acted towards you with so much gentle love.

The text, however, not only sets forth patience on God's part, but it teaches *perseverance on our part.* "Doth the ploughman plough all day?" Yes, he does; then if I am seeking Christ, ought I to be discouraged because I do not immediately find him? The promise is, "He that asketh, receiveth; and he that seeketh, findeth; and to him that knocketh it shall be opened." There may be reasons why the door is not opened at our first knock. What then? "Doth the ploughman plough all day?" Then will I knock all day. It may be at the first seeking I may not find; what then? "Doth the ploughman plough all day?" Then will I seek all day. It may happen that at my first asking I shall not receive; what then? "Doth the ploughman plough all day?" Then will I ask all day. Friends, if you have begun to seek the Lord, the short way is, "Believe on the Lord Jesus Christ, and thou shalt be saved." Do that at once. In the name of God do it at once, and you are saved at once. May the Spirit of God bring you to faith in Jesus, and you are at once in the kingdom of Christ. But if peradventure in seeking the Lord, you are ignorant of this, or do not see your way, never give up seeking; get to the foot of the cross, lay hold of it, and cry, "If I perish I will perish here. Lord, I come to thee in Jesus Christ for mercy, and if thou art not pleased to look at me immediately, and forgive my sins, I will cry to thee till thou dost." When God's Holy Spirit brings a man to downright earnest prayer which will not take a denial, he is not far from peace. Careless indifference and shilly-shallying with God hold men in bondage. They find peace when their hearts are roused to strong resolve to seek until they find. I like to see men search the Scriptures till they learn the way of salvation, and hear the gospel till their souls live by it. If they are resolved to drive the plough through doubts, and fears, and difficulties, till they come to salvation, they shall soon come to it by the grace of God.

The same is true in seeking the salvation of others. "Doth the ploughman plough all day?" Yes, when it is ploughing-time. Then, so will I work on, and on, and on. I will pray and preach, or pray and teach, however long the day may be that God shall appoint me, for—

> "'Tis all my business here below
> The precious gospel seed to sow."

Brother worker, are you getting a little weary? Never mind, rouse yourself, and plough on for the love of Jesus, and dying men. Our day of work has in it only the appointed hours, and while they last let us fulfil our task. Ploughing is hard work; but as there will be no harvest without it, let us just put forth all our strength, and never flag till we have performed our Lord's will, and by his Holy Spirit wrought conviction in men's souls. Some soils are very stiff, and cling together, and the labour is heart-breaking; others are like the unreclaimed waste, full of roots and tangled bramble; they need a steam-plough, and we must pray the Lord to make us such, for we cannot leave them untilled, and therefore we must put forth more strength that the labour may be done.

I heard some time ago of a minister who called to see a poor man who was dying, but he was not able to gain admittance; he called the next morning, and some idle excuse was made so that he could not see him; he called again the next morning, but he was still refused; he went on till he called twenty times in vain, but on the twenty-first occasion he was permitted to see the sufferer, and by God's grace he saved a soul from death. "Why do you tell your child a thing twenty times?" asked some one of a mother. "Because," said she, "I find nineteen times is not enough." Now, when a soul is to be ploughed, it may so happen that hundreds of furrows will not do it. What then? why, plough all day till the work is done. Whether you are ministers, missionaries, teachers, or private soul-winners, never grow weary, for your work is noble, and the reward of it is infinite. The grace of God is seen in our being permitted to engage in such holy service; it is greatly magnified in sustaining us in it and it will be pre-eminently conspicuous in enabling us to hold out till we can say, "I have finished the work which thou gavest me to do."

We prize that which costs us labour and service, and we shall set all the higher value upon the saved ones when the Lord grants them to our efforts. It is good for us to learn the value of our sheaves by going forth weeping to the sowing. When you think of the ploughman's ploughing all day, be moved to plod on in earnest efforts to win souls. Seek—

> "With cries, entreaties, tears to save
> And snatch them from the fiery wave."

Doth the ploughman plough all day for a little bit of oats or barley, and will not you plough all day for souls that shall live for ever, if saved, to adore the grace of God, or shall live for ever if unsaved, in outer darkness and woe? Oh, by the terrors of the wrath to come, and the glory that is to be revealed, gird up your loins, and plough all day.

I would beg all the members of our churches to keep

their hands on the gospel plough, and their eyes straight before them. "Doth the ploughman plough all day?" let Christians do the same. Start close to the hedge, and go right down to the bottom of the field. Plough as close to the ditch as you can, and leave small headlands. What though there are fallen women, thieves, and drunkards in the slums around, do not neglect any of them; for if you leave a stretch of land to the weeds they will soon spread amongst the wheat. When you have gone right to the end of the field once, what shall you do next? Why, just turn round, and make for the place you started from. And when you have thus been up and down, what next? Why, up and down again. And what next? Why, up and down again. You have visited that district with tracts; do it again, fifty-two times in the year—multiply your furrows. We must learn how to continue in well doing. Your eternal destiny is to go on doing good for ever and ever, and it is well to go through a rehearsal here. So just plough on, plough on, and look for results as the reward of continued perseverance. Ploughing is not done with a skip and a jump: the ploughman ploughs all day. Dash and flash are all very fine in some things, but not in ploughing: there the work must be steady, persistent, regular. Certain persons soon give it up, it wears out their gloves, blisters their soft hands, tires their bones, and makes them eat their bread rather more in the sweat of their face than they care for. Those whom the Lord fills with his grace will keep to their ploughing year after year, and verily I say unto you, they shall have their reward. "Doth the ploughman plough all day?" Then let us do the same, being assured that one day every hill and valley shall be tilled and sown, and every desert and wilderness shall yield a harvest for our Lord, and the angel reapers shall descend, and the shouts of the harvest-home shall fill both earth and heaven.

II. But, now, somewhat briefly, THE TEXT MAY BE ANSWERED IN THE NEAGTIVE. "Doth the ploughman plough all day to sow?" No, he does not always plough. After he has ploughed he breaks the clods, sows, reaps, and threshes. In the chapter before us you will see that other works of husbandry are mentioned, The ploughman has many other things to do beside ploughing. There is an advance in what he does; this teaches us that there is the like on God's part, and should be the like on ours.

First, *on God's part, there is an advance in what he does.* "Doth the ploughman plough all day?" No, he goes forward to other matters. It may be that in the case of some of you the Lord has been using certain painful agencies to plough you. You are feeling the terrors of the law, the bitterness of sin, the holiness of God, the weakness of the flesh, and the shadow of the wrath to come. Is this going to last for ever? Will it continue till the spirit fails and the soul expires? Listen: "Doth the ploughman plough all day?" No, he is preparing for something else—he ploughs to sow. Thus doth the Lord deal with you; therefore be of good courage, there is an end to the wounding and slaying, and better things are in store for you. You are poor and needy, and you seek water, and there is none, and your tongue faileth for thirst; but the Lord will hear you, and deliver you. He will not contend for ever, neither will he be always wroth. He will turn again, and he will have compassion upon us. He will not always make furrows by his chiding, he will come and cast in the precious corn of consolation, and water it with the dews of heaven, and smile upon it with the sunlight of his grace; and there shall soon be in you, first the blade, then the ear, after that the full corn in the ear, and in due season you shall joy as with the joy of harvest. O ye who are sore wounded in the place of dragons, I hear you cry, Doth God always send terror and conviction of sin? Listen to this,—"If ye be willing and obedient ye shall eat the good of the land," and what is the call of God to the willing and obedient but this, "Believe on the Lord Jesus Christ and thou shalt be saved"? Thou shalt be saved now, find peace now, if thou wilt have done with thyself and all looking to thine own good works to save thee, and wilt turn to him who paid the ransom for thee upon the tree. The Lord is gentle and tender and full of compassion, be will not always chide, neither will he keep his anger for ever. Many of your doubts and fears come of unbelief, or of Satan, or of the flesh, and are not of God at all. Blame him not for what he does not send, and does not wish you to suffer. His mind is for your peace, not for your distress; for thus he speaks— "Comfort ye, comfort ye my people, saith your God. Speak ye comfortably to Jerusalem, and cry unto her, that her warfare is accomplished, that her iniquity is pardoned." "I have blotted out, as a thick cloud, thy transgressions, and, as a cloud, thy sins: return unto me; for I have redeemed thee." He has smitten, but he will smile; he has wounded, but he will heal; he has slain, but he will make alive; therefore turn unto him at once and receive comfort at his hands. The ploughman does not plough for ever; else would he reap no harvest; and God is not always heart-breaking, he also draws near on heart-healing errands.

You see, then, that the great husbandman advances from painful agencies, and I want you to mark that he goes on to *productive work* in the hearts of his people. He will take away the furrows, you shall not see them, for the corn will cover them with beauty. As she that was in travail remembers no more her sorrow for joy that a man is born into the world, so shall you, who are under the legal rod, remember no more the misery of conviction, for God will sow you with grace, and make your soul, even your poor, barren soul to bring forth fruit unto his praise and glory. "Oh!" says one, "I wish that would come true to me." It will. "Doth the ploughman plough all day to sow?" You expect by-and-by to see ploughed fields clothed with springing corn; and you may look to see repentant hearts gladdened with forgiveness. Therefore, be of good courage.

You shall advance, also, to a *joyful experience.* See that ploughman; he whistles as he ploughs, he does not own much of this world's goods, but yet he is merry. He looks forward to the day when he will be on the top of the big waggon, joining in the shout of the harvest home, and so he ploughs in hope, expecting a crop. And, dear soul, God will yet joy and rejoice over you when you believe in Jesus Christ, and you, too, shall be brimful of joy. Be of good cheer, the better portion is yet to come, press forward to it. Gospel sorrowing leads on to gospel hoping, believing, rejoicing, and the rejoicing knows no end. God will not chasten all day, but he will lead you on from strength to strength, from glory unto glory, till you shall be like himself. This, then, is the advance that there is in God's work among men, from painful agencies to productive work and joyful experience.

But what if the ploughing should never lead to sowing; what if you should be disturbed in conscience, and should go on to resist it all? Then God will make another advance, but it will be to put up the plough, and to command the clouds that they rain no rain upon the land, and then its end is to be burned. Oh! man, there is nothing more awful than for your soul to be left to go out of cultivation; God himself giving you up. Surely that is hell. He that is unholy will be unholy still. The law of fixity of character will operate eternally, and no hand of the merciful One shall come near to till the soul again. What worse than this can happen?

We conclude by saying that *this advance is a lesson to us;* for we, too, are to go forward. "Doth the ploughman plough all day?" No, he ploughs to sow, and in due time he sows. Some churches seem to think that all they have to do is to plough; at least, all they attempt is a kind of scratching of the soil, and talking of what they are going to do. It is fine talk, certainly; but doth the ploughman plough all day? You may draw up a large programme and promise great things; but pray do not stop there. Don't be making furrows all day; do get to your sowing. I fancy that those who promise most perform the least. Men who do much in the world have no programme at first, their course works itself out by its own inner force by the grace of God: they do not propose, but perform. They do not plough all day to sow, but they are like our Lord's servant in the parable, of whom he saith, "the sower went forth to sow."

Let the ministers of Christ also follow the rule of advance. *Let us go from preaching the law to preaching the gospel.* " Doth the ploughman plough all day?" He does plough: he would not sow in hope if he had not first prepared the ground. Bobbie Flockart, who preached for years in the Edinboro' streets, says, "It is in vain to sew with the silk thread of the gospel, unless you use the sharp needle of the law." Some of my brethren do not care to preach eternal wrath and its terrors. This is a cruel mercy, for they ruin souls by hiding from them their ruin. If they must needs try to sew without a needle, I cannot help it; but I do not mean to be so foolish myself; my needle may be old-fashioned, but it is sharp, and when it carries with it the silken thread of the gospel, I am sure good work is done by it. You cannot get a harvest if you are afraid of disturbing the soil, nor can you save souls if you never warn them of hell fire. We must tell the sinner what God has revealed about sin, righteousness, and judgment to come. Still, brethren, we must not plough all day. No, no, the preaching of the law is only preparatory to the preaching of the gospel. The stress of our business lies in proclaiming glad tidings. We are not followers of John the Baptist, but of Jesus Christ; we are not rugged prophets of woe, but joyful heralds of grace. Be not satisfied with revival services, and stirring appeals, but preach the doctrines of grace so as to bring out the full compass of covenant truth. Ploughing has had its turn, now for planting and watering. Reproof may now give place to consolation. We are first to make disciples of men, and then to teach them to observe all things whatsoever Jesus has commanded us. We must pass on from the rudiments to the higher truths, from laying foundations to further upbuilding.

And now, another lesson to those of you who are as yet hearers and nothing more. I want you to go from ploughing to something better, namely, *from hearing and fearing to believing.* How many years some of you have been hearing the gospel! Do you mean to continue in that state for ever? Will you never believe in him of whom you hear so much? You have been stirred up a good deal; the other night you went home almost broken-hearted; I should think you are

ploughed enough by this time; and yet you have not
received the seed of eternal life, for you have not
believed in the Lord Jesus. It is dreadful to be always
on the brink of everlasting life, and yet never to be
alive. It will be an awful thing to be almost in heaven,
and yet for ever shut out. It is a wretched thing to
rush into a railway-station just in time to see the train
steaming out; I had much rather be half-an-hour
behind time. To lose a train by half-a-second is most
annoying. Alas, if you go on as you have done for years,
you will have your hand on the latch of heaven and
yet be shut out. You will be within a hair's breadth of
glory, and yet be covered with eternal shame. O
beware of being so near to the kingdom, and yet lost;
almost, but not altogether saved. God grant that you
may not be among those who are ploughed, and
ploughed, and ploughed, and yet never sown. It will
be of no avail at the last to cry, "Lord, we have eaten
and drunk in thy presence, and thou hast taught in
our streets. We had a seat at the chapel, we attended
the services on week-nights as well as on Sundays,
we went to prayer-meetings, we joined a Bible-class,
we distributed tracts, we subscribed our guinea to the
funds, we gave up every open sin, we used a form of
prayer, and read a chapter of the Bible every day."
All these things may be done, and yet there may be
no saving faith in the Lord Jesus. Take heed lest your
Lord should answer, "With all this, your heart never
came to me; therefore, depart from me, I never knew
you." If Jesus once knows a man he always knows
him. He can never say to *me*, "I never knew you," for
he has known me as his poor dependent, a beggar for
years at his door. Some of you have been all that is
good except that you never came into contact with
Christ, never trusted him, never knew him. Ah me,

how sad your state! Will it be always so?

Lastly, I would say to you who are being ploughed, and are agitated about your souls, Go at once to the next stage of believing. Oh! if people did but know how simple a thing believing is, surely they would believe. Alas, they do not know it, and it becomes all the more difficult to them because in itself it is so easy. The difficulty of believing lies in there being no difficulty in it. "If the prophet had bid thee do some great thing, wouldst thou not have done it?" Oh, yes, you would have done it, and you would have thought it easy too; but when he simply says, "Wash, and be clean," there is a difficulty with pride and self. If you can truly say that you are willing to abase your pride, and do anything which the Lord bids you, then I pray you understand that there is no further preparation required, and believe in Jesus at once. May the Holy Spirit make you sick of self, and ready to accept the gospel. The word is nigh thee, let it be believed; it is in thy mouth, let it be swallowed down; it is in thy heart, let it be trusted. With your heart believe in Jesus, and with your mouth make confession of him, and you shall be saved. A main part of faith lies in the giving up of all other confidences. O give up at once every false hope. I tried once to show what faith was by quoting Dr. Watts' lines

> "A guilty, weak, and helpless worn,
>   On thy kind arms I fall.
>   Be thou my strength, and righteousness,
>   My Jesus and my all."

I tried to represent faith as failing into Christ's arms, and I thought I made it so plain that the wayfaring man could not err therein. When I had finished preaching, a young man came to me and said,

"But, sir, I cannot fall upon Christ's arms." I replied at once, "Tumble into them anyhow; faint away into Christ's arms, or die into Christ's arms, so long as you get there." Many talk of what they can do and what they cannot do, and I fear they miss the vital point. Faith is leaving off can-ing and cannot-ing, and leaving it all to Christ, for *he* can do all things, though you can do nothing. "Doth the ploughman plough all day to sow?" No, he makes progress, and goes from ploughing to sowing. Go, and do thou likewise: sow unto the Spirit the precious seed of faith in Christ, and the Lord will give thee a joyous harvest.

Ploughing the Rock

"Shall horses run upon the rock? will one plow there with oxen?"—Amos vi. 12.

THESE expressions are proverbs, taken from the familiar sayings of the east country. A proverb is generally a sword with two edges, or, if I may so say, it has many edges, or is all edge, and hence it may be turned this way and that way, and every part of it will have force and point. A proverb has often many bearings, and you cannot always tell what was the precise meaning of him who uttered it. The connection would abundantly tolerate two senses in this place. An ancient commentator asserts that it has seven meanings, and that any one of them would be consistent with the context. I cannot deny the assertion, and if it be correct it is only one among many instances of the manifold wisdom of the Word of God. Like those curiously carved Chinese balls in

which there is one ball within another, so in many a
holy text there is sense within sense, teaching within
teaching, and each one worthy of the Spirit of God.

The first sense of the text upon which I would say
just a word or two is this: the prophet is expostulating
with ungodly men upon their *pursuit of happiness
where it never can be found.* They were endeavouring
to grow rich and great and strong by oppression. The
prophet says, "Ye have turned judgment into gall, and
the fruit of righteousness into hemlock." Justice was
bought and sold among them, and the book of the law
was made the instrument of fraud. "Yet," says the
prophet, "there is no gain to be gotten this way—no
real profit, no true happiness. As well may horses run
upon a rock, and oxen plough the sand: it is labour
in vain."

If any of you try to content yourselves with this
world, and hope to find a heaven in the midst of your
business and your family without looking upward for
it, you labour in vain. If you hope to find pleasure in
sin, and think that it will go well with you if you
despise the law of God, you will make a great mistake.
You might as well seek for roses in the grottoes of the
sea, or look for pearls on the pavements of the city.
You will find what your soul requires nowhere but in
God. To seek after happiness in evil deeds is to plough
a rock of granite. To labour after true prosperity by
dishonest means is as useless as to till the sandy
shore. "Wherefore do you spend your money for that
which is not bread, and your labour for that which
satisfieth not?" Young man, you are killing yourself
with ambition; you seek your own honour and
emolument, and this is a poor, poor object for an
immortal soul. And you, too, sir, are wearing out your
life with care; your mind and body both fail you in

endeavouring to amass riches, as if a man's life consisted in the abundance of the things which he possesses: you are ploughing a rock; your cares will not bring you joy of heart or content of spirit; your toil will end in failure. And you, too, who labour to weave a righteousness by your works apart from Christ, and fancy that with the diligent use of outward ceremonies you may be able to do the work of the Holy Spirit upon your own heart, you, too, are ploughing thankless rock. The strength of fallen nature exerted at its utmost can never save a soul. Why, then, plough the rock any longer? Give over the foolish task.

So far, I believe, we have not misread the text, but have mentioned a very probable meaning of the words; still, another strikes me, which I think equally suitable, and upon it I shall dwell, by God's help.

It is this. *God will not always send his ministers to call men to repentance.* When men's hearts remain obdurate, and they do not and will not repent, then God will not always deal with them in mercy. "My Spirit shall not always strive with man." There is a time of ploughing, but when it is evident that the heart is wilfully hardened, then wisdom itself suggests to mercy that she should give over her efforts. "Shall horses run upon the rock? will one plow there with oxen?" No, there is a limit to the efforts of kindness, and in fulness of time the labour ceases, and the rock remains unploughed henceforth and for ever.

I. Taking that sense, we shall speak upon it, and remark, first, that MINISTERS LABOUR TO BREAK UP MEN'S HEARTS: the wise preacher tries by the power of the Holy Ghost to break up the hard clods of the heart, so that it may receive the heavenly seed.

Many truths are used like sharp ploughshares to

break up the heart. Men must be made to feel that
they have sinned, and they must be led to repent of
sin. They must receive Christ, not with the head only,
but with the heart; for with the heart man believeth
unto righteousness. There must be emotion: we must
cut into the heart with the ploughshare of the law. A
farmer who is too tender-hearted to tear up and
harrow the land will never see a harvest. Here is the
failing of certain divines, they are afraid of hurting
anyone's feelings, and so they keep clear of all the
truths which are likely to excite fear or grief. They have
not a sharp ploughshare on their premises, and are
never likely to have a stack in their rickyard. They
angle without hooks for fear of hurting the fish, and
fire without bullets out of respect to the feelings of
the birds. This kind of love is real cruelty to men's
souls. It is much the same as if a surgeon should
permit a patient to die because he would not pain him
with the lancet, or by the necessary removal of a limb.
It is a terrible tenderness which leaves men to sink
into hell rather than distress their minds. It is pleasant
to prophesy smooth things, but woe unto the man who
thus degrades himself. Is this the spirit of Christ? Did
he conceal the sinner's peril? Did he cast doubts upon
the unquenchable fire and the undying worm? Did he
lull souls into slumber by smooth strains of flattery?
Nay, but with honest love and anxious concern he
warned men of the wrath to come, and bade them
repent or perish. Let the servant of the Lord Jesus in
this thing follow his Master, and plough deep with a
sharp ploughshare, which will not be baulked by the
hardest clods. This we must school ourselves to do. If
we really love the souls of men, let us prove it by
honest speech. The hard heart must be broken, or it
will still refuse the Saviour who was sent to bind up

the broken-hearted. There are some things which men may or may not have, and yet may be saved; but those things which go with the ploughing of the heart are indispensable; there must be a holy fear and a humble trembling before God, there must be an acknowledgment of guilt and a penitent petition for mercy; there must, in a word, be a thorough ploughing of the soul before we can expect the seed to bring forth fruit.

II. But the text indicates to us that AT TIMES MINISTERS LABOUR IN VAIN. "Shall horses run upon the rock? will one plow there with oxen?" In a short time a ploughman feels whether the plough will go or not, and so does the minister. He may use the very same words in one place which he has used in another, but he feels in the one place great joy and hopefulness in preaching, while with another audience he has heavy work, and little hope. The plough in the last case seems to jump out of the furrow; and a bit of the share is broken off now and then. He says to himself, "I do not know how it is, but I do not get on at this," and he finds that his Master has sent him to work upon a particularly heavy soil. All labourers for Christ know that this is occasionally the case. You must have found it so in a Sunday-school class, or in a cottage meeting, or in any other gathering where you have tried to teach and preach Jesus. You have said to yourself every now and then, "Now I am ploughing a rock. Before, I turned up rich mould which a yoke of oxen might plough with ease, and a horse might even run at the work; but now the horse may tug, and the oxen may wearily toil till they gall their shoulders, but they cannot cut a furrow; the rock is stubborn to the last degree."

There are such hearers in all congregations. They

are as iron, and yet they are side by side with a fine
plot of ground. Their sister, their brother, their son,
their daughter, all these have readily felt the power of
the gospel; but *they* do not feel it. They hear it
respectfully; and they so far allow it free course that
they permit it to go in at one ear and out at the other,
but they will have nothing more to do with it. They
would not like to be Sabbath-breakers and stop away
from worship; they therefore do the gospel the
questionable compliment of coming when it is
preached and then refusing to regard it. They are hard,
hard, hard bits of rock, the plough does not touch
them.

Many, on the other hand, are equally hard; but it
is in another way. The impression made by the word
is not deep or permanent. They receive it with joy, but
they do not retain it, They listen with attention, but it
never comes to practice with them. They hear about
repentance, but they never repent. They hear about
faith, but they never believe. They are good judges of
what the gospel is, and yet they have never accepted
it for themselves. They will not eat; but still they insist
that good bread shall be put on the table. They are
great sticklers for the very things which they
personally reject. They are moved to feeling; they shed
tears occasionally, but still their hearts are not really
broken up by the word. They go their way, and forget
what manner of men they are. They are rocky-hearted
through and through: all our attempts to plough them
are failures.

Now this is all the worse, because certain of these
rocky-hearted people have been ploughed for years,
and have become harder instead of softer. Once or
twice ploughing, and a broken share or two, and a
disappointed ploughman or two, we might not mind,

if they would yield at last; but these have since their childhood known the gospel and never given way before its power. It is a good while since their childhood now with some of them. Their hair is turning grey, and they themselves are getting feeble with years. They have been entreated and persuaded times beyond number, but labour has been lost upon them. In fact, they used to feel the word, in a certain fashion, far more years ago than they do now. The sun, which softens wax, hardens clay, and the same gospel which has brought others to tenderness and repentance has exercised a contrary effect upon them, and made them more careless about divine things than they were in their youth. This is a mournful state of things, is it not?

Why are certain men so extremely rocky? Some are so from a *peculiar stolidity of nature.* There are many people in the world whom you cannot very well move, they have a great deal of granite in their constitution, and are more nearly related to Mr. Obstinate than to Mr. Pliable. Now, I do not think badly of these people, because one knows what it is to preach to an excitable people, and to get them all stirred, and to know that in the end they are none the better; whereas some of the more solid and immovable people when they are moved are moved indeed; when they do feel they feel intensely, and they retain any impression that is made. A little chip made in granite by very hard blows will abide there, while the lashing of water, which is easy enough, will leave no trace even for a moment. It is a grand thing to get hold of a fine piece of rock and to exercise faith about it. The Lord's own hammer has mighty power to break, and in the breaking great glory comes to the Most High.

Worse still, certain men are hard because of their

infidelity—not heart-infidelity all of it, but an infidelity which springs out of a desire not to believe, which has helped then to discover difficulties. These difficulties exist, and were meant to exist, for there would be no room for faith if everything were as plain as the nose on one's face. These persons have gradually come to doubt or to think that they doubt, essential truths, and this renders them impervious to the gospel of Christ.

A much more numerous body are orthodox enough, but hard-hearted for all that. *Worldliness* hardens a man in every way. It often dries up all charity to the poor, because the man must make money, and he thinks that the poor-rates are sufficient excuse for neglecting the offices of charity. He has no time to think of the next world; he must spend all his thoughts upon the present one. Money is tight, and therefore he must hold it tight; and when money brings in little interest he finds therein a reason for being the more niggardly. He has no time for prayer, he *must* get down to the counting-house. He has no time for reading his Bible, his ledger wants him. You may knock at his door, but his heart is not at home; it is in the counting-house, wherein he lives and moves and has his being. His god is his gold, his bliss is his business, his all in all is himself. What is the use of preaching to him? As well may horses run upon a rock, or oxen drag a plough across a field sheeted with iron a mile thick.

With some, too, there is a hardness, produced by what I might almost call the opposite of stern worldliness, namely, a *general levity*. They are naturally butterflies flitting about and doing nothing. They never think or want to think. Half a thought exhausts them, and they must needs be diverted, or their feeble minds will utterly weary. They live in a round of amusement. To them the world is a stage, and all the men and women only players. It is of little use to preach to them: there is no depth of earth in their superficial nature; beneath a sprinkling of shifting, worthless sand lies an impenetrable rock of utter stupidity and senselessness. I might thus multiply reasons why some are harder than others, but it is a well assured fact that they are so, and there I leave the matter.

III. I shall now ask everybody to judge whether the running of horses upon a rock, and the ploughing there with oxen, shall always be continued. I assert that IT IS UNREASONABLE TO EXPECT THAT GOD'S SERVANTS SHOULD ALWAYS CONTINUE TO LABOUR IN VAIN. These people have been preached to, taught, instructed, admonished, expostulated with, and advised; shall this unrecompensed work be always performed? We have given them a fair trial; what do reason and prudence say? Are we bound to persevere till we are worn out by this unsuccessful work? We will ask it of men who plough their own farms; do they recommend perseverance when failure is certain? Shall horses run upon the rock? Shall one plough there with oxen? Surely not for ever.

I think we shall all agree that labour in vain cannot be continued for ever if we consider *the ploughman.* He does not want to be much considered; but still his Master does not overlook him. See how weary he grows when the work discourages him. He goes to his Master with, "Who hath believed our report, and to whom is the arm of the Lord revealed?" "Why hast thou sent me," says he, "to a people that have ears but hear not? They sit as thy people sit, and they hear as thy people hear, and then they go their way and they forget every word that is spoken, and they obey not the voice of the Lord." See how disappointed the preacher becomes. It is always hard work when you appear to get no further forward, although you do your utmost. No man, whoever he may be, likes to be set upon work which appears to be altogether a waste of time and effort. To his own mind it seems to have a touch of the ridiculous about it, and he fears that he will be despised of his fellows for aiming at the impossible. Shall it always be the lot of God's ministers to be trifled with? Will the great Husbandman bid his ploughmen spill their lives for nought? Must his preachers continue to cast pearls before swine? If the consecrated workers are so bidden by their Lord they will persevere in their painful task; but their Master is considerate of them, and I ask *you* also to consider whether it is reasonable to expect a zealous heart to be for ever occupied with the salvation of those who never respond to its anxiety? Shall the horses always plough upon the rock? Shall the oxen always labour there?

Again, there is *the Master* to be considered. The Lord—is he always to be resisted and provoked? Many of you have had eternal life set before you as the result of believing in Jesus; and you have refused to believe. It is a wonder that my Lord has not said to me, "You have done your duty with them; never set Christ before them again; my Son shall not be insulted." If you offer a beggar in the street a shilling and he will not have it, you cheerfully put it into your purse and go your way; you do not entreat him to have his wants relieved. But behold, our God in mercy begs sinners to come to him, and implores them to accept his Son. In his condescension he even stands like a salesman in the market crying, "Ho, every one that thirsteth, come ye to the waters, and he that hath no money; come, buy wine and milk without money and without price." In another place he says of himself, "All day long have I stretched out my hands to a disobedient and gainsaying generation." If the Lord of mercy has been refused so long in the sight of you who reverence him, does not some indignation mingle with your pity, and while you love sinners and would have them saved, do you not feel in your heart that there must be an end to such insulting behaviour? I ask even the careless to think of the matter in this light, and if they do not respect the ploughman, yet let them have regard to his Master.

And then, again, there are so many *other people* who are needing the gospel, and who would receive it if they had it, that it would seem to be wise to leave off wearying oneself about those who despise it. What did our Lord say? He said that if the mighty things which had been done in Bethsaida and Chorazin had been done in Tyre and Sidon, they would have repented. What is more wonderful still, he says that if he had wrought the same miracles in Sodom and Gomorrah which were wrought in Capernaum, they would have repented in sackcloth and ashes. Does it not occur to us at once to give the word to those who will have it and leave the despisers to perish in their own wilfulness? Does not reason say, "Let us send this medicine where there are sick people who will value it"? Thousands of people are willing to hear the gospel. See how they crowd wherever the preacher goes—how they tread upon one another in their anxiety to listen to him; and if these people who hear him every day will not receive his message, "in God's name," saith he, "let me go where there is a probability of finding soil that can be ploughed." "Shall horses

run upon the rock? Will one plough there with oxen?"
Must I work always where nothing comes of it? Does
not reason say, let the word go to China, to Hindostan,
or to the utmost parts of the earth, where they will
receive it for those who have it preached in the corners
of their streets despise it?

I shall not lengthen this argument, but shall
solemnly put the question again. Would any of you
continue to pursue an object when it has proved to
be hopeless? Do you wonder that when the Lord has
sent his servants to speak kind gracious, tender
words, and men have not heard, he says to them,
"They are joined unto their idols; let them alone"?
There is a boundary to the patience of men, and we
soon arrive at it; and assuredly there is a limit, though
it is long before we outrun it, to the patience of God.
"At length," he says, "it is enough. My Spirit shall no
longer strive with them." If the Lord says this, can any
of us complain? Is not this the way of wisdom? Does
not prudence itself dictate it? Any thoughtful mind
will say, "Ay, ay, a rock cannot be ploughed for ever."

IV. Fourthly. THERE MUST BE AN ALTERATION, then and
that speedily. The oxen shall be taken off from such
toil. It can be easily done, and done soon. It can be
effected in three ways.

First, the unprofitable hearer can be removed so
that he shall no more hear the gospel from the lips of
his best approved minister. There is a preacher who
has some sort of power over him; but as he rejects
his testimony, and remains impenitent the man shall
be removed to another town, where he shall hear
monotonous discourses which will not touch his
conscience. He shall go where he shall be no longer
persuaded and entreated; and there he will sleep

himself into hell. That may be readily enough done; perhaps some of you are making arrangements even now for your own removal from the field of hope.

Another way is to take away the ploughman. He has done his work as best he could, and he shall be released from his hopeless task. He is weary. Let him go home. The soil would not break up, but he could not help that; let him have his wage. He has broken his plough at the work; let him go home and hear his Lord say, "Well done." He was willing to keep on at the disheartening labour as long as his Master bade him; but it is evidently useless, therefore let him go home, for his work is done. He has been sore sick, let him die, and enter into his rest. This is by no means improbable.

Or, there may happen something else. The Lord may say, "That piece of rock shall never trouble the ploughman any more. I will take it away." And he may take it away in this fashion: the man who has heard the gospel, but rejected it, will die. I pray my Master that he will not suffer any one of you to die in your sins, for then we cannot reach you any more, or indulge the faintest hope for you. No prayers of ours can follow you into eternity. There is one name by which you may be saved, and that name is sounded in your ears—the name of Jesus; but if you reject him now, even that name will not save you. If you do not take Jesus to be your Saviour he will appear as your judge. I pray you, do not destroy your own souls by continuing to be obstinate against almighty love.

God grant that some better thing may happen. Can nothing else be done? This soil is rock; can we not sow it without breaking it? No. Without repentance there is no remission of sin. But is there not a way of saving men without the grace of God? The Lord Jesus

did not say so; but he said, "He that believeth and is
baptized shall be saved, but he that believeth not shall
be damned." He did not hint at a middle course or
hold out a "larger hope," but he declared, "He that
believeth not shall be damned," *and so he must be.*
Dream not of a back door to heaven, for the Lord has
provided none.

What then? Shall the preacher continue his
fruitless toil? If there is only half a hope left him, he
is willing to go on and say, "Hear, ye deaf, and see, ye
blind, and live, ye dead." He will even so speak this
day, for his Master bids him preach the gospel to every
creature; but it will be hard work to repeat the word
of exhortation for years to those who will not hear it.

Happily there is one other turn which affairs may
take. There is a God in heaven, let us pray to him to
put forth his power. Jesus is at his side, let us invoke
his interposition. The Holy Ghost is almighty, let us
call for his aid. Brothers who plough and sisters who
pray, cry to the Master for help. The horse and the ox
evidently fail, but there remains One above who is able
to work great marvels. Did he not once speak to the
rock, and turn the flint into a stream of water? Let us
pray him to do the same now.

And, oh, if there is one who feels and mourns that
his heart is like a piece of rock, I am glad he feels it;
for he who feels that his heart is a rock gives some
evidence that the flint is being transformed. O rock,
instead of smiting thee, as Moses smote the rock in
the wilderness and erred therein, I would speak to
thee. O rock, wouldst thou become like wax? O rock,
wouldst thou dissolve into rivers of repentance?
Hearken to God's voice! O rock, break with good desire!
O rock, dissolve with longing after Christ, for God is
working upon thee now. Who knows but at this very

moment thou shalt begin to crumble down. Dost thou feel the power of the Word? Does the sharp ploughshare touch thee just now? Break and break again, till by contrition thou art dissolved, for then will the good seed of the gospel come to thee, and thou shalt receive it into thy bosom, and we shall all behold the fruit thereof.

And so I will fling one more handful of good corn, and have done. If thou desirest eternal life, trust Jesus Christ and thou art saved at once. "Look unto me, and be ye saved, all the ends of the earth," says Christ, "for I am God, and beside me there is none else." He that believeth in him hath everlasting life. "Like as Moses lifted up the serpent in the wilderness, even so must the Son of man be lifted up: that whosoever believeth in him should not perish, but have eternal life."

O Lord, break up the rock, and let the seed drop in among its broken substance, and get thou a harvest from the dissolved granite, at this time, for Jesus Christ's sake. Amen.

The Parable of the Sower

"And when much people were gathered together, and were come to him out of every city, he spake by a parable: a sower went out to sow his seed: and as he sowed, some fell by the way side; and it was trodden down, and the fowls of the air devoured it. And some fell upon a rock; and as soon as it was sprung up, it withered away, because it lacked moisture. And some fell among thorns; and the thorns sprang up with it, and choked it. And other fell on good ground, and sprang up, and bare fruit an hundredfold. And when he had said these things, he cried, He that hath ears to hear, let him hear."—Luke viii. 4-8.

N our country, when a sower goes forth to his work, he generally enters into an enclosed field, and scatters the seed from his basket along every ridge and furrow; but in the East, the corn-growing country, hard by a small town, is usually an open area. It is divided into different properties, but there are no visible divisions, except the ancient landmarks, or perhaps ridges of stones. Through these open lands there are footpaths, the most frequented being called the highways. You must not imagine these highways to be like our macadamised roads; they are merely paths, trodden tolerably hard. Here and there you notice bye-ways, along which travellers who wish to avoid the public road may journey with a little more safety when the main road is infested with robbers: hasty travellers also strike out short cuts for themselves, and so open fresh tracks for others. When the sower goes forth to sow he finds a plot of ground scratched over with the primitive Eastern plough; he aims at scattering his seed there most plentifully; but a path runs through the centre of his field, and unless he is willing to leave a broad headland, he must throw a handful upon it. Yonder, a rock crops out in the midst of the ploughed land, and the seed falls on its shallow soil. Here is a corner full of the roots of nettles and thistles, and he flings a little here; the corn and the nettles come up together, and the thorns being the stronger soon choke the seed, so that it brings forth no fruit unto perfection. The recollection that the Bible was written in the East, and that its metaphors and allusions must be explained to us by Eastern travellers, will often help us to understand a passage far better than if we think of English customs.

The preacher of the gospel is like the sower. He does not make his seed; it is given him by his divine Master. No man could create the smallest grain that ever grew upon the earth, much less the celestial seed of eternal life. The minister goes to his Master in secret, and asks him to teach him his gospel, and thus he fills his basket with the good seed of the kingdom. He then goes forth in his Master's name and scatters precious truth. If he knew where the best soil was to be found, perhaps he might limit himself to that which had been prepared by the plough of conviction; but not knowing men's hearts, it is his business to preach the gospel to every creature—to throw a handful on the hardened heart, and another on the mind which is overgrown with the cares and pleasures of the world. He has to leave the seed in the care of the Lord who gave it to him, for he is not responsible for the harvest, he is only accountable for the care and industry with which he does his work. If no single ear should ever make glad the reaper, the sower will be rewarded by his Master if he had planted the right seed with careful hand. If it were not for this fact with what despairing agony should we utter the cry of Esaias. "Who hath believed our report? and to whom is the arm of the Lord revealed?"

Our duty is not measured by the character of our hearers, but by the command of our God. We are bound to preach the gospel, whether men will hear, or whether they will forbear. It is ours to sow beside all waters. Let men's hearts be what they may the minister must preach the gospel to them; he must sow the seed on the rock as well as in the furrow, on the highway as well as in the ploughed field.

I shall now address myself to the four classes of hearers mentioned in our Lord's parable. We have, first of all, those who are represented by the *way-side,* those who are "hearers only"; then those represented by the *stony-ground;* these are transiently impressed, but the word produces no lasting fruit; then, those *among thorns*, on whom a good impression is produced, but the cares of this life, and the deceitfulness of riches, and the pleasures of the world choke the seed; and, lastly, that small class—God be pleased to multiply it exceedingly—that small class of *good-ground* hearers, in whom the Word brings forth abundant fruit.

I. First of all, I address myself to those hearts which are like the WAY-SIDE—"Some fell by the wayside; and it was trodden down, and the fowls of the air devoured it." Many of you do not go to the place of worship desiring a blessing. You do not intend to worship God, or to be affected by anything that you hear. You are like the highway, which was never intended to be a cornfield. If a single grain of truth should fall into your heart and grow it would be as great a wonder as for corn to grow up in the street. If the seed shall be dextrously scattered, some of it will fall upon you, and rest for a while upon your thoughts. 'Tis true you will not understand it; but, nevertheless, if it be placed before you in an interesting style, you will talk about it till some more congenial entertainment shall attract you. Even this slender benefit is brief, for in a little season you will forget all that you have heard. Would to God we could hope that our words would tarry with you, but we cannot hope it for the soil of your heart is so hard beaten by continual traffic, that there is no hope of the seed finding a living root-hold. Satan is constantly passing over your heart with his company of blasphemies, lusts, lies, and vanities. The chariots of pride roll along it, and the feet of greedy mammon tread it till it is hard as adamant. Alas! for the good seed, it finds not a moment's respite; crowds pass and repass; in fact your soul is an exchange, across which continually hurry the busy feet of those who make merchandise of the souls of men. You are buying and selling, but you little think that you are selling the truth, and that you are buying your soul's destruction. You have no time, you say, to think of religion. No, the road of your heart is such a crowded thoroughfare, that there is no room for the wheat to spring up. If it did begin to germinate, some rough foot would crush the green blade ere it could come to perfection. The seed has occasionally lain long enough to begin to sprout, but just then a new place of amusement has been opened, and you have entered there, and as with an iron heel, the germ of life that was in the seed was crushed out. Corn could not grow in Cornhill or Cheapside, however excellent the seed might be: your heart is just like those crowded thoroughfares; for so many cares and sins throng it and so many proud, vain, evil, rebellious thoughts against God pass through it, that the seed of truth cannot grow.

We have looked at this hard road-side, let us now describe what becomes of the good word, when it falls upon such a heart. It would have grown if it had fallen on right soil, but it has dropped into the wrong place, and it remains as dry as when it fell from the sower's hand. The word of the gospel lies upon the surface of such a heart, but never enters it. Like the snow, which sometimes falls upon our streets, drops upon the wet pavement, melts, and is gone at once, so is it with this man. The word has not time to quicken in his soul: it lies there an instant but it never strikes root, or takes the slightest effect.

Why do men come to hear if the word never enters their hearts? That has often puzzled us. Some hearers would not be absent on the Sunday on any account; they are delighted to come up with us to worship, but yet the tear never trickles down their cheek, their soul never mounts up to heaven on the wings of praise, nor do they truly join in our confessions of sin. They do not think of the wrath to come, nor of the future state of their souls. Their heart is as iron; the minister might as well speak to a heap of stones as preach to them. What brings these senseless sinners here? Surely we are as hopeful of converting lions and leopards as these untamed, insensible hearts. Oh feeling! thou art fled to brutish beasts, and men have lost their reason! Do these people come to our assemblies because it is respectable to attend a place of worship? Or is it that their coming helps to make them comfortable in their sins? If they stopped away conscience would prick them; but they come hither that they may flatter themselves with the notion that they are religious. Oh! my hearers, your case is one that might make an angel weep! How sad to have the sun of the gospel shining on your face; and yet to have blind eyes that never see the light. The music of heaven is lost upon you, for you have no ears to hear. You can catch the turn of a phrase, you can appreciate the poetry of an illustration, but the hidden meaning, the divine life you do not perceive. You sit at the marriage-feast, but you eat not of the dainties; the bells of heaven ring with joy over ransomed spirits, but you live unransomed, without God, and without Christ. Though we plead with you, and pray for you, and weep over you, you still remain as hardened, as careless, and as thoughtless as ever you were. May God have mercy on you, and break up your hard hearts, that his word may abide in you.

We have not, however, completed the picture. The passage tells us that the fowls of the air devoured the seed. Is there here a way-side hearer? Perhaps he did not mean to hear this sermon, and when he has heard it he will be asked by one of the wicked to come into company. He will go with the tempter, and the good seed will be devoured by the fowls of the air. Plenty of evil ones are ready to take away the gospel from the heart. The devil himself, that prince of the air, is eager at any time to snatch away a good thought. And then the devil is not alone—he has legions of helpers. He can set a man's wife, children, friends, enemies, customers, or creditors, to eat up the good seed, and they will do it effectually. Oh, sorrow upon sorrow, that heavenly seed should become devil's meat; that God's corn should feed foul birds!

O my hearers, if you have heard the gospel from your youth, what waggon-loads of sermons have been wasted on you! In your younger days, you heard old Dr. So-and-so, and the dear old man was wont to pray for his hearers till his eyes were red with tears! Do you recollect those many Sundays when you said to yourself, "Let me go to my chamber and fall on my knees and pray"? But you did not: the fowls of the air ate up the seed, and you went on to sin as you had sinned before. Since then, by some strange impulse, you are very rarely absent from God's house; but now the seed of the gospel falls into your soul as if it dropped upon an iron floor, and nothing comes of it. The law may be thundered at you; you do not sneer at it, but it never affects you. Jesus Christ may be lifted up; his dear wounds may be exhibited; his streaming blood may flow before your very eyes, and you may be bidden with all earnestness to look to him and live; but it is as if one should sow the sea-shore. What shall I do for you? Shall I stand here and rain tears upon this hard highway? Alas! my tears will not break it up; it is trodden too hard for that. Shall I bring the gospel plough? Alas! the ploughshare will not enter ground so solid. What shall we do? O God, thou knowest how to melt the hardest heart with the precious blood of Jesus. Do it now, we beseech thee, and thus magnify thy grace, by causing the good seed to live, and to produce a heavenly harvest.

II. I shall now turn to the second class of hearers:— "And some fell upon a ROCK; and as soon as it was sprung up, it withered away, because it lacked moisture." You can easily picture to yourselves that piece of rock in the midst of the field thinly veiled with soil; and of course the seed falls there as it does everywhere else. It springs up, it hastens to grow, it withers, it dies. None but those who love the souls of men can tell what hopes, what joys, and what bitter disappointments these stony places have caused us. We have a class of hearers whose hearts are hard, and yet they are apparently the softest and most impressible of men. While other men see nothing in the sermon, these men weep. Whether you preach the terrors of the law or the love of Calvary, they are alike stirred in their souls, and the liveliest impressions are apparently produced. Such may be listening now. They have resolved, but they have procrastinated. They are not the sturdy enemies of God who clothe themselves in steel, but they seem to bare their breasts, and lay them open to the minister. Rejoiced in heart, we shoot our arrows there, and they appear to penetrate; but, alas, a secret armour blunts every dart, and no wound is felt. The parable speaks of this character thus— "Some fell upon stony places, where they had not much earth: and forthwith they sprung up, because they had no deepness of earth." Or as another passage explains it: "And these are they likewise which are sown on stony ground; who, when they have heard the word, immediately receive it with gladness; and have no root in themselves, and so endure but for a time: afterward, when affliction or persecution ariseth for the word's sake, immediately they are offended." Have we not thousands of hearers who receive the word with joy? They have no deep convictions, but they leap into Christ on a sudden, and profess an instantaneous faith in him, and that faith has all the appearance of being genuine. When we look at it, the seed has really sprouted. There is a kind of life in it, there is apparently a green blade. We thank God that a sinner is brought back, a soul is born to God. But our joy is premature: they sprang up on a sudden, and received the word with joy, because they had no depth of earth, and the self-same cause which hastened their reception of the seed also causes them, when the sun is risen with his fervent heat to wither away. These men we see every day in the week. They come to join the church; they tell us a story of how they heard us preach on such-and-such an occasion, and, oh, the word was so blessed to them, they never felt so happy in their lives! "Oh, sir, I thought I must leap from my seat when I heard about a precious Christ, and I believed on him there and then; I am sure I did." We question them as to whether they were ever convinced of sin. They think they were; but one thing they know, they feel a great pleasure in religion. We put it to them, "Do you think you will hold on?" They are confident that they shall. They hate the things they once loved, they are sure they do. Everything has become new to them. And all this is on a sudden. We enquire when the good work began. We find it began when it ended, that is to say, there was no previous work, no ploughing of the soil, but on a sudden they sprang from death to life, as if a field should be covered with wheat by magic. Perhaps we receive them into the church; but in a week or two they are not so regular as they used to be. We gently reprove them, and they explain that they meet with such opposition in religion, that they are obliged to yield a little. Another month and we lose them altogether. The reason is that they have been laughed at or exposed to a little opposition, and they have gone back. And what, think you, are the feelings of the minister? He is like the husbandman, who sees his field all green and flourishing, but at night a frost nips every shoot and his hoped-for gains are gone. The minister goes to his chamber, and casts himself on his face before God, and cries, "I have been deceived; my converts are fickle, their religion has withered as the green herb." In the ancient story Orpheus is said to have had such skill upon the lyre, that he made the oaks and stones to dance around him. It is a poetical fiction, and yet hath it sometimes happened to the minister, that not only have the godly rejoiced, but men, like oaks and stones, have danced from their places. Alas! they have been oaks and stones still. Hushed is the lyre. The oak returns to its rooting-place, and the stone casts itself heavily to the earth. The sinner, who, like Saul, was among the prophets, goes back to plan mischief against the Most High.

If it is bad to be a wayside hearer, I cannot think it is much better to be like the rock. This second class of hearers certainly gives us more joy than the first. A certain company always comes round a new minister; and I have often thought it is an act of God's kindness that he allows these people to gather at the first, while the minister is young, and has but few to stand by him: these persons are easily moved, and if the minister preaches earnestly they feel it, and they love him, and rally round him, much to his comfort. But time, that proves all things, proves them. They seemed to be made of true metal; but when they are put into the fire to be tested, they are consumed in the furnace. Some of the shallow kind are here now. I have looked at you when I have been preaching, and I have often thought, "That man one of these days will come out from the world, I am sure he will." I have thanked God for him. Alas, he is the same as ever. Years and years have we sowed him in vain, and it is to be feared it will be so to the end, for he is without depth, and without the moisture of the Spirit. Shall it be so? Must I stand over the mouth of your open sepulchre, and think, "Here lies a shoot which never became an ear, a man in whom grace struggled but never reigned, who gave some hopeful spasms of life and then subsided into eternal death"? God save you! Oh! may the Spirit deal with you effectually, and may you, even you, yet bring forth fruit unto God, that Jesus may have a reward for his sufferings.

III. I shall briefly treat of the third class, and may the Spirit of God assist me to deal faithfully with you. "And some fell among THORNS; and the thorns sprang up with it and choked it." Now, this was good soil. The two first characters were bad: the wayside was not the proper place, the rock was not a congenial situation for the growth of any plant; but this is good soil, for it grows thorns. Wherever a thistle will spring up and flourish, there would wheat flourish too. This was fat fertile soil; it was no marvel therefore that the husbandman dealt largely there, and threw handful after handful upon that corner of the field. See how happy he is when in a month or two he visits the spot. The seed has sprung up. True, there's a suspicious little plant down there of about the same size as the wheat. "Oh!" he thinks, "that's not much, the corn will out-grow *that*. When it is stronger it will choke these few thistles that have unfortunately mixed with it." Ay, Mr. Husbandman, you do not understand the force of evil, or you would not thus dream! He comes again, and the seed has grown, there is even the corn in the ear; but the thistles, the thorns, and the briars have become intertwisted with one another, and the poor wheat can hardly get a ray of sunshine. It is so choked with thorns every way, that it looks quite yellow: the plant is starved. Still it perseveres in growing, and it does seem as if it would bring forth a little fruit. Alas, it never comes to anything. With it the reaper never fills his arm.

We have this class very largely among us. These hear the word and understand what they hear. They take the truth home; they think it over; they even go the length of making a profession of religion. The wheat seems to spring and ear; it will soon come to perfection. Be in no hurry, these men and women have a great deal to see after; they have the cares of a large concern; their establishment employs so many hundred hands; do not be deceived as to their godliness—they have no time for it. They will tell you that they must live; that they cannot neglect this world; that they must anyhow look out for the present and as for the future, they will render it all due attention by-and-by. They continue to attend gospel-preaching, and the poor little stunted blade of religion keeps on growing after a fashion. Meanwhile they have grown rich, they come to the place of worship in a carriage, they have all that heart can wish. Ah! now the seed will grow, will it not? No, no. They have no cares now; the shop is given up, they live in the country; they have not to ask, "Where shall the money come from to meet the next bill?" or "how shall they be able to provide for an increasing family." Now they have too much instead of too little, for they have riches, and they are too wealthy to be gracious. "But" says one, "they might spend their riches for God." Certainly they might, but they do not, for riches are deceitful. They have to entertain much company, and chime in with the world, and so Christ and his church are left in the lurch.

Yes, but they begin to spend their riches, and they have surely got over that difficulty, for they give largely to the cause of Christ and they are munificent in charity; the little blade will grow, will it not? No, for now behold the thorns of pleasure. Their liberality to others involves liberality to themselves; their pleasures, amusements, and vanities choke the wheat of true religion: the good grains of gospel truth cannot grow because they have to attend that musical party, that ball, and that soirée, and so they cannot think of the things of God. I know several specimens of this class. I knew one, high in court circles, who has confessed to me that he wished he were poor, for then he might enter the kingdom of heaven. He has said to me, "Ah! sir, these politics, these politics, I wish I were rid of them, they are eating the life out of my heart; I cannot serve God as I would." I know of another, overloaded with riches, who has said to me, "Ah! sir, it is an awful thing to be rich; one cannot keep close to the Saviour with all this earth about him."

Ah! my dear readers, I will not ask for you that God may lay you on a bed of sickness, that he may strip you of all your wealth, and bring you to beggary; but oh, if he were to do it and you were to save your souls, it would be the best bargain you could ever make. If those mighty ones who now complain that the thorns choke the seed could give up all their riches and pleasures, if they that fare sumptuously every day could take the place of Lazarus at the gate, it were a happy change for them if their souls might be saved. A man may be honourable and rich, and yet go to heaven; but it will be hard work, for "It is easier for a camel to go through the eye of a needle, than for a rich man to enter into the kingdom of heaven." God does make some rich men enter the kingdom of heaven, but hard is their struggle. Steady, young man, steady! Hurry not to climb to wealth! It is a place where many heads are turned. Do not ask God to make you popular; they that have popularity are wearied by it. Cry with Agur—"Give me neither poverty nor riches." God give me to tread the golden mean, and may I ever have in my heart that good seed, which shall bring forth fruit a hundredfold to his own glory.

IV. I now close with the last character, namely, the GOOD GROUND. Of the good soil, as you will mark, we have but one in four. Will one in four of our hearers, with well-prepared heart, receive the Word?

The ground is described as "good": not that it was good by nature, but it had been made good by grace. God had ploughed it; he had stirred it up with the plough of conviction, and there it lay in ridge and furrow as it should lie. When the gospel was preached, the heart received it, for the man said, "That is just the blessing I want. Mercy is what a needy sinner requires." So that the preaching of the gospel was THE thing to give comfort to this disturbed and ploughed soil. Down fell the seed to take good root. In some cases it produced fervency of love, largeness of heart, devotedness of purpose of a noble kind, like seed which produces a hundredfold. The man became a mighty servant for God, he spent himself and was spent. He took his place in the vanguard of Christ's army, stood in the hottest of the battle, and did deeds of daring which few could accomplish—the seed produced a hundredfold. It fell into another heart of like character;—the man could not do the most, but still he did much. He gave himself to God, and in his business he had a word to say for his Lord; in his daily walk he quietly adorned the doctrine of God his Saviour,—he brought forth sixty-fold. Then it fell on another, whose abilities and talents were but small; he could not be a star, but he would be a glow-worm; he could not do as the greatest, but he was content to do something, however humble. The seed had brought forth in him tenfold, perhaps twentyfold. How many are there of this sort here? Is there one who prays within himself, "God be merciful to me a sinner"? The seed has fallen in the right spot. Soul, thy prayer shall be heard. God never sets a man longing for mercy without intending to give it. Does another whisper, "Oh that I might be saved"? Believe on the Lord Jesus Christ, and thou, even thou, shalt be saved. Hast thou been the chief of sinners? Trust Christ and thy enormous sins shall vanish as the millstone sinks beneath the flood. Is there no one here that will trust the Saviour? Can it be possible that the Spirit is entirely absent? that he is not moving in one soul? not begetting life in one spirit? We will pray that he may now descend, that the word may not be in vain.

The Principal Wheat

"The principal wheat."—Isaiah xxviii. 25.

HE prophet mentions it as a matter of wisdom on the part of the husbandman, that HE KNOWS WHAT IS THE PRINCIPAL THING TO CULTIVATE, and makes it his principal care. The text with the connection, runs thus,— "Does not the husbandman cast in the principal wheat?" He does not go to the granary and take out wheat and cummin, and barley, and rye, and fling these about right and left, but he estimates the value of each grain, and arranges them in his mind accordingly. He does not think that cummin, and carroway, which he merely grows to give a flavour to his meal, are of half such importance as his bread-corn; and, though rye and barley have their values, yet he does not reckon that even these are equal to what he calls "the principal wheat." He is a man of discretion, he arranges things; he places the most important crop in the front rank, and spends upon it the most care.

Here let us learn a lesson. Do keep things distinct in your minds—not huddled and muddled by a careless thoughtlessness. Do not live a confused life, without care and discretion, running all things into one; but sort things out and divide and distinguish between the precious and the vile. See what this is worth, and what the other is worth, and set your matters in rank and order, making some of them principal, and others of them inferior. I suggest to you young people especially that, in starting life, you say to yourselves, "What shall we live for? There is a principal thing for which we ought to live, what shall it be?" Have you turned over that question, or have you gone at it hit or miss? What are you living for? What is your principal aim? Is it going to be that of the old gentleman in Horace who said to his boy, "Get money: get it honestly, if you can; but, by all means, get money." Will you be a money-spinner? Shall coin be your principal corn? Or will you choose a life of pleasure—"a short life and a merry one," as so many fools have said to their great sorrow? Is it in dissipation that your life is to be spent? Are thistles to be your principal crop? Because there is a pleasure in looking at a Scotch thistle, do you intend to grow acres of pleasurable vice? And will you make your bed upon them when you come to die? Search and see what is worthy of being the principal object in life; and, when you have found it out, then beseech the Holy Spirit to help you to choose that one thing, and to give all your powers and faculties to the cultivation of it. The farmer who finds that wheat ought to be his principal crop, makes it so, and lays himself out with that end in view: learn from this to have a main object, and to give your whole mind to it.

This farmer was wise, because *he counted that to be principal which was the most needful.* His family could do without cummin, which was but a flavouring. Perhaps the mistress might complain, or the cook might grumble, but that did not signify so much as it would do if the children cried for bread. They certainly must have wheat, for bread is the staff of life. It is bread that strengtheneth man's heart, and therefore the farmer must grow wheat if he does not grow anything else. That which is necessary he regarded as the principal thing. Is not this common sense? If we were wisely to sit down and estimate, should we not say, "To be forgiven my sins, to be right with God, to be holy, to be fit to live eternally in heaven, is the greatest the most needful thing for me, and therefore I will make it the principal object of my pursuit." A creature cannot be satisfied unless he is answering the end for which he is created; and the end of every intelligent creature is first, to glorify God, and next, to enjoy God. What a bliss it must be to enjoy God himself for ever and ever. Other things may be desirable, but this thing is needful. A competence of income, a measure of esteem among men, a degree of health—all these are the flavouring of life, but to be saved in the Lord with an everlasting salvation is life itself. Jesus Christ is the bread by which our soul's best life is sustained. Oh, that we were all wise enough to feel that to be one with Christ is the one thing needful; that to be at peace with God is the principal thing; that to be brought into harmony with the Most High is the true music of our being. Other herbs may take their place in due order, but grace is the principal wheat, and we must cultivate it.

This farmer was wise, because *he made that to be the principal thing which was the most fit to be so.* Of course, barley is useful as food, for nations have lived on barley bread, and lived healthily too; and rye has been the nutriment of millions: neither have they starved on oats, and other grains. Still, give me a piece of wheaten bread, for it is the best staff for life's journey. This farmer knew that wheat was the most fitting food for man, and so he did not put the inferior grain, which might act as a substitute, into the prominent place; but he gave his wheat the preference. He did not say, "the principal barley," or "the principal rye," much less "the principal cummin," or "the principal fitches," but "the principal wheat."

And what is there, brethren, that is so fit for the heart, the mind, the soul of man, as to know God and his Christ? Other mental foods, such as the fruits of knowledge, and the dainties of science, excellent though they may be—are inferior nutriment and unsuitable to build up the inner manhood. In my God and my Saviour, I find my heaven and my all. My soul sits down to a crumb of truth about Jesus, and finds great satisfaction in living upon it. The more we can know God, and enjoy God, and become like to God, and the more Christ is our daily bread, the more do we perceive the fitness of all this to our new-born natures. O beloved, make that to be your principal object which is the fittest pursuit of an immortal mind.

> "Religion is the chief concern
>   Of mortals here below;
> May I its great importance learn,
>   Its sovereign virtue know!
>
> "More needful this than glittering wealth,
>   Of aught the world bestows;
> Not reputation, food, or health,
>   Can give us such repose."

Moreover, this farmer was wise, because *he made that the principal thing which was the most profitable.* Under certain circumstances, in our own country, wheat is not the most profitable thing which a man can grow; but ordinarily, it is the best crop that the earth yields, and therefore the text speaks of "the principal wheat." Our grandfathers used to rely upon the wheat stack to pay their rent. They looked to their corn as the arm of their strength; and though it is not so now, it always was so of old, and perhaps it may yet be so again. Anyhow, the figure holds good with regard to true religion. That is the most profitable thing. I am told that rich men find it very hard to get hold of anything which yields five per cent. nowadays; but this blessed fear of the Lord is an extraordinarily profitable investment, for it does not yield a hundred per cent. or a thousand per cent., but a man begins with nothing and all things become his by faith. Being freely discharged of our sins, we are by overflowing grace greatly enriched, so that we number among our possessions heaven itself, Christ himself, God himself. All things are ours. Oh, what a blessed crop to sow! What a harvest comes of it! Godliness is profitable for the life that now is, and for that which is to come. Godliness is a blessing to a man's body, it keeps him from drunkenness and vice; and it is a blessing to his soul, it makes him sweet and pure. It is a blessing to him every way. If I had to die like a dog, I would like to live like a Christian. If there were no hereafter, yet still, for comfort and for joy, give me the life of one who strives to live like Christ. There is a practical everyday truth in the verse—

> "'Tis religion that can give
> Sweetest pleasures while we live;
> 'Tis religion must supply
> Solid comfort when we die."

Only that religion must not be of the common sort; it must have for its root a hearty faith in Jesus Christ. See ye to it. Our religion must be either everything or nothing, either first or nowhere. Make it "the principal wheat," and it will richly repay you.

II. Secondly, the husbandman is a lesson to us because HE GIVES THIS PRINCIPAL THING THE PRINCIPAL PLACE. I find that the Hebrew is rendered by some eminent scholars, "He puts the wheat into the principal place." That little handful of cummin for the wife to flavour the cakes with he grows in a corner; and the various herbs he places in their proper borders. The barley he sets in its plot, and the rye in its acre; but if there is a good bit of rich soil—the best he has—he appropriates it to the principal wheat. He gives his choicest fields to that which is to be the main means of his living.

Now, here is a lesson for you and for me. Let us give to true godliness our principal powers and abilities. Let us give to the things of God our best and *most intense thought.* I pray you, do not take religion at second hand from what I tell you, or from what somebody else tells you; but think it over. Read, mark, learn, and inwardly digest the word of God. The thoughtful Christian is the growing Christian. Remember, the service of God deserves our first consideration and endeavour. We are poor things at our prime, but we ought to give the Lord nothing short of our best. God would not have us serve him heedlessly, but he would have us use all the brain and intellect and mind that we have in studying and practising his word. "Acquaint now thyself with him, and be at peace." "Meditate upon these things. Give thyself wholly to them." If your mind is more clear and active at one time than at another, then sow the principal wheat. If you feel more fresh and more inclined to think at one time of the day than at another, let your mind then go towards the best things.

Be sure, also, to yield to this subject *your most earnest love.* The best field in the little estate of manhood is not the head, but the heart; sow the principal wheat there. Oh, to have true religion in the heart; to love what we know—intensely to love it; to hold it fast as with the grip of life and death—never to let it go! The Lord says, "My son, give me thy heart;" and he will not be contented with anything less than our heart. Oh, when your zeal is most burning, and your love is most fervent, let the warmth and the fervency all go towards the Lord your God, and to the service of him who has redeemed you with his precious blood. Let the principal wheat have the principal part of your nature. Towards God and his Christ also turn your *most fervent desires.* When you enlarge your desire, desire Christ; when you become ambitious let your ambition be all for God. Let your hunger and your thirst be after righteousness. Let your aspirations and your longings be all towards holiness, and the things that shall make you like to Christ. Give to this principal wheat your principal desires.

Then let the Lord have *the attentive respect of your life.* Let the principal wheat be sown in every action. If we are truly Christians we must be as much Christians outside the church as in it. We shall try to make our eating and our drinking, and everything we do, tend to the glory of God. Draw no line between the secular and the religious part of your conduct but let the secular be made religious by a devout desire to glorify God in the one as much as in the other. Let us worship God in the commonest duties of life, even as they do who stand before his throne. So it ought to be. Let us sow the principal wheat in all the fields of our conversation, in business, in the family, among our friends, and with our children. May we each one feel, "For me to live is Christ. I cannot live without Christ, or for anything but Christ." Let your whole nature yield itself to Jesus, and to none else.

We should give to this principal wheat *our most earnest labours.* We should spend ourselves for the spread of the gospel. A Christian man ought to lay himself out to serve Jesus. I hate to see a professing man zealous in politics and lukewarm in devotion; all on fire at a parish vestry, and chill as winter when he comes to a prayer-meeting. Some fly like eagles when they are serving the world, but they have a broken wing in the service of God. This should not be. If anything could rouse us up, and make the lion within us roar in his strength, it should be when we confront the foes of Jesus or fight in his cause. Our Lord's service is the principal wheat, let us labour most in connection with it.

This, I think, should also take possession of us so as to lead to *our greatest sacrifices.* The love of Christ ought to be so strong as to swallow up self, and make sacrifice our daily joy. For Christ's name's sake we should be willing to endure poverty, reproach, slander, exile, death. Nothing should be dear to a Christian in comparison with Christ. Now, I will put it to you whether it is so or no. Is the love of Jesus the principal wheat with us? Are we giving our religion the chief place or not? I am afraid some people treat religion as certain gentlemen treat an off-hand farm; they put a bailiff into it and only give an eye to it now and then. Their minister is the bailiff, and they expect him to see to it for them. These off-hand farms are losing concerns. Look at these half-and-half brethren. They have religion? Certainly. But they are like the man of whom the child spoke at the Sunday-school. "Is your father a Christian?" said the teacher. "Yes," said the child, "but he has not worked much at it lately." I could point out several of this sort, who are sowing their wheat very sparingly, and choosing the most barren patch to sow it in. They profess to be Christians, but religion is a tenth-rate article on their farm. Some have a large acreage for the world, and a poor little plot for

Christ. They are growers of worldly pleasure and self-indulgence, and they sow a little religion by the roadside for appearance sake. This will not do. God will not thus be mocked. If we despise him and his truth we shall be lightly esteemed. O come let us give our principal time, talent, thought, effort to that which is the chief concern of immortal spirits. May we imitate the husbandman who gives the principal wheat the principal place in his farm.

III. Let us learn a third lesson. THE HUSBANDMAN SELECTS THE PRINCIPAL SEED-CORN WHEN HE IS SOWING HIS WHEAT. When a farmer is setting aside wheat for sowing, he does not choose the tail corn and the worst of his produce, but if he is a sensible man he likes to sow the best wheat in the world. Many farmers search the country round for a good sample of wheat for sowing, for they do not expect to get a good harvest out of bad seed. The husbandman is taught of God to put into the ground "the principal wheat." Let me learn that if I am going to sow to the Lord and to be a Christian, I should sow the best kind of Christianity.

I should try to do this, first, *by believing the weightiest doctrines.* I would believe not this "ism," nor that, but the unadulterated truth which Jesus taught; for a holy character will only grow by the Spirit of God out of true doctrine. Falsehood breeds sin: truth begets and fosters holiness. You and I therefore ought to select our seed carefully, and cast out all error. If we are wise we shall think most of the most important truths, for I have known people attach the greatest importance to the smallest things. They fight over the fitches, and leave the wheat to the crows. As for me, those who will may dispute over vials and trumpets, I shall mainly preach the doctrine of the precious blood and the glorious truths of substitution and atonement. These doctrines are the principal wheat and therefore these shall have my choice.

Next to that, we ought to sow *the noblest examples.* Many men are dwarfed because they choose a bad model to start with. They imitate dear old Mr. So-and-so till they grow wonderfully like him with the best of him left out. A minister happens to be of a gloomy turn of mind, and he preaches the deep experience of the children of God, and in consequence a band of good people think it their duty to be melancholy. Why need they fall into a ditch because their leader has splashed himself? We should never copy any man's infirmities. To be like Paul there is no need to have weak eyes; to be like Thomas there is no necessity to doubt. If you copy any good man, there is a point at which you ought to stop short. If I must have a human model, I would prefer one of the bravest of the saints of God; but oh how much better to follow that perfect pattern which you have in Christ Jesus!

We should sow the best wheat by seeing that we have *the purest spirit.* Alas! how soon do spirits become soiled by self or pride, or despondency or sloth, or some earthly taint. But what a grand thing it is to live in the spirit of Christ. May we be humble, lowly, bold, self-sacrificing, pure, chaste, and holy.

And, then, there is one more mode of sowing selected seed. We should endeavour to live in *the closest communion with God.* A dear brother prayed just now that we might have as much grace as we were capable of receiving, and that God would bring us into such a state that we might not hinder him in anything which he willed to do by us. This is a good prayer. It should be our desire to rise to the highest form of spiritual life. If you sow this principal wheat, get the best sort of it. There is a spirit and a spirit; and there are doctrines and doctrines; the best is the best for you. O young men, if you mean to have piety, go in for it thoroughly. Do not sneak through the world as if you were ashamed of your Lord. If you are Christ's show your colours. Rally to his banner, gather to his trumpet call, and then stand up, stand up for Jesus. If there is any manhood in you, this great cause calls for it all; exhibit it, and may the Spirit of God help you so to do.

IV. Fourthly, THE HUSBANDMAN GROWS THE PRINCIPAL WHEAT WITH THE PRINCIPAL CARE. Some critics say that the proper translation is that the husbandman plants his wheat in rows. It is said that the large crops in Palestine in olden time were due to the fact that they planted the wheat. They set it in lines, so that it was not checked or suffocated by its being too thick in one place, neither was there any fear of its being too thin in another. The wheat was planted, and then streams of water were turned by the foot to each particular plant. No wonder, therefore, that the land brought forth abundantly.

We should give our principal care to the principal thing. Our godliness should be carried out with discretion and care. Brethren, are we careful enough as to our religious walk? Have you ever searched to the bottom of your profession? Why do you happen to be members of a certain church? Your mother was so. Well, there is some good in that reason, but not enough to justify you in the sight of God. I pray you judge your standing. If any Christian minister is afraid to urge you to this duty I stand in doubt of him. I am not at all afraid. I beg you to examine all that I teach you, for I would not like to be responsible for another man's creed. Like the Bereans, search and see whether these things be according to Scripture or not. One of the greatest blessings that could come upon the church would be a searching spirit which would refer everything to the Holy Scriptures. If they speak not according to this word it is because there is no light in them. Do your service to God as carefully as the eastern farmer planted his wheat, when he set it in rows with great orderliness and exactness. You serve a precise God, therefore serve him precisely. He is a jealous God, therefore be jealous of the least taint of error or will-worship.

Take care, also, that you water every part of your religion, as the farmer watered each plant. Pray for grace from on high that you may never be parched and dried up. Perform to your faith, to your hope, to your love, and to all the plants that are in your soul every other service which the husbandman renders to his wheat. Give grace your principal care, for it deserves it.

V. With this I close. Do this, because FROM THIS YOU MAY EXPECT YOUR PRINCIPAL CROP. If religion be the principal thing, you may look to religion for your principal reward. The harvest will come to you in various ways. You will make the greatest success in this life if you wholly live to the glory of God. Success or failure must much depend upon the fitness of our object. It is of no use *my* attempting to sing, for I shall never be able to conduct a choir. I could not succeed in that, but if I preach, I may succeed, for that is my work. Now you, Christian man, if you try to live to the world you will not prosper, for you are not fitted for it. Grace has spoiled you for sin. If you live to God with all your heart you will succeed in it, for God has made you on purpose for it. As he made the fish for the water, and the birds for the air, so he made the believer for holiness, and for the service of God; and you will be out of your element, a fish out of water, or a bird in the stream, if you leave the service of God. The Eastern painter's prosperity hinges on his wheat, and yours upon your devotion to God. It is to Godliness that you must look for your joy. Is there any bliss like the bliss of knowing that you are in Christ, and are the beloved of the Lord? It is to your religion that you must look for comfort on a sick and dying bed, and you may be there very soon.

In the world to come what a crop, what a harvest will come of serving the Lord! What will come out of all else? What but mere smoke? A man has made a million of money, and he is dead. What has he got by his wealth? A man's fame rings throughout the earth as a great and successful warrior, and he is dead. What has he as the result of all his honours? To live to the world is like playing with boys in the street for halfpence, or with babes for bits of platter and oyster shells. Life for God is real and substantial, but all else is waste. Let us think so, and gird up our loins to serve the Lord. May the divine Spirit help us to sow "the principal wheat," and to live in joyful expectation of reaping a happy harvest according to the promise, "They that sow in tears shall reap in joy."

Spring in the Heart

"Thou waterest the ridges thereof abundantly: thou settlest the furrows thereof: thou makest it soft with showers: thou blessest the springing thereof."—Psalm lxv. 10.

HOUGH other seasons excel in fulness, spring must always bear the palm for freshness and beauty. We thank God when the harvest hours draw near, and the golden grain invites the sickle, but we ought equally to thank him for the rougher days of spring, for these prepare the harvest. April showers are mothers of the sweet May flowers, and the wet and cold of winter are the parents of the splendour of summer. God blesses the springing thereof, or else it could not be said, "Thou crownest the year with thy goodness." There is as much necessity for divine benediction in spring as for heavenly bounty in summer; and, therefore, we should praise God all the year round.

Spiritual spring is a very blessed season in a

church. Then we see youthful piety developed, and on every hand we hear the joyful cry of those who say, "We have found the Lord." Our sons are springing up as the grass and as willows by the watercourses. We hold up our hands in glad astonishment and cry, "who are these that fly as a cloud and as doves to their windows?" In the revival days of a Church, when God is blessing her with many conversions, she has great cause to rejoice in God and to sing, "Thou blessest the springing thereof."

I intend to take the text in reference to individual cases. There is a time of springing of grace, when it is just in its bud, just breaking through the dull cold earth of unregenerate nature. I desire to talk a little about that, and concerning the blessing which the Lord grants to the green blade of new-born godliness, to those who are beginning to hope in the Lord.

I. First, I shall have a little to say about THE WORK PREVIOUS TO THE SPRINGING THEREOF.

It appears from the text that there is work for God alone to do before the springing comes, and we know that there is work for God to do through us as well.

There is work for us to do. Before there can be a springing up in the soul of any, there must be ploughing, harrowing, and sowing. There must be a ploughing, and we do not expect that as soon as ever we plough we shall reap the sheaves. Blessed be God, in many cases, the reaper overtakes the ploughman, but we must not always expect it. In some hearts God is long in preparing the soul by conviction: the law with its ten black horses drags the ploughshare of conviction up and down the soul till there is no one part of it left unfurrowed. Conviction goes deeper than any plough to the very core and centre of the spirit, till the spirit is wounded. The ploughers make deep furrows indeed when God puts his hand to the work: the soil of the heart is broken in pieces in the presence of the Most High.

Then comes the *sowing*. Before there can be a springing up it is certain that there must be something put into the ground, so that after the preacher has used the plough of the law, he applies to his Master for the seed-basket of the gospel. Gospel promises, gospel doctrines, especially a clear exposition of free grace and the atonement, these are the handfuls of corn which we scatter broadcast. Some of the grain falls on the highway, and is lost; but other handfuls fall where the plough has been, and there abide.

Then comes the *harrowing* work. We do not expect to sow seed and then leave it: the gospel has to be prayed over. The prayer of the preacher and the prayer of the Church make up God's harrow to rake in the seed after it is scattered, and so it is covered up within the clods of the soul, and is hidden in the heart of the hearer.

Now there is a reason why I dwell upon this, namely, that I may exhort my dear brethren who have not seen success, not to give up the work but to hope that they have been doing the ploughing, and sowing, and harrowing work, and that the harvest is to come. I mention this for yet another reason, and that is, by way of warning to those who expect to have a harvest without this preparatory work. I do not believe that much good will come from attempts at sudden revivals made without previous prayerful labour. A revival to be permanent must be a matter of growth, and the result of much holy effort, longing, pleading, and watching. The servant of God is to preach the gospel whether men are prepared for it or not; but in order to large success, depend upon it there is a preparedness necessary amongst the hearers. Upon some hearts warm earnest preaching drops like an unusual thing which startles but does not convince; while in other congregations, where good gospel preaching has long been the rule, and much prayer has been offered, the words fall into the hearers' souls and bring forth speedy fruit. We must not expect to have results without work. There is no hope of a church having an extensive revival in its midst unless there is continued and importunate waiting upon God, together with earnest labouring, intense anxiety, and hopeful expectation.

But there is also a work to be done which is beyond our power. After ploughing, sowing, and harrowing, there must come the shower from heaven. "Thou visitest the earth and waterest it;" says the Psalmist. In vain are all our efforts unless God shall bless us with the rain of his Holy Spirit's influence. O Holy Spirit! thou, and thou alone, workest wonders in the human heart, and thou comest from the Father and the Son to do the Father's purposes, and to glorify the Son.

Three effects are spoken of. First, we are told he *waters the ridges.* As the ridges of the field become well saturated through and through with the abundant rain, so God sends his Holy Spirit till the whole heart of man is moved and influenced by his divine operations. The understanding is enlightened, the conscience is quickened, the will is controlled, the affections are inflamed; all these powers, which I may call the ridges of the heart, come under the divine working. It is ours to deal with men as men, and bring to bear upon them gospel truth, and to set before them motives that are suitable to move rational creatures; but after all, it is the rain from on high which alone can water the ridges: there is no hope of the head being savingly affected except by divine operations.

Next, it is added, *"Thou settlest the furrows,"* by which some think it is meant that the furrows are drenched with water. Others think there is an allusion here to the beating down of the earth by heavy rain till the ridges become flat, and by the soaking of the water are settled into a more compact mass. Certain it is that the influences of God's Spirit have a humbling and settling effect upon a man. He was unsettled once like the earth that is dry and crumbly, and blown about and carried away with every wind of doctrine; but as the earth when soaked with wet is compacted and knit together, so the heart becomes solid and serious under the power of the Spirit. As the high parts of the ridge are beaten down into the furrows, so, the lofty ideas, the grand schemes, and carnal boastings of the heart begin to level down, when the Holy Spirit comes to work upon the soul. Genuine humility is a very gracious fruit of the Spirit. To be broken in heart is the best means of preparing the soul for Jesus. "A broken and a contrite heart, O God, thou wilt not despise." Brethren, always be thankful when you see high thoughts of man brought down; this settling the furrows is a very gracious preparatory work of grace.

Yet again, it is added, *"Thou makest it soft with showers?"* Man's heart is naturally hardened against the gospel; like the Eastern soil, it is hard as iron if there be no gracious rain. How sweetly and effectively does the Spirit of God soften the man through and through! He is no longer towards the Word what he used to be: he feels everything, whereas once he felt nothing. The rock flows with water; the heart is dissolved in tenderness, the eyes are melted into tears.

All this is God's work. I have said already that God works through us, but still it is God's immediate work to send down the rain of his grace from on high. Perhaps he is at work upon some of you, though as yet there is no springing up of spiritual life in your souls. Though your condition is still a sad one, we will hope for you that ere long there shall be seen the living seed of grace sending up its tender green shoot above the soil, and may the Lord bless the springing thereof.

II. In the second place, let us deliver A BRIEF DESCRIPTION OF THE SPRINGING THEREOF.

After the operations of the Holy Spirit have been quietly going on for a certain season as pleaseth the great Master and Husbandman, then there are signs of grace. Remember the apostle's words, "First the blade, then the ear, then the full corn in the ear." Some of our friends are greatly disturbed because they cannot see the full corn in the ear in themselves. They suppose that, if they were the subjects of a divine work, they would be precisely like certain advanced Christians with whom it is their privilege to commune, or of whom they may have read in biographies. Beloved, this is a very great mistake. When first grace enters the heart, it is not a great tree covering with its shadow whole acres, but it is the least of all seeds, like a grain of mustard seed. When it first rises upon the soul, it is not the sun shining at high noon, but it is the first dim ray of dawn. Are you so simple as to expect the harvest before you have passed through the springing-time? I shall hope that by a very brief description of the earliest stage of Christian experience you may be led to say, "I have gone as far as that," and then I hope you may be able to take the comfort of the text to yourselves: "Thou blessest the springing thereof."

What then is the springing up of piety in the heart? We think it is first seen in *sincerely earnest desires after salvation.* The man is not saved, in his own apprehension, but he longs to be. That which was once a matter of indifference is now a subject of intense concern. Once he despised Christians, and thought them needlessly earnest; he thought religion a mere trifle, and he looked upon the things of time and sense as the only substantial matters; but now how changed he is! He envies the meanest Christian, and would change places with the poorest believer if he might but be able to read his title clear to mansions in the skies. Now worldly things have lost dominion over him, and spiritual things are uppermost. Once with the unthinking many, he cried, "Who will show us any good?" but now he cries, "Lord, lift thou up the light of thy countenance upon me." Once it was the corn and the wine to which he looked for comfort, but now he looks to God alone. His rock of refuge must be God, for he finds no comfort elsewhere. His holy desires, which he had years ago, were like smoke from the chimney, soon blown away; but now his longings are permanent, though not always operative to the same degree. At times these desires amount to a hungering and a thirsting after righteousness, and yet he is not satisfied with these desires, but wishes for a still more anxious longing after heavenly things. These desires are among the first springings of divine life in the soul.

"The springing thereof" shows itself next in *prayer.* It *is* prayer now. Once it was the mocking of God with holy sounds unattended by the heart; but now, though the prayer is such that he would not like a human ear to hear him, yet God approves it, for it is the talking of a spirit to a Spirit, and not the muttering of lips to an unknown God. His prayers, perhaps, are not very long: they do not amount to more than this, "Oh!" "Ah!" "Would to God!" "Lord have mercy upon me, a sinner!" and such-like short ejaculations; but, then, they *are* prayers. "Behold he prayeth," does not

refer to a long prayer; it is quite as sure a proof of
spiritual life within, if it only refers to a sigh or to a
tear. These "groanings that cannot be uttered," are
amongst "the springings thereof."

There will also be manifest *a hearty love for the
means of grace,* and the house of God. The Bible, long
unread, which was thought to be of little more use
than an old almanac, is now treated with great
consideration; and though the reader finds little in it
that comforts him just now, and much that alarms
him, yet he feels that it is the book for him, and he
turns to its pages with hope. When he goes up to God's
house, he listens eagerly, hoping that there may be a
message for him. Before he attended worship as a sort
of pious necessity incumbent upon all respectable
people; but now he goes up to God's house that he
may find the Saviour. Once there was no more religion
in him than in the door which turns upon its hinges;
but now he enters the house praying, "Lord meet with
my soul," and if he gets no blessing, he goes away
sighing, "O that I knew where I might find him, that I
might come even to his seat." This is one of the blessed
signs of "the springing thereof."

Yet more cheering is another, namely, that the soul
in this state has *faith in Jesus Christ,* at least in some
degree. It is not a faith which brings great joy and
peace, but still it is a faith which keeps the heart from
despair and prevents its sinking under a sense of sin.
I have known the time when I do not believe any man
living could see faith in me, and when I could scarcely
perceive any in myself, and yet I was bold to say, with
Peter, "Lord, thou knowest all things, *thou* knowest
that I love Thee." What man cannot see, Christ can
see. Many people have faith in the Lord Jesus Christ,
but they are so much engaged looking at it that they
do not see it. If they would look to Christ and not to

their own faith, they not only see Christ but see their own faith too; but they measure their faith, and it seems so little when they contrast it with the faith of full-grown Christians, that they fear it is not faith at all. Oh, little one, if thou hast faith enough to receive Christ, remember the promise, "To as many as received him, to them gave he power to become the sons of God." Poor simple, weak-hearted, and troubled one, look to Jesus and answer, Can such a Saviour suffer in vain? Can such an atonement be offered in vain? Canst thou trust him, and yet be cast away? It cannot be. It never was in the Saviour's heart to shake off one that did cling to his arm. However feeble the faith he blesses "the springing thereof." The difficulty arises partly from misapprehension and partly from want of confidence in God. I say misapprehension: now if like some Londoners you had never seen corn when it is green, you would cry out, "What! Do you say that yonder green stuff is wheat?" "Yes," the farmer says, "that is wheat." You look at it again and you reply, "Why, man alive, that is nothing but grass. You do not mean to tell me that this grassy stuff will ever produce a loaf of bread such as I see in the baker's window; I cannot conceive it." No, you could not conceive it, but when you get accustomed to it, it is not at all wonderful to see the wheat go through certain stages; first the blade, then the ear, and afterwards the full corn in the ear. Some of you have never seen growing grace, and do not know anything about it. When you are newly converted you meet with Christians who are like ripe golden ears, and you say, "I am not like them." True, you are no more like them than that grassy stuff in the furrows is like full-grown wheat; but you will grow like them one of these days. You must expect to go through the blade period before you get to the ear period, and in the ear period you

will have doubts whether you will ever come to the
full corn in the ear; but you will arrive at perfection
in due time. Thank God that you are in Christ at all.
Whether I have much faith or little faith, whether I
can do much for Christ or little for Christ is not the
first question; I am saved, not on account of what I
am, but on account of what Jesus Christ is; and if I
am trusting to him, however little in Israel I may be, I
am as safe as the brightest of the saints.

I have said, however, that mixed with
misapprehension there is a great deal of unbelief. I
cannot put it all down to an ignorance that may be
forgiven: for there is sinful unbelief too. O sinner, why
do you not trust Jesus Christ? Poor quickened,
awakened conscience, God gives you his word that he
who trusts in Christ is not condemned, and yet you
are afraid that you are condemned! This is to give God
the lie! Be ashamed and confounded that you should
ever have been guilty of doubting the veracity of God.
All your other sins do not grieve Christ so much as
the sin of thinking that he is unwilling to forgive you,
or the sin of suspecting that if you trust him he will
cast you away. Do not slander his gracious character.
Do not cast a slur upon the generosity of his tender
heart. He saith, "Him that cometh to me I will in no
wise cast out." Come in the faith of his promise, and
he will receive you just now.

I have thus given some description of "the springing
thereof."

III. Thirdly, according to the text, THERE IS ONE WHO
SEES THIS SPRINGING. Thou, Lord—*thou* blessest the
springing thereof.

I wish that some of us had quicker eyes to see the
beginning of grace in the souls of men; for want of
this we let slip many opportunities of helping the

weaklings. If a woman had the charge of a number of children that were not her own, I do not suppose she would notice all the incipient stages of disease; but when a mother nurses her own dear children, as soon as ever upon the cheek or in the eye there is a token of approaching sickness, she perceives it at once. I wish we had just as quick an eye, because just as tender a heart, towards precious souls. I do not doubt that many young people are weeks and even months in distress, who need not be, if you who know the Lord were a little more watchful to help them in the time of their sorrow. Shepherds are up all night at lambing time to catch up the lambs as soon as they are born, and take them in and nurse them; and we, who ought to be shepherds for God, should be looking out for all the lambs, especially at seasons when there are many born into God's great fold, for tender nursing is wanted in the first stages of the new life. God, however, when his servants do not see "the springing thereof," sees it all.

Now, you silent retired spirits, who dare not speak to father or mother, or brother or sister, this text ought to be a sweet morsel to you. *"Thou* blessest the springing thereof," which proves that God sees you and your new-born grace. The Lord sees the first sign of penitence. Though you only say to yourself, "I will arise, and go to my Father," your Father hears you. Though it is nothing but a desire, your Father registers it. "Thou puttest my tears into thy bottle. Are they not in thy book?" He is watching your return; he runs to meet you, and puts his arms about you, and kisses you with the kisses of his accepting love. O soul, be encouraged with that thought, that up in the chamber or down by the hedge, or wherever it is that thou hast sought secrecy, God is there. Dwell on the thought, "Thou God seest me." That is a precious text,—"All my desire is before thee;" and here is another sweet one, "The Lord taketh pleasure in them that fear him, in them that hope in his mercy." He can see you when you only hope in his mercy, and he takes pleasure in you if you have only begun to fear him. Here is a third choice word, "Thou wilt perfect that which concerneth me." Have you a concern about these things? Is it a matter of soul-concern with you to be reconciled to God, and to have an interest in Jesu's precious blood? It is only "the springing thereof," but he blesses it. It is written, "A bruised reed he will not break, and the smoking flax he will not quench, till he bring forth judgment unto victory." There shall be victory for you, even before the judgment-seat of God, though as yet you are only like the flax that smokes and gives no light, or like the reed that is broken, and yields no music. God sees the first springing of grace.

IV. A few words upon a fourth point: WHAT A MISERY IT WOULD BE, IF IT WERE POSSIBLE, TO HAVE THIS SPRINGING WITHOUT GOD'S BLESSING!

The text says, "Thou *blessest* the springing thereof." We must, just a moment, by way of contrast, think of how the springing would have been without the blessing. Suppose we were to see a revival amongst us without God's blessing. It is my conviction that there are revivals which are not of God at all, but are produced by excitement merely. If there be no blessing from the Lord, it will be all a delusion, a bubble blown up into the air for a moment, and then gone to nothing. We shall only see the people stirred, to become the more dull and dead afterwards; and this is a great mischief to the church.

In the individual heart, if there should be a springing up without God's blessing, there would be no good in it. Suppose you have good desires, but no blessing on these desires, they will only tantalise and worry you; and then, after a time, they wilt be gone, and you will be more impervious than you were before to religious convictions; for, if religious desires are not of God's sending, but are caused by excitement, they will probably prevent your giving a serious hearing to the Word of God in times to come. If convictions do not soften they will certainly harden. To what extremities have some been driven who have had springings of a certain sort which have not led them to Christ! Some have been crushed by despair. They tell us that religion crowds the madhouse: it is not true; but there is no doubt whatever that religiousness of a certain kind has driven many a man out of his mind. The poor souls have felt their wound but have not seen the balm. They have not known Jesus. They have had a sense of sin and nothing more. They have not fled for refuge to the hope which God has set before them. Marvel not if men do go mad when they refuse the Saviour. It may come as a judicial visitation of God upon those men who, when in great distress of mind, will not fly to Christ. I believe it is with some just this— you must either fly to Jesus, or else your burden will become heavier and heavier until your spirit will utterly fail. This is not the fault of religion, it is the fault of those who will not accept the remedy which religion presents. A springing up of desires without God's blessing would be an awful thing, but we thank him that we are not left in such a case.

V. And now I have to dwell upon THE COMFORTING THOUGHT THAT GOD DOES BLESS "THE SPRINGING THEREOF." I wish to deal with you who are tender and troubled; I want to show that God *does* bless your springing. He does it in many ways.

Frequently he does it by the cordials which he

brings. You have a few very sweet moments: you cannot say that you are Christ's, but at times the bells of your heart ring very sweetly at the mention of his name. The means of grace are very precious to you. When you gather to the Lord's worship you feel a holy calm, and you go away from the service wishing that there were seven Sundays in the week instead of one. By the blessing of God the Word has just suited your case, as if the Lord had sent his servants on purpose to you: you lay aside your crutches for awhile, and you begin to run. Though these things have been sadly transient they are tokens for good.

On the other hand, if you have had none of these comforts, or few of them, and the means of grace have not been consolations to you, I want you to look upon that as a blessing. It may be the greatest blessing that God can give us to take away all comforts on the road, in order to quicken our running towards the end. When a man is flying to the City of Refuge to be protected from the man-slayer, it may be an act of great consideration to stay him for a moment that he may quench his thirst and run more swiftly afterwards; but perhaps, in a case of imminent peril, it may be the kindest thing neither to give him anything to eat or to drink, nor invite him to stop for a moment, in order that he may fly with undiminished speed to the place of safety. The Lord may be blessing you in the uneasiness which you feel. Inasmuch as you cannot say that you are in Christ, it may be the greatest blessing which heaven can give to take away every other blessing from you, in order that you may be compelled to fly to the Lord. You perhaps have a little of your self-righteousness left, and while it is so you cannot get joy and comfort. The royal robe which Jesus gives will never shine brilliantly upon us till every rag of our own goodness is gone. Perhaps you are not empty enough, and God will never fill you with Christ till you are. Fear often drives men to faith. Have you never heard of a person walking in the fields into whose bosom a bird has flown because pursued by the hawk! Poor timid thing, it would not have ventured there had not a greater fear compelled it. All this may be so with you; your fears may be sent to drive you more swiftly and more closely to the Saviour, and if so, I see in these present sorrows the signs that God is blessing "the springing thereof."

In looking back upon my own "springing" I sometimes think God blessed me then in a lovelier way than now. Though I would not willingly return to that early stage of my spiritual life, yet there were many joys about it. An apple tree when loaded with apples is a very comely sight; but give me, for beauty, the apple tree in bloom. The whole world does not present a more lovely sight than an apple blossom. Now, a full-grown Christian laden with fruit is a comely sight, but still there is a peculiar loveliness about the young Christian. Let me tell you what that blessedness is; you have probably now a greater horror of sin than professors who have known the Lord for years; they might wish that they felt your tenderness of conscience. You have now a graver sense of duty, and a more solemn fear of the neglect of it than some who are further advanced. You have also a greater zeal than many: you are now doing your first works for God, and burning with your first love; nothing is too hot or too heavy for you: I pray that you may never decline, but always advance.

And now to close. I think there are three lessons for us to learn. First, *let older saints be very gentle and kind to young believers.* God blesses the springing thereof—mind that you do the same. Do not throw cold water upon young desires: do not snuff out young believers with hard questions. While they are babes and need the milk of the Word, do not be choking them with your strong meat; they will eat strong meat by-and-by, but not just yet. Remember, Jacob would not overdrive the lambs; be equally prudent. Teach and instruct them, but let it be with gentleness and tenderness, not as their superiors, but as nursing fathers for Christ's sake. God, you see, blesses the springing thereof—may he bless it through you!

The next thing I have to say is, *fulfil the duty of gratitude.* Beloved, if God blesses the springing thereof we ought to be grateful for a little grace. If you have only seen the first shoot peeping up through the mould be thankful, and you shall see the green blade waving in the breeze; be thankful for the ankle-deep verdure and you shall soon see the commencement of the ear; be thankful for the first green ears and you shalt see the flowering of the wheat, and by-and-by its ripening, and the joyous harvest.

The last lesson is one of *encouragement.* If God blesses "the springing thereof," dear beginners, what will he not do for you in after days? If he gives you such a meal when you break your fast, what dainties will be on your table when he says to you, "Come and dine"; and what a banquet will he furnish at the supper of the Lamb! O troubled one! let the storms which howl and the snows which fall, and the wintry blasts that nip your springing, all be forgotten in this one consoling thought that God blesses your springing, and whom God blesses none can curse. Over your head, dear, desiring, pleading, languishing soul, the Lord of heaven and earth pronounces the blessing of the Father, and the Son, and the Holy Spirit. Take that blessing and rejoice in it evermore. Amen.

Farm Labourers

"I have planted, Apollos watered but God gave the increase. So then neither is he that planteth any thing, neither he that watereth; but God that giveth the increase. Now he that planteth and he that watereth are one: and every man shall receive his own reward according to his own labour. For we are labourers together with God: ye are God's husbandry."—1 Corinthians iii. 6-9.

I SHALL begin at the end of my text, because I find it to be the easiest way of mapping out my discourse. We shall first remark that *the church is God's farm:* "Ye are God's husbandry." In the margin of the revised version we read, "Ye are God's tilled ground," and that is the very expression for me. "Ye are God's tilled ground," or farm. After we have spoken of the farm we will next say a little upon the fact that *the Lord employs labourers* on his estate: and when we have looked at the labourers—such poor fellows as they are—we will remember that *God himself is the great worker:* "We are labourers together with God."

I. We begin by considering that THE CHURCH IS GOD'S FARM. The Lord has made the church his own by his sovereign *choice.* He has also secured it unto himself by *purchase,* having paid for it a price immense. "The Lord's portion is his people; Jacob is the lot of his inheritance." Every acre of God's farm cost the Saviour a bloody sweat, yea, the blood of his heart. He loved us, and gave himself for us: that is the price he paid. Henceforth the church is God's freehold, and he holds the title deeds of it. It is our joy to feel that we are not our own, we are bought with a price. The church is God's farm by choice and purchase.

And now he has made it his by *enclosure.* It lay exposed aforetime as part of an open common, bare and barren, covered with thorns and thistles, and the haunt of every wild beast; for we were "by nature the children of wrath, even as others." Divine foreknowledge surveyed the waste, and electing love marked out its portion with a full line of grace, and thus set us apart to be the Lord's own estate for ever. In due time effectual grace came forth with power, and separated us from the rest of mankind, as fields are hedged and ditched to part them from the open heath. Hath not the Lord declared that he hath chosen his vineyard and fenced it?

> "We are a garden wall'd around,
>   Chosen and made peculiar ground;
>   A little spot, enclosed by grace
>   Out of the world's wide wilderness."

The Lord has also made this farm evidently his own by *cultivation.* What more could he have done for his farm? He has totally changed the nature of the soil: from being barren he hath made it a fruitful land. He hath ploughed it, and digged it, and fattened it, and watered it and planted it with all manner of flowers and fruits. It hath already brought forth to him many a pleasant cluster, and there are brighter times to come, when angels shall shout the harvest home, and Christ shall see of the travail of his soul, and shall be satisfied."

This farm is preserved by the Lord's continual protection. Not only did he enclose it, and cultivate it by his miraculous power, to make it his own farm, but he continually maintains possession of it. "I the Lord do keep it; I will water it every moment: lest any hurt it, I will keep it night and day." If it were not for God's continual power her hedges would soon be thrown down, and wild beasts would devour her fields. Wicked hands are always trying to break down her walls and lay her waste again, so that there should be no true church in the world; but the Lord is jealous for his land, and will not allow it to be destroyed. A church would not long remain a church if God did not preserve it unto himself. What if God should say, "I will take away the hedge thereof, and it shall be eaten up; and break down the wall thereof, and it shall be trodden down"? What a wilderness it would become. What saith he? "Go ye now unto my place which was in Shiloh, where I set my name at the first, and see what I did to it for the wickedness of my people Israel." Go ye to Jerusalem, where of old was the city of his glory and the shrine of his indwelling, and what is left there today? Go ye to Rome, where once Paul preached the gospel with power: what is it now but the centre of idolatry? The Lord may remove the candlestick, and leave a place that was bright as day to become black as darkness itself. Hence God's farm remains a farm because he is ever in it to prevent its returning to its former wildness. Omnipotent power is as needful to keep the fields of the church under cultivation as to reclaim them at the first.

Inasmuch as the church is God's own farm, *he expects to receive a harvest from it.* The world is waste, and he looks for nothing from it; but we are tilled land, and therefore a harvest is due from us. Barrenness suits the moorland, but to a farm it would be a great discredit. Love looks for returns of love; grace given demands gracious fruit. Watered with the drops of the Saviour's bloody sweat, shall we not bring forth a hundredfold to his praise? Kept by the eternal Spirit of God, shall there not be produced in us fruits to his glory? The Lord's husbandry upon us has shown a great expenditure of cost, and labour, and thought; ought there not to be a proportionate return? Ought not the Lord to have a harvest of obedience, a harvest of holiness, a harvest of usefulness, a harvest of praise? Shall it not be so? I think some churches forget that an increase is expected from every field of the Lord's farm, for they never have a harvest or even look for one. Farmers do not plough their lands or sow their fields for amusement; they mean business, and plough and sow because they desire a harvest. If this fact could but enter into the heads of some professors, surely they would look at things in a different light; but of late it has seemed as if we thought that God's church was not expected to produce anything, but existed for her own comfort and personal benefit. Brethren, it must not be so; the great Husbandman must have some reward for his husbandry. Every field must yield its increase, and the whole estate must bring forth to his praise. We join with the bride in the Song in saying, "My vineyard, which is mine, is before me: thou, O Solomon, must have a thousand, and those that keep the fruit thereof two hundred."

But I come back to the place from which I started. This farm is, by choice, by purchase, by enclosure, by cultivation, by preservation, entirely the Lord's. See, then, the injustice of allowing any of the labourers to call even a part of the estate his own. When a great man has a large farm of his own, what would he think if Hodge the ploughman should say, "Look here, I plough this farm, and therefore it is mine: I shall call this field Hodge's Acres"? "No," says Hobbs, "I reaped that land last harvest, and therefore it is mine, and I shall call it Hobbs's Field." What if all the other labourers became Hodgeites and Hobbsites, and so parcelled out the farm among them? I think the landlord would soon eject the lot of them. The farm belongs to its owner, and let it be called by his name but it is absurd to call it by the names of the men who labour upon it. Shall insignificant nobodies rob God of his glory? Remember how Paul put it: "Who then is Paul, and who is Apollos?" "Is Christ divided? was Paul crucified for you? or were ye baptized in the name of Paul?" The entire church belongs to him who has chosen it in his sovereignty, bought it with his blood, fenced it by his grace, cultivated it by his wisdom, and preserved it by his power. There is but one church on the face of the earth, and those who love the Lord should keep this truth in mind. Paul is a labourer, Apollos is a labourer, Cephas is a labourer; but the farm is not Paul's, not so much as a rood of it, nor does a single parcel of land belong to Apollos, or the smallest allotment to Cephas; for "Ye are Christ's." The fact is that in this case the labourers belong to the land, and not the land to the labourers: "For all things are yours; whether Paul, or Apollos, or Cephas." "We preach not ourselves, but Christ Jesus the Lord; and ourselves your servants for Jesus' sake."

II. We have now to notice, as our second head, that
THE GREAT HUSBANDMAN EMPLOYS LABOURERS. *By human
agency God ordinarily works out his designs.* He can,
if he pleases, by his Holy Spirit get directly at the
hearts of men, but that is his business, and not ours;
we have to do with such words as these: "It pleased
God by the foolishness of preaching to save them that
believe." The Master's commission is not, "Sit still and
see the Spirit of God convert the nations;" but, "Go ye
into all the world, and preach the gospel to every
creature." Observe God's method in supplying the race
with food. In answer to the prayer, "Give us this day
our daily bread," he might have bidden the clouds drop
manna, morning by morning, at each man's door; but
he sees that it is for our good to work, and so he uses
the hands of the ploughman and the sower for our
supply. God might cultivate his chosen farm, the
church, by miracle, or by angels; but in great
condescension he blesses her through her own sons
and daughters. He employs us for our own good; for
we who are labourers in his fields receive much more
good for ourselves than we bestow. Labour develops
our spiritual muscle and keeps us in health. "Unto
me," says Paul, "who am less than the least of all
saints, is this grace given, that I should preach among
the Gentiles the unsearchable riches of Christ."

Our great Master means that every labourer on his
farm should receive some benefit from it for he never
muzzles the mouth of the ox that treadeth out the corn.
The labourer's daily bread comes out of the soil.
Though he works not for himself, but for his Master,
yet still he has his portion of food. In the Lord's granary
there is seed for the sower, but there is also bread for
the eater. However disinterestedly we may serve God
in the husbandry of his church we are ourselves

partakers of the fruit. It is a great condescension on God's part that he uses us at all, for we are poor tools at the best and more hindrance than help.

The labourers employed by God are all *occupied upon needful work.* Notice: "I have planted, Apollos watered." Who beat the big drum, or blew his own trumpet? Nobody. On God's farm none are kept for ornamental purposes. I have read some sermons which could only have been meant for show, for there was not a grain of gospel in them. They were ploughs with the share left out, drills with no wheat in the box, clod-crushers made of butter. I do not believe that our God will ever pay wages to men who only walk about his grounds to show themselves. Orators who display their eloquence in the pulpit are more like gypsies who stray on the farm to pick up chickens, than honest labourers who work to bring forth a crop for their master. Many of the members of our churches live as if their only business on the farm was to pluck blackberries or gather wild flowers. They are great at finding fault with other people's ploughing and mowing; but not a hand's turn will they do themselves. Come on, my good fellows. Why stand ye all the day idle? The harvest is plenteous, and the labourers are few. You who think yourselves more cultivated than ordinary people, if you are indeed Christians, must not strut about and despise those who are hard at work. If you do, I shall say, "That person has mistaken his master; he may probably be in the employ of some gentleman farmer, who cares more for show than profit; but our great Lord is practical, and on his estate his labourers attend to needful labour." When you and I preach or teach it will be well if we say to ourselves, "What will be the use of what I am going to do? I am about to teach a difficult subject: will it do any good? I have chosen an abstruse point of theology: will it serve any purpose?" Brethren, a labourer may work very hard at a whim of his own, and yet it may be all waste labour. Some discourses do little more than show the difference between tweedle-*dum* and tweedle-*dee*, and what is the use of that? Suppose we sow the fields with sawdust, or sprinkle them with rosewater, what of that? Will God bless our moral essays, and fine compositions, and pretty passages? Brethren, we must aim at usefulness: we must as labourers together with God be occupied with something that is worth doing. "I," says one, "have planted": it is well, for planting must be done. "I," answers another, "have watered": that also is good and necessary. See to it that ye can each bring in a solid report; but let no man be content with the mere child's-play of oratory, or the getting up of entertainments and such like.

On the Lord's farm *there is a division of labour.* Even Paul did not say, "I have planted and watered." No, Paul planted. And certainly Apollos could not say, "I have planted as well as watered." No, it was enough for him to attend to the watering. No man has all gifts. How foolish, then, are they who say, "I enjoy So-and-so's ministry because he edifies the saints in doctrine; but when he was away the other Sunday I could not profit by the preacher because he was all for the conversion of sinners." Yes, he was planting; you have been planted a good while, and do not need planting again; but you ought to be thankful that others are made partakers of the benefit. One soweth and another reapeth, and therefore instead of grumbling at the honest ploughman because he did not bring a sickle with him, you ought to have prayed for him that he might have strength to plough deep and break up hard hearts.

Observe that, on God's farm, *there is unity of*

purpose among the labourers. Read the text. "Now he that planteth and he that watereth are one." One Master has employed them, and though he may send them out at different times, and to different parts of the farm, yet they are all one in being used for one end, to work for one harvest. In England we do not understand what is meant by watering, because the farmer could not water all his farm; but in the East a farmer waters almost every inch of his ground. He would have no crop if he did not use all means for irrigating the fields. If you have ever been in Italy, Egypt, or Palestine, you will have seen a complete system of wells, pumps, wheels, buckets, channels, little streamlets, pipes, and so on, by which the water is carried all over the garden to every plant, otherwise in the extreme heat of the sun it would be dried up. Planting needs wisdom, watering needs quite as much, and the piecing of these two works together needs that the labourers should be of one mind. It is a bad thing when labourers are at cross purposes, and work against each other, and this evil is worse in the church than anywhere else. How can I plant with success if my helper will not water what I have planted; or what is the use of my watering if nothing is planted? Husbandry is spoiled when foolish people undertake it, and quarrel over it; for from sowing to reaping the work is one, and all must be done to one end. Let us pull together all our days, for strife brings barrenness.

We are called upon to notice in our text that *all the labourers put together are nothing at all.* "Neither is he that planteth any thing, neither he that watereth." The workmen are nothing at all without their master. All the labourers on a farm could not manage it if they had no one at their head, and all the preachers and Christian workers in the world can do nothing unless

God be with them. Remember that every labourer on
God's farm has derived all his qualifications from God.
No man knows how to plant or water souls except the
Lord teaches him from day to day. All these holy gifts
are grants of free grace. All the labourers work under
God's direction and arrangement, or they work in vain.
They would not know when or how to do their work if
their Master did not guide them by his Spirit, without
whose help they cannot even think a good thought.
All God's labourers must go to him for their seed, or
else they will scatter tares. All good seed comes out of
God's granary. If we preach, it must be the true word
of God, or nothing can come of it. More than that, all
the strength that is in the labourer's arm to sow the
heavenly seed must be given by the Master. We cannot
preach except God be with us. A sermon is vain talk
and dreary word-spinning unless the Holy Spirit
enlivens it. He must give us both the preparation of
the heart and the answer of the tongue, or we shall be
as men who sow the wind. When the good seed is sown
the whole success of it rests with God. If he withhold
the dew and the rain the seed will never rise from the
ground; and unless he shall shine upon it the green
ear will never ripen. The human heart will remain
barren, even though Paul himself should preach,
unless God the Holy Ghost shall work with Paul and
bless the word to those that hear it. Therefore, since
the increase is of God alone, put the labourers into
their place. Do not make too much of us; for when we
have done all we are unprofitable servants.

Yet, though inspiration calls the labourers nothing,
it says that *they shall be rewarded.* God works our
good works in us, and then rewards us for them. Here
we have mention of a personal service, and a personal
reward: "Every man shall receive his own reward

according to his own labour." The reward is proportionate, not to the success, but to the labour. Many discouraged workers may be comforted by that expression. You are not to be paid by results, but by endeavours. You may have a stiff bit of clay to plough, or a dreary plot of land to sow, where stones, and birds, and thorns, and travellers, and a burning sun may all be leagued against the seed; but you are not accountable for these things; your reward shall be according to your work. Some put a great deal of labour into a little field, and make much out of it. Others use a great deal of labour throughout a long life, and yet they see but small result, for it is written, "One soweth, and another reapeth"; but the reaping man will not get all the reward, the sowing man shall receive his portion of the joy. The labourers are nobodies, but they shall enter into the joy of their Lord.

Unitedly, according to the text, *the workers have been successful,* and that is a great part of their reward. "I have planted, Apollos watered; but God gave the increase." Frequently brethren say in their prayers, "A Paul may plant, an Apollos may water, but it is all in vain unless God gives the increase." This is quite true; but another truth is too much overlooked, namely, that, when Paul plants and Apollos waters, God does give the increase. We do not labour in vain. There would be no increase without God; but then we are not without God: when such men as Paul and Apollos plant and water, there is sure to be an increase; they are the right kind of labourers, they work in a right spirit, and God is certain to bless them. This is a great part of the labourers' wages.

III. So much upon the labourers. Now for the main point again. GOD HIMSELF IS THE GREAT WORKER. He may use what labourers he pleases, but the increase comes alone from him. Brethren, you know it is so in natural things: the most skilful farmer cannot make the wheat germinate, and grow, and ripen. He cannot even preserve a single field till harvest time, for the farmer's enemies are many and mighty. In husbandry there's many a slip 'twixt the cup and the lip; and when the farmer thinks, good easy man, that he shall reap his crop, there are blights and mildews lingering about to rob him of his gains. God must give the increase. If any man is dependent on God it is the husbandman, and through him we are all of us dependent upon God from year to year for the food by which we live. Even the king must live by the produce of the field. God gives the increase in the barn and the hayrick; and in the spiritual farm it is even more so, for what can man do in this business? If any of you think that it is an easy thing to win a soul I should like you to attempt it. Suppose that without divine aid you should try to save a soul—you might as well attempt to make a world. Why, you cannot create a fly, how can you create a new heart and a right spirit? Regeneration is a great mystery, it is out of your reach. "The wind bloweth where it listeth, and thou hearest the sound thereof, but canst not tell whence it cometh, and whither it goeth: so is everyone that is born of the Spirit." What can you and I do in this matter? it is far beyond our line. We can tell out the truth of God; but to apply that truth to the heart and conscience is quite another thing. I have preached Jesus Christ with my whole heart, and yet I know that I have never produced a saving effect upon a single unregenerate man unless the Spirit of God has opened the heart and placed the living seed of truth within it. Experience teaches us this. Equally is it the Lord's work to keep the seed alive when it springs up. We think we have converts, and we are not long before we are disappointed in them. Many are like blossoms on our apple trees; they are fair to look upon, but they do not come to anything; and others are like the many little apples which fall off long before they have come to any size. He who presides over a great church, and feels an agony for the souls of men, will soon be convinced that if God does not work there will be no work done: we shall see no conversion, no sanctification, no final perseverance, no glory brought to God, no satisfaction for the passion of the Saviour, unless the Lord be with us. Well said our Lord, "Without me ye can do nothing."

Briefly I would draw certain practical lessons out of this important truth: the first is, if the whole farm of the church belongs exclusively to the great Master Worker, and the labourers are worth nothing without him, *let this promote unity among all whom he employs.* If we are all under one Master, do not let us quarrel. It is a miserable business when we cannot bear to see good being done by those of a different denomination who work in ways of their own. If a new labourer comes on the farm, and he uses a hoe of a new shape, shall I become his enemy? If he does his work better than I do mine, shall I be jealous? Do you not remember reading in the Scriptures that, upon one occasion, the disciples could not cast out a devil? This ought to have made them humble; but to our surprise we read a few verses further on that they saw one casting out devils in Christ's name, and they forbade him because he followed not with their company. *They* could not cast out the devil themselves, and they forbade those who could. A certain band of people are going about winning souls, but because they are not doing it in our fashion, we do not like it. It is true they have odd ways; but they do really save souls, and that is the main point. Instead of cavilling, let us encourage all on Christ's side. Wisdom is justified of her children, though some of them are far from handsome. The labourers ought to be satisfied with the new ploughman if their Master smiles upon him. Brother, if the great Lord has employed you, it is no business of mine to question his choice. Can I lend you a hand? Can I show you how to work better? Or can you show me how I can improve? This is the proper behaviour of one workman to another.

This truth, however, ought to *keep all the labourers very dependent.* Are you going to preach, young man? "Yes, I am going to do a great deal of good." Are you? Have you forgotten that you are nothing? "Neither is he that planteth anything." A divine is coming brimful of the gospel to comfort the saints. If he is not coming in strict dependence upon God, he, too, is nothing. "Neither is he that watereth anything." Power belongeth unto God. Man is vanity and his words are wind; to God alone belongeth power and wisdom. If we keep our places in all lowliness our Lord will use us; but if we exalt ourselves he will leave us to our nothingness.

Next notice that *this fact ennobles everybody who labours in God's husbandry.* My soul is lifted up with joy when I mark these words, "For we are labourers together with God:" mere labourers on his farm, and yet labourers *with him.* Does the Lord work with its? We know he does by the signs following. "My Father worketh hitherto, and I work," is language for all the sons of God as well as for the great Firstborn. God is with you, my brethren, when you are serving him with all your heart. Speaking to your class concerning Jesus, it is God that speaks by you; picking up that stranger on the way, and telling him of salvation by faith, Christ is speaking through you even as he spoke with the woman at the well; addressing the rough crowd in the open air, young man, if you are preaching pardon through the atoning blood, it is the God of Peter who is testifying of his Son, even as he did on the day of Pentecost.

But, lastly, *how this should drive us to our knees.* Since we are nothing without God, let us cry mightily unto him for help in this our holy service. Let both sower and reaper pray together, or they will never rejoice together. If the blessing be withheld, it is because we do not cry for it and expect it. Brother labourers, come to the mercy-seat and we shall yet see the reapers return from the fields bringing their sheaves with them, though, perhaps, they went forth weeping to the sowing. To our Father, who is the husbandman be all glory, for ever and ever. Amen.

What the Farm Labourers can do and what they cannot do

"And he said, So is the kingdom of God, as if a man should cast seed into the ground; and should sleep, and rise night and day, and the seed should spring and grow up, he knoweth not how. For the earth bringeth forth fruit of herself; first the blade, then the ear, after that the full corn in the ear. But when the fruit is brought forth, immediately he putteth in the sickle, because the harvest is come."—Mark iv. 26-29.

HERE is a lesson for labourers together with God. It is a parable for all who are concerned in the kingdom of God. It will be of little value to those who are in the kingdom of darkness for they are not bidden to sow the good seed: "Unto the wicked God saith, What hast thou to do to declare my statutes?" But all who are commissioned to scatter seed for the Royal Husbandman, will be glad to know how the harvest is preparing for him whom they serve. Listen, then, ye that sow beside all waters; ye that with holy diligence seek to fill the garners of heaven,—listen, and may the Spirit of God speak into your ears as you are able to bear it.

I. We shall, first learn from our text WHAT WE CAN DO AND WHAT WE CANNOT DO. Let this stand as our first head.

"So is the kingdom of God, as if a man should cast seed into the ground:" this the gracious worker can do. "And the seed should spring and grow up, he knoweth not how:" this is what he cannot do: seed once sown is beyond human jurisdiction, and man can neither make it spring nor grow. Yet ere long the worker comes in again:—"When the fruit is brought forth, immediately he putteth in the sickle." We can reap in due season, and it is both our duty and our privilege to do so. You see, then, that there is a place for the worker at the beginning, and though there is no room for him in the middle passage, yet another opportunity is given him farther on when that which he sowed has actually yielded fruit.

Notice, then, that *we can sow.* Any man who has received the knowledge of the grace of God in his heart can teach others. I include under the term "man" all who know the Lord, be they male or female. We cannot all teach alike, for all have not the same gifts; to one is given one talent, and to another ten; neither have we all the same opportunities, for one lives in obscurity and another has far-reaching influence; yet there is not within the family of God an infant hand which may not drop its own tiny seed into the ground. There is not a man among us who needs to stand idle in the market-place, for work suitable to his strength is waiting for him. There is not a saved woman who is left without a holy task; let her do it and win the approving word, "She hath done what she could."

We need never quarrel with God because we cannot do everything, if he only permits us to do this one thing; for sowing the good seed is a work which will need all our wit, our strength, our love, our care. Holy seed sowing should be adopted as our highest pursuit and it will be no inferior object for the noblest life. You will need heavenly teaching that you may carefully select the wheat, and keep it free from the darnel of error. You will require instruction to winnow out of it your own thoughts and opinions; for these may not be according to the mind of God. Men are not saved by our word, but by God's word. We need grace to learn the gospel aright and to teach the whole of it. To different men we must, with discretion, bring forward that part of the word of God which will best bear upon their consciences; for much may depend upon the word being *in season.*

Having selected the seed, we shall have plenty of work if we go forth and sow it broadcast everywhere, for every day brings its opportunity, and every company furnishes its occasion. "In the morning sow thy seed, and in the evening withhold not thy hand." "Sow beside all waters."

Still, wise sowers discover favourable opportunities for sowing, and gladly seize upon them. There are times when it would clearly be a waste to sow; for the soil could not receive it, it is not in a fit condition. After a shower, or before a shower, or at some such time as he that hath studied husbandry prefers, then must we be up and doing. While we are to work for God always, yet there are seasons when it were casting pearls before swine to talk of holy things, and there are other times when to be silent would be a great sin. Sluggards in the time for ploughing and sowing are sluggards indeed, for they not only waste the day, but throw away the year. If you watch for souls, and use hours of happy vantage, and moments of sacred softening, you will not complain of the scanty space allowed for agency. Even should you never be called to water, or to reap, your office is wide enough if you fulfil the work of the sower.

For little though it seem to teach the simple truth of the gospel, yet it is essential. How shall men hear without a teacher? Servants of God, the seed of the word is not like thistle-down, which is borne by every wind; but the wheat of the kingdom needs a human hand to sow it and without such agency it will not enter into men's hearts, neither can it bring forth fruit to the glory of God. The preaching of the gospel is the necessity of every age; God grant that our country may never be deprived of it. Even if the Lord should send us a famine of bread and of water, may he never send us a famine of the word of God. Faith cometh by hearing, and how can there be hearing if there is no teaching? Scatter ye, scatter ye, then, the seed of the kingdom, for this is essential to the harvest.

This seed should be sown often, for many are the foes of the wheat, and if you repeat not your sowing you may never see a harvest. The seed must be sown everywhere, too, for there are no choice corners of the world that you can afford to let alone, in the hope that they will be self-productive. You may not leave the rich and intelligent under the notion that surely the gospel will be found among them, for it is not so: the pride of life leads them away from God. You may not leave the poor and illiterate, and say, "Surely they will of themselves feel their need of Christ." Not so: they will sink from degradation to degradation unless you uplift them with the gospel. No tribe of man, no peculiar constitution of the human mind, may be neglected by us; but everywhere we must preach the word in season and out of season. I have heard that Captain Cook, the celebrated circumnavigator, in whatever part of the earth he landed, took with him a little packet of English seeds, and scattered them in suitable places. He would leave the boat and wander up from the shore. He said nothing, but quietly scattered the seeds wherever he went, so that he belted the world with the flowers and herbs of his native land. Imitate him wherever you go; sow spiritual seed in every place that your foot shall tread upon.

Let us now think of what you cannot do. *You cannot, after the seed has left your hand, cause it to put forth life.* I am sure you cannot make it grow, for you do not know how it grows. The text saith, "And the seed should spring and grow up, he knoweth not how:" That which is beyond the range of our knowledge is certainly beyond the reach of our power. Can you make a seed germinate? You may place it under circumstances of damp and heat which will cause it to swell and break forth with a shoot, but the germination itself is beyond you. How is it done? We know not. After the germ has been put forth, can you make it further grow, and develop its life into leaf and stem? No; that too, is out of your power. And when the green, grassy blade has been succeeded by the ear, can you ripen it? It will be ripened; but can *you* do it? You know you cannot; you can have no finger in the actual process, though you may promote the conditions under which it is carried on. Life is a mystery; growth is a mystery; ripening is a mystery: and these three mysteries are as fountains sealed against all intrusion. How comes it that there is within the ripe seed the preparations for another sowing and another growth? What is this vital principle, this secret reproducing energy? Knowest thou anything about this? The philosopher may talk about chemical combinations, and he may proceed to quote analogies from this and that; but still the growth of the seed remains a secret, it springs up, he knoweth not how. Certainly this is true of the rise and progress of the life of God in the heart. It enters the soul, and roots itself we know not how. Naturally men hate the word, but it enters and it changes their hearts, so that they come to love it; yet we know not how. Their whole nature is renewed, so that instead of producing sin it yields repentance, faith, and love; but we know not how. How the Spirit of God deals with the mind of man, how he creates the new heart and the right spirit, how we are begotten again unto a lively hope, we cannot tell. The Holy Ghost enters into us; we hear not his voice, we see not his light, we feel not his touch; yet he worketh an effectual work upon us, which we are not long in perceiving. We know that the work of the Spirit is a new creation, a resurrection, a quickening from the dead; but all these words are only covers to our utter ignorance of the mode of his working, with which it is not in our power to meddle. We do not know how he performs his miracles of love, and, not knowing how he works, we may be quite sure that we cannot take the work out of his hands. We cannot create, we cannot quicken, we cannot transform, we cannot regenerate, we cannot save.

This work of God having proceeded in the growth of the seed, what next? *We can reap the ripe ears.* After a season God the Holy Spirit uses his servants again. As soon as the living seed has produced first of all the blade of thought, and afterwards the green ear of conviction, and then faith, which is as full corn in the ear, then the Christian worker comes in for further service, for *he can reap.* "When the fruit is brought forth, immediately he putteth in the sickle." This is not the reaping of the last great day, for that does not come within the scope of the parable, which evidently relates to a human sower and reaper. The kind of reaping which the Saviour here intends is that which he referred to when he said to his disciples, "Lift up your eyes, and look on the fields; for they are white already to harvest." After he had been sowing the seed in the hearts of the Samaritans and it had sprung up, so that they began to evince faith in him, the Lord Jesus cried, "The fields are white to harvest." The apostle saith, "One soweth, and another reapeth." Our Lord said to the disciples, "I sent you to reap that whereon ye bestowed no labour." Is there not a promise, "In due season we shall reap, if we faint not"?

Christian workers begin their harvest work by watching for signs of faith in Christ. They are eager to see the blade, and delighted to mark the ripening ear. They often hope that men are believers, but they long to be sure of it; and when they judge that at last the fruit of faith is put forth, they begin to encourage, to congratulate, and to comfort. They know that the young believer needs to be housed in the barn of Christian fellowship, that he may be saved from a thousand perils. No wise farmer leaves the fruit of the field long exposed to the hail which might beat it out or to the mildew which might destroy it, or to the birds which might devour it. Evidently no believing man should be left outside of the garner of holy fellowship; he should be carried into the midst of the church with all the joy which attends the home-bringing of sheaves. The worker for Christ watches carefully, and when he discerns that his time is come, he begins at once to fetch in the converts, that they may be cared for by the brotherhood, separated from the world, screened from temptation, and laid up for the Lord. He is diligent to do it at once, because the text saith, "immediately he putteth in the sickle." He does not wait for months in cold suspicion; he is not afraid that he shall encourage too soon when faith is really present. He comes with the word of promise and the smile of brotherly love at once, and he says to the new believer, "Have you confessed your faith? Is not the time come for an open confession? Hath not Jesus bidden the believer to be baptized? If you love him, keep his commandments." He does not rest till he has introduced the convert to the communion of the faithful. For our work, beloved, is but half done when men are made disciples and baptized. We have then to encourage, to instruct, to strengthen, to console, and succour in all times of difficulty and danger. What saith the Saviour? "Go ye therefore, and make disciples of all the nations, baptizing them into the name of the Father, and of the Son, and of the Holy Ghost: teaching them to observe all things whatsoever I have commanded you."

Observe, then, the sphere and limit of agency. We can introduce the truth to men, but that truth the Lord himself must bless; the living and growing of the word within the soul is of God alone. When the mystic work of growth is done, we are able to garner the saved ones in the church. For Christ to be formed in men the hope of glory is not of our working, that remains with God; but, when Jesus Christ is formed in them, to discern the image of the Saviour and to say, "Come in, thou blessed of the Lord, wherefore standest thou without?" this is our duty and delight. To create the divine life is God's, to cherish it is ours. To cause the hidden life to grow is the work of the Lord; to see the uprising and development of that life, and to harvest it is the work of the faithful, even as it is written, "When the fruit is brought forth, immediately he putteth in the sickle, because the harvest is come."

This, then, is our first lesson; we see what we can do and what we cannot do.

II. Our second head is like unto the first, and consists of WHAT WE CAN KNOW AND WHAT WE CANNOT KNOW.

First, *what we can know.* We can know when we have sown the good seed of the word that it will grow; for God has promised that it shall do so. Not every grain in every place; for some will go to the bird, and some to the worm, and some to be scorched by the sun; but, as a general rule, God's word shall not return unto him void, it shall prosper in the thing whereto he hath sent it. This we can know. And we can know that the seed when once it takes root will continue to grow; that it is not a dream or a picture that will disappear, but a thing of force and energy, which will advance from a grassy blade to corn in the ear, and under God's blessing will develop to actual salvation, and be as the full corn in the ear." God helping and blessing it, our work of teaching will not only lead men to thought and conviction, but to conversion and eternal life.

We also can know, because we are told so, that the reason for this is mainly because there is life in the word. In the word of God itself there is life, for it is written—"The word of God is quick and powerful,"— that is, "living and powerful." It is "the incorruptible seed which liveth and abideth for ever." It is the nature of living seeds to grow; and the reason why the word of God grows in men's hearts is because it is the living word of the living God, and where the word of a king is there is power. We know this, because the Scriptures teach us so. Is it not written, "Of his own will begat he us by the word of truth"?

Moreover, the earth, which is here the type of the man, "bringeth forth fruit of herself." We must mind what we are at in expounding this, for human hearts do not produce faith of themselves; they are as hard rock on which the seed perishes. But it means this,— that as the earth under the blessing of the dew and the rain is, by God's secret working upon it, made to take up and embrace the seed, so the heart of man is made ready to receive and enfold the gospel of Jesus Christ within itself. Man's awakened heart wants exactly what the word of God supplies. Moved by a divine influence the soul embraces the truth, and is embraced by it, and so the truth lives in the heart, and is quickened by it. Man's love accepts the love of God; man's faith wrought in him by the Spirit of God believes the truth of God; man's hope wrought in him by the Holy Ghost lays hold upon the things revealed, and so the heavenly seed grows in the soil of the soul. The life comes not from you who preach the word, but it is placed within the word which you preach by the Holy Spirit. The life is not in your hand, but in the heart which is led to take hold upon the truth by the Spirit of God. Salvation comes not from the personal authority of the preacher, but through the personal conviction, personal faith, and personal love of the hearer. So much as this we may know, and is it not enough for all practical purposes?

Still, there is *a something which we cannot know,* a secret into which we cannot pry. I repeat what I have said before: you cannot look into men's inward parts and see exactly how the truth takes hold upon the heart, or the heart takes hold upon the truth. Many have watched their own feelings till they have become blind with despondency, and others have watched the feelings of the young till they have done them rather harm than good by their rigorous supervision. In God's work there is more room for faith than for sight. The heavenly seed grows secretly. You must bury it out of sight or there will be no harvest. Even if you keep the seed above ground, and it does sprout, you cannot discover *how* it grows; even though you microscopically watched its swelling and bursting, you could not see the inward vital force which moves the seed. Thou knowest not the way of the Spirit. His work is wrought in secret. "Explain the new birth," says somebody. My answer is, "Experience the new birth, and you shall know what it is." There are secrets into which we cannot enter, for their light is too bright for mortal eyes to endure. O man, thou canst not become omniscient for thou art a creature, and not the Creator. For thee there must ever be a region not only unknown but unknowable. So far shall thy knowledge go, but no further; and thou mayest thank God it is so, for thus he leaves room for faith, and gives cause for prayer. Cry mightily unto the Great Worker to do what thou canst not attempt to perform, that so, when thou seest men saved, thou mayest give the Lord all the glory evermore.

III. Thirdly, our text tells us WHAT WE MAY EXPECT IF WE WORK FOR GOD, AND WHAT WE MAY NOT EXPECT. According to this parable *we may expect to see fruit.* The husbandman casts his seed into the ground: the seed springs and grows, and he naturally expects a harvest. I wish I could say a word to stir up the expectations of Christian workers; for I fear that many work without faith. If you had a garden or a field, and you sow seed in it, you would he very greatly surprised and grieved if it did not come up at all; but many Christian people seem quite content to work on without expectation of result. This is a pitiful kind of working— pulling up empty buckets by the year together. Surely, I must either see some result for my labour and be glad, or else, failing to see it, I must be ready to break my heart if I be a true servant of the great Master. We

ought to have expected results; if we had expected
more we should have seen more; but a lack of
expectation has been a great cause of failure in God's
workers.

*But we may not expect to see all the seed which we
sow spring up the moment we sow it.* Sometimes glory
be to God, we have but to deliver the word, and
straightway men are converted: the reaper overtakes
the sower, in such instances; but it is not always so.
Some sowers have been diligent for years upon their
plots of ground, and yet apparently all has been in
vain; at last the harvest has come, a harvest which,
speaking after the manner of men, had never been
reaped if they had not persevered to the end. This
world, as I believe, is to be converted to Christ; but
not today, nor tomorrow, peradventure not for many
an age; but the sowing of the centuries is not being
lost, it is working on towards the grand ultimatum. A
crop of mushrooms may soon be produced; but a forest
of oaks will not reward the planter till generations of
his children have mouldered in the dust. It is ours to
sow, and to hope for quick reaping; but still we ought
to remember that "the husbandman waiteth for the
precious fruit of the earth, and hath long patience for
it, until he receive the early and latter rain," and so
must we. We are to expect results, but not to be
dispirited if we have to wait for them.

We are also to expect to see the good seed grow,
but *not always after our fashion.* Like children, we are
apt to be impatient. Your little boy sowed mustard and
cress yesterday in his garden. This afternoon Johnny
will be turning over the ground to see if the seed is
growing. There is no probability that his mustard and
cress will come to anything, for he will not let it alone
long enough for it to grow. So is it with hasty workers;

they must see the result of the gospel directly, or else they distrust the blessed word. Certain preachers are in such a hurry that they will allow no time for thought, no space for counting the cost, no opportunity for men to consider their ways and turn to the Lord with full purpose of heart. All other seeds take time to grow, but the seed of the word must grow before the speaker's eyes like magic, or he thinks nothing has been done. Such good brethren are so eager to produce blade and ear there and then, that they roast their seed in the fire of fanaticism, and it perishes. They make men think that they are converted, and thus effectually hinder them from coming to a saving knowledge of the truth. Some men are prevented from being saved by being told that they are saved already, and by being puffed up with a notion of perfection when they are not even broken in heart. Perhaps if such people had been taught to look for something deeper they might not have been satisfied with receiving seed on stony ground; but now they exhibit a rapid development, and an equally rapid decline and fall. Let us believingly expect to see the seed grow; but let us look to see it advance after the manner of the preacher,—firstly, secondly, thirdly: first the blade, then the ear, then the full corn in the ear.

We may expect also to see the seed ripen. Our works will by God's grace lead up to real faith in those he hath wrought upon by his word and Spirit; but *we must not expect to see it perfect at first.* How many mistakes have been made here. Here is a young person under impression, and some good, sound brother talks with the trembling beginner, and asks profound questions. He shakes his experienced head, and knits his furrowed brows. He goes into the corn-field to see how the crops are prospering, and though it is early in the year, he laments that he cannot see an ear of corn; indeed, he perceives nothing but mere grass. "I cannot see a trace of corn," says he. No, brother, of course you cannot; for you will not be satisfied with the blade as an evidence of life, but must insist upon seeing everything at full growth at once. If you had looked for the blade you would have found it; and it would have encouraged you. For my own part, I am glad even to perceive a faint desire, a feeble longing, a degree of uneasiness, or a measure of weariness of sin, or a craving after mercy. Will it not be wise for you, also, to allow things to begin at the beginning, and to be satisfied with their being small at the first? See the blade of desire, and then watch for more. Soon you shall see a little more than desire; for there shall be conviction and resolve, and after that a feeble faith, small as a mustard seed, but bound to grow. Do not despise the day of small things. Do not examine the new-born babe to see whether he is sound in doctrine after your idea of soundness; ten to one he is a long way off sound, and you will only worry the dear heart by introducing difficult questions. Speak to him about his being a sinner, and Christ a Saviour, and you will in this way water him so that his grace in the ear will become the full corn in the ear. It may be that there is not much that looks like wheat about him yet; but by-and-by you shall say, "Wheat! ah, that it is, if I know wheat. This man is a true ear of corn, and gladly will I place him among my Master's sheaves." If you cut down the blades, where will the ears come from? Expect grace in your converts; but do not look to see glory in them just yet.

IV. Under the last head we shall consider WHAT SLEEP WORKERS MAY TAKE, AND WHAT THEY MAY NOT TAKE; for it is said of this sowing man, that he sleeps and rises night and day, and the seed springs and grows up he knoweth not how. They say a farmer's trade is a good one because it is going on while he is abed and asleep; and surely ours is a good trade, too, when we serve our Master by sowing good seed; for it is growing even while we are asleep.

But how may a good workman for Christ lawfully go to sleep? I answer, first, he may sleep the sleep of *restfulness* born of confidence. You are afraid the kingdom of Christ will not come, are you? Who asked you to tremble for the ark of the Lord? Afraid for the infinite Jehovah that his purposes will fail? Shame on you! Your anxiety dishonours your God. Shall Omnipotence be defeated? You had better sleep than wake to play the part of Uzzah. Rest patiently; God's purpose will be accomplished, his kingdom will come, his chosen will be saved, and Christ shall see of the travail of his soul. Take the sweet sleep which God gives to his beloved, the sleep of perfect confidence, such as Jesus slept in the hinder part of the ship when it was tossed with tempest. The cause of God never was in jeopardy, and never will be; the seed sown is insured by omnipotence, and must produce its harvest. In patience possess your soul, and wait till the harvest comes, for the pleasure of the Lord must prosper in the hands of Jesus.

Also take that sleep of *joyful expectancy* which leads to a happy waking. Get up in the morning and feel that the Lord is ruling all things for the attainment of his own purposes, and the highest benefit of all who put their trust in him. Look for a blessing by day, and close your eyes at night calmly expecting to meet with better things tomorrow. If you do not sleep you will not wake up in the morning refreshed, and ready for more work. If it were possible for you to sit up all night and eat the bread of carefulness you would be unfit to attend to the service which your Master appoints for the morning; therefore take your rest and be at peace, and work with calm dignity, for the matter is safe in the Lord's hands. Is it not written, "So he giveth his beloved sleep"?

Take your rest because you have consciously resigned your work into God's hands. After you have spoken the word, resort to God in prayer, and commit the matter into God's hand, and then do not fret about it. It cannot be in better keeping, leave it with him who worketh all in all.

But do not sleep the sleep of unwatchfulness. The farmer sows his seed, but he does not therefore forget it. He has to mend his fences, to drive away birds, to remove weeds, or to prevent floods. He does not watch the growth of the seed, but he has plenty else to do. He sleeps, but it is only in due time and measure, and is not to be confounded with the sluggard's slumbers. He never sleeps the sleep of indifference, or even of inaction, for each season has its demand upon him. He has sown one field, but he has another to sow. He has sown, but he has also to reap; and if reaping is done, he has to thresh and to winnow. A farmer's work is never done, for in one part or the other of the farm he is needed. His sleep is but a pause that gives him strength to continue his occupation. The parable teaches us to do all that lies within our province, but not to intrude into the domain of God: in teaching to the ear we are to labour diligently, but with regard to the secret working of truth upon man's mind, we are to pray and rest, looking to the Lord for the inward power.

The Sheep before the Shearers

"As a sheep before her shearers is dumb, so he openeth not his mouth."—Isaiah liii. 7.

OUR Lord Jesus so took our place that we are in this chapter compared to sheep; "All we like sheep have gone astray," and he is compared to a sheep also,—"As a sheep before her shearers is dumb." It is wonderful how complete was the interchange of positions between Christ and his people, so that he became what they were in order that they might become what he is. We can well understand how we should be the sheep and he the shepherd; but to liken the Son of the Highest to a sheep would have been unpardonable presumption had not his own Spirit employed the condescending figure.

Though the emblem is very gracious, its use in this place is by no means singular, for our Lord had been long before Isaiah's day typified by the lamb of the

Passover. Since then he has been proclaimed as "the Lamb of God which taketh away the sin of the world;" and indeed even in his glory he is the Lamb in the midst of the throne.

I. In opening up this divine emblem I would invite you to consider, first, OUR SAVIOUR'S PATIENCE, set forth under the figure of a sheep dumb before her shearers. Our Lord was brought to the shearers that he might be shorn of his comfort, and of his honour, shorn even of his good name, and shorn at last of life itself; but when under the shearers he was as silent as a sheep. How patient he was before Pilate, and Herod, and Caiaphas, and on the cross. You have no record of his uttering any exclamation of impatience at the pain and shame which he received at the hands of these wicked men. You hear not one bitter word. Pilate cries, "Answerest thou nothing? Behold how many things they witness against thee"; and Herod is woefully disappointed, for he expected to see some miracle wrought by him. All that our Lord does say is in submissive tones, like the bleating of a sheep, though infinitely more full of meaning. He utters sentences like these,—"For this purpose was I born, and came into the world, that I might bear witness to the truth," and, "Father, forgive them, for they know not what they do." Otherwise he is all patience and silence.

Remember, first, that our Lord was dumb and opened not his mouth *against his adversaries,* and did not accuse one of them of cruelty or injustice. They slandered him, but he replied not; false witnesses arose, but he answered them not. One would have thought he must have spoken when they spat in his face. Might he not have said, "Friend, why doest thou this? For which of all my works dost thou insult me?"

But the time for such expostulations was over. When they smote him on the face with the palms of their hands, it would not have been wonderful if he had said, "Wherefore do you smite me so?" But no; he is as though he heard not their revilings. He brings no accusation to his Father. He needed only to have lifted his eye to heaven and legions of angels would have chased away the ribald soldiery; one flash of a seraph's wing and Herod had been eaten by worms, and Pilate had died the death he well deserved as an unjust judge. The hill of the cross might have become a volcano's mouth to swallow up the whole multitude who stood there jesting and jeering at him: but no, there was no display of power, or rather there was so great a display of power over himself that he restrained Omnipotence itself with a strength which never can be measured.

Again, as he did not utter a word against his adversaries, so he did not say a word *against any one of us.* You remember how Zipporah said to Moses, "Surely a bloody husband art thou to me," as she saw her child bleeding; and surely Jesus might have said to his church, "Thou art a costly spouse to me, to bring me all this shame and bloodshedding." But he giveth liberally, he openeth the very fountain of his heart, and he upbraideth not. He had reckoned on the uttermost expenditure, and therefore he endured the cross, despising the shame.

> "This was compassion like a God,
> That when the Saviour knew,
> The price of pardon was his blood,
> His pity ne'er withdrew."

No doubt he looked across the ages; for that eye of his was not dim, even when bloodshot on the tree: he must have foreseen your indifference and mine, our coldness of heart, and base unfaithfulness, and he might have left on record some such words as these: "I am suffering for those who are utterly unworthy of my regard; their love will be a miserable return for mine. Though I give my whole heart for them, how lukewarm is their love to me! I am sick of them, I am weary of them, and it is woe to me that I should be laying down my heart's blood for such a worthless race as these my people are." But there is not a hint of such a feeling. No. "Having loved his own which were in the world, he loved them unto the end," and he did not utter a syllable that looked like murmuring at his suffering on their behalf, or regretting that he had commenced the work.

And again, as there was not a word against his adversaries, nor a word against you nor me, so there was not a word *against his Father,* nor a syllable of repining at the severity of the chastisement laid upon him for our sakes. You and I have murmured when under a comparatively light grief, thinking ourselves hardly done by. We have dared to cry out against God, "My face is foul with weeping, and on my eyelids is the shadow of death; not for any injustice in mine hands: also my prayer is pure." But not so the Saviour; in his mouth were no complaints. It is quite impossible for us to conceive how the Father pressed and bruised him, yet was there no repining. "My God, my God, why hast thou forsaken me?" is an exclamation of astonished grief, but it is not the voice of complaint. It shows manhood in weakness, but not manhood in revolt. Many are the Lamentations of Jeremiah, but few are the lamentations of Jesus. Jesus wept, and Jesus sweat great drops of blood, but he never murmured nor felt rebellion in his heart.

Behold your Lord and Saviour lying in passive resignation beneath the shearers, as they take away everything that is dear to him, and yet he openeth not his mouth. I see in this our Lord's *complete submission.* He gives himself up; there is no reserve about it. The sacrifice did not need binding with cords to the horns of the altar. How different from your case and mine! He stood there willing to suffer, to be spit upon, to be shamefully entreated, and to die, for in him there was a complete surrender. He was wholly given to do the Father's will, and to work out our redemption. There was *complete self-conquest* too. In him no faculty arose to plead for liberty, and ask to be exempted from the general strain; no limb of the body, no portion of the mud, no faculty of the spirit started, but all submitted to the divine will: the whole Christ gave up his whole being unto God, that he might perfectly offer himself without spot for our redemption.

There was not only self-conquest, but *complete absorption in his work.* The sheep, lying there, thinks no more of the pastures, it yields itself up to the shearer. The zeal of God's house did eat up our Lord in Pilate's hall as well as everywhere else, for there he witnessed a good confession. No thought had he but for the clearing of the divine honour, and the salvation of God's elect. Brethren, I wish we could arrive at this, to submit our whole spirit to God, to learn self-conquest, and the delivering up of conquered self entirely to God.

The wonderful serenity and submissiveness of our Lord are still better set forth by our text if it be indeed true that sheep in the East are even more docile than with us. Those who have seen the noise and roughness of many of our washings and shearings will hardly believe the testimony of that ancient writer Philo-

Judæus when he affirms that the sheep came voluntarily to be shorn. He says; "Woolly rams laden with thick fleeces put themselves into the shepherd's hands to have their wool shorn, being thus accustomed to pay their yearly tribute to man, their king by nature. The sheep stands in a silent inclining posture, unconstrained under the hand of the shearer. These things may appear strange to those who do not know the docility of the sheep, but they are true." Marvellous indeed was this submissiveness in our Lord's case; let us admire and imitate.

II. Thus I have feebly set forth the patience of our beloved Master. Now I want you to follow me, in the second place, to VIEW OUR OWN CASE UNDER THE SAME METAPHOR AS THAT WHICH IS USED IN REFERENCE TO OUR LORD.

Did I not begin by saying that because we were sheep he deigns to compare himself to a sheep? Let us look from another point of view: our Lord was a sheep under the shearers, and as he is so are we also in this world. Though we shall never be offered up like lambs in the temple by way of expiation, yet the saints for ages were the flock of slaughter, as it is written, "For thy sake we are killed all the day long, we are accounted as sheep for the slaughter!" Jesus sends us forth as sheep in the midst of wolves, and we are to regard ourselves as living sacrifices, ready to be offered up. I dwell however more particularly upon the second symbol: we are brought as sheep under the shearers' hands.

Just as a sheep is taken by the shearer, and its wool is all cut off, so doth the Lord take his people and shear them, taking away all their earthly comforts, and leaving them bare. I wish when it came to our turn to undergo this operation it could be said of us as of our Lord, "As a sheep before her shearers is dumb, so he openeth not his mouth." I fear that we open our mouths a great deal, and make no end of complaining without any apparent cause, or with the very slenderest reason. But now to the figure.

First, remember that a *sheep rewards its owner for all his care and trouble by being shorn.* There is nothing else that I know of that a sheep can do. It yields food when it is killed, but while it is alive the one payment that the sheep can make to the shepherd is to yield its fleece in due season. Some of God's people can give to Christ a tribute of gratitude by active service, and they should do so gladly every day of their lives; but many others cannot do much in active service, and about the only reward they can give to their Lord is to render up their fleece by suffering when he calls upon them to suffer, submissively yielding to be shorn of their personal comfort when the time comes for patient endurance.

Here comes the shearer; he takes the sheep and begins to cut, cut, cut, cut, taking away the wool wholesale. Affliction is often used as the big shears. The husband, or perhaps the wife, is removed, little children are taken away, property is shorn off, and health is gone. Sometimes the shears cut off the man's good name; slander follows; comforts vanish. Well, this is your shearing time, and it may be that you are not able to glorify God to any very large extent except by undergoing this process. If this be the fact, do you not think that we, like good sheep of Christ, should surrender ourselves cheerfully, feeling, "I lay myself down with this intent, that thou shouldst take from me anything and everything, and do what thou wilt with me; for I am not mine own, I am bought with a price"?

Notice that the sheep is itself *benefited by the operation of shearing.* Before they begin to shear the sheep the wool is long and old, and every bush and briar tears off a bit of the wool, until the sheep looks ragged and forlorn. If the wool were left, when the heat of summer came the sheep would not be able to bear itself, it would be so overloaded with clothing that it would be as uncomfortable as we are when we have kept on our borrowed wool, our flannels and broadcloths, too late. So brethren, when the Lord shears us, we do not like the operation any more than the sheep do; but first, it is for *his glory;* and secondly, it is for *our benefit,* and therefore we are bound most willingly to submit. There are many things which we should have liked to have kept which, if we had kept them, would not have proved blessings but curses. A stale blessing is a curse. The manna, though it came from heaven, was only good so long as God's command made it a blessing, but when they kept it over its due time it bred worms and stank, and then it was no blessing. Many persons would keep their mercies till they turn to corruption; but God will not have it so. Up to a certain point for you to be wealthy was a blessing; it would not have been a blessing any longer, and so the Lord took your riches away. Up to that point your child was a boon, but it would have been no longer so, and therefore it fell sick and died. You may not be able to see it, but it is so, that God, when he withdraws a blessing from his people, takes it away because it would not be a blessing any longer.

Before sheep are shorn *they are always washed.* Were you ever present at the scene when they drive them down to the brook? Men are placed in rows, leading to the shepherd who stands in the water. The sheep are driven down, and the men seize them, throw them into the pool, keeping their faces above water, and swirl them round and round and round to wash the wool before they clip it off. You see them come out on the other side frightened to death, poor things, wondering whatever is coming. I want to suggest to you, brethren that whenever a trial threatens to overtake you, you should entreat the Lord to sanctify it to you. If the good Shepherd is going to clip your wool, ask him to wash it before he takes it off; ask to be cleansed in spirit, soul, and body. That is a very good custom Christian people have of asking a blessing on their meals before they eat bread. Do you not think it is even more necessary to ask a blessing on our troubles before we get into them? Here is your dear child likely to die; will you not, dear parents, meet together and ask God to bless the death of that child, if it is to happen? The harvest fails; would it not be well to say—"Lord, sanctify this poverty, this loss, this year's bad harvest: cause it to be a means of grace to us." Why not ask a blessing on the cup of bitterness as well as upon the cup of thanksgiving? Ask to be washed before you are shorn, and if the shearing must come, let it be your chief concern to yield clean wool.

After the washing, when the sheep has been dried, it actually *loses what was its comfort.* The sheep is thrown down, and the shearers get to work; the poor creature is losing its comfortable fleece. You also will have to part with your comforts. Will you recollect this? The next time you receive a fresh blessing call it a loan. Poor sheep, there is no wool on your back but what will have to come off; child of God, there is no earthly comfort in your possession but what will either leave you, or you will leave it. Nothing is our own except our God. "Why," says one, "not our sin?" Sin was our own, but Jesus has taken it upon himself, and it is gone. There is nothing our own but our God, for all his gifts are held on lease, terminate at his sovereign will. We foolishly consider that our mercies belong to us, and when the Lord takes them away we half grumble. A loan, they say, should go laughing home, and so should we rejoice when the Lord takes back that which he had lent us. All our possessions are but brief favours borrowed for the hour. As the sheep yields up its wool and so loses its comfort, so must we yield up all our earthly properties; or if they remain with us till we die, we shall part with them then, we shall not take so much as one of them across the stream of death.

The shearers *take care not to hurt the sheep:* they clip as close as they can, but they do not cut the skin. If possible, they will not draw blood, even in the smallest degree. When they do make a gash, it is because the sheep does not lie still: but a careful shearer has bloodless shears. Of this Thomson sings in his Seasons, and the passage is so good an illustration of the whole subject that I will adorn my discourse with it:—

> "How meek, how patient, the mild creature lies!
> What softness in its melancholy face,
> What dumb complaining innocence appears!
> Fear not, ye gentle tribes! 'tis not the knife
> Of horrid slaughter that is o'er you waved;
> No, 'tis the tender swain's well guided shears,
> Who having now, to pay his annual care,
> Borrow'd your fleece, to you a cumbrous load,
> Will send you bounding to your hills again."

It is the kicking and the struggling that make the shearing work at all hard, but if we are dumb before the shearers no harm can come. The Lord may clip wonderfully close: I have known him clip some so close that they did not seem to have a bit of wool left, for they were stripped entirely, even as Job when he cried, "Naked came I out of my mother's womb, and naked shall I return thither." Still, like Job, they have added, "The Lord gave, and the Lord hath taken away; blessed be the name of the Lord."

Notice that the shearers always *shear at a suitable time.* It would be a very wicked, cruel, and unwise thing to begin sheepshearing in winter time. There is a proverb which talks about God "tempering the wind to the shorn lamb." It may be so, but it is a very cruel practice to shear lambs while winds need tempering. Sheep are shorn when it is warm, genial weather, when they can afford to lose their fleeces, and are all the better for being relieved of them. As the summer comes on sheepshearing time comes. Have you ever noticed that whenever the Lord afflicts us he selects the best possible time? There is a prayer that he put into his disciples' mouths, "Pray that your flight be not in the winter": the spirit of that prayer may be seen in the seasonableness of our sorrows. He will not send us our worst troubles at our worst times. If your soul is depressed the Lord does not send you a very heavy burden; he reserves such a load for times when you have joy in the Lord to be your strength. It has come to be a kind of feeling with us that when we have much delight a trial is near, but when sorrow thickens deliverance is approaching. The Lord does not send us two burdens at a time; or, if he does, he sends double strength. His shearing time is chosen with tender discretion.

There is another thing to remember. It is with us as with the sheep, *there is new wool coming.* Whenever the Lord takes away our earthly comforts with one

hand, one, two, three, he restores with the other hand
six, a score, a hundred; we are crying and whining
about the little loss and yet it is necessary in order
that we may be able to receive the great gain. Yes, it
will be so, we shall yet have cause for rejoicing, "joy
cometh in the morning." If we have lost one position,
there is another for us: if we have been driven out of
one place, a better refuge is prepared. Providence
opens a second door when it shuts the first. If the
Lord takes away the manna, as he did from his people
Israel, it is because they have the old corn of the land
of Caanan to live upon. If the water of the rock did
not follow the tribes any longer, it was because they
drank of the Jordan, and of the brooks. O sheep of
the Lord's fold, there is new wool coming: therefore
do not fret at the shearing. I have given these thoughts
in brief, that we may come to the last word.

III. Let us, in the third place, endeavour to IMITATE
THE EXAMPLE OF OUR BLESSED LORD WHEN OUR TURN COMES
TO BE SHORN. Let us be dumb before the shearers,
submissive, quiescent, even as he was.

I have been giving, in everything I have said, a
reason for so doing. I have shown that our shearing
by affliction glorifies God, rewards the Shepherd, and
benefits ourselves. I have shown that the Lord
measures and tempers our affliction, and sends the
trial at the right time. I have shown you in many ways
that it will be wise to submit ourselves, as the sheep
does to the shearer, and that the more completely we
do so the better.

We struggle far too much, and we are apt to make
excuses for so doing. Sometimes we say, "Oh, this is
so painful, I cannot be patient! I could have borne
anything else but this." When a father is going to correct

his child, does he select something pleasant? No. The painfulness of the punishment is the essence of it, and even so the bitterness of our sorrow is the soul of our chastening. By the blueness of the wound the heart will be made better. Do not repine because your trial seems strange and sharp. That would in fact be saying, "If I have it all my own way I will, but if everything does not please me I will rebel"; and that is not a fit spirit for a child of God.

Sometimes we complain because of our great weakness. "Lord, were I stronger I would not mind this heavy loss; but I am frail as a sere leaf driven of the tempest." But who is to be the judge of the suitability of your trial? You or God? Since the Lord judges this trial to be suitable to your weakness, you may be sure that it is so. Lie still! Lie still! "Alas," you say, "my grief comes from the most cruel quarter; this trouble did not arise directly from God, it came through my cousin or my brother who ought to have treated me with gratitude. It was not an enemy: then I could have borne it." My brother, let me assure you that in reality trial comes not from an enemy after all. God is at the bottom of all your tribulation; look through the second causes to the great First Cause. It is a great mistake when we fret over the human instrument which smites us, and forget the hand which uses the rod. If I strike a dog, he bites my stick; poor creature, he knows no better: but if he could think a little he would bite *me,* or else take the blow submissively. Now, you must not begin biting the stick. After all, it is your heavenly Father that uses the staff; though it be of ebony or of blackthorn, it is in his hand. It is well to have done with picking and choosing our trials, and to leave the whole matter in the hand of infinite wisdom. A sweet singer has put this matter very prettily; let me quote the lines:—

"But when my Lord did ask me on what side
             I were content,
The grief whereby I must be purified,
             To me was sent,

"As each imagined anguish did appear,
             Each withering bliss
Before my soul, I cried, 'Oh! spare me here,
             Oh, no, not this!'

"Like one that having need of, deep within,
             The surgeon's knife,
Would hardly bear that it should graze the skin,
             Though for his life.

"Nay, then, but he, who best doth understand
             Both what we need,
And what can bear, did take my case in hand,
             Nor crying heed."

This is the pith of my sermon: oh, believer, yield thyself! Lie passive in the hands of God! Yield thee, and struggle not! There is no use in struggling, for our great Shearer, if he means to shear, will do it. Did I not say just now that the sheep, by struggling, might be cut by the shears! So you and I, if we struggle against God, will get two strokes instead of one; and after all there is not half so much trouble in a trouble as there is in kicking against the trouble. The Eastern ploughman has a goad, and pricks the ox to make it move more actively; he does not hurt it much by his gentle prodding, but suppose the ox flings out its leg the moment it touches him, he drives the goad into himself, and bleeds. So it is with us, we shall find it hard to kick against the pricks; we shall endure much more pain by rebelling than would have come if we had yielded to the divine will. What good comes of fretting? We cannot make one hair white or black. You that are troubled, rest with us, for you cannot make shower or shine, foul or fair, with all your groaning. Did you ever bring a penny into the till by fretting, or put a loaf on the table by complaint? Murmuring is wasted breath, and fretting is wasted time. To lie passive in the hand of God brings a blessing to the soul. I would myself be more quiet, calm, and self-possessed. I long to cry habitually, "Lord, do what thou wilt, when thou wilt, as thou wilt, with me, thy servant: appoint me honour or dishonour, wealth or poverty, sickness or health, exhilaration or depression, and I will take all right gladly from thy hand." A man is not far from the gates of heaven when he is fully submissive to the Lord's will.

You that have been shorn have, I hope, received comfort through the ever blessed Spirit of God. May God bless you. Oh that the sinner, too, would humble himself under the mighty hand of God! Submit yourselves unto God, let every thought be brought into captivity to him, and the Lord send his blessing, for Christ's sake. Amen.

In the Hay Field

"He causeth the grass to grow for the cattle."—Psalm civ. 14.

AT the appointed season all the world is busy with ingathering the grass crop, and you can scarcely ride a mile in the country without scenting the delicious fragrance of the new-mown hay and hearing the sharpening of the mower's scythe. There is a gospel in the hay-field, and that gospel we intend to bring out as we may be enabled by the Holy Spirit.

Our text conducts us at once to the spot, and we shall therefore need no preface. "He causeth the grass to grow for the cattle"—three things we shall notice; first, that *grass is in itself instructive;* secondly, that *grass is far more so when God is seen in it;* and thirdly, that *by the growth of grass for the cattle, the ways of grace may be illustrated.*

I. First, then, "He causeth the grass to grow for the

cattle." Here we have SOMETHING WHICH IS IN ITSELF
INSTRUCTIVE. Scarcely any emblem, with the exception
of water and light, is more frequently used by
inspiration than the grass of the field.

In the first place, the grass may be instructively
looked upon as *the symbol of our mortality.* "All flesh is
grass." The whole history of man may be seen in the
meadow. He springs up green and tender, subject to
the frosts of infancy, which imperil his young life; he
grows, he comes to maturity, he puts on beauty even
as the grass is adorned with flowers; but after a while
his strength departs and his beauty is wrinkled, even
as the grass withers and is followed by a fresh
generation, which withers in its turn. Like ourselves,
the grass ripens but to decay. The sons of men come to
maturity in due time, and then decline and wither as
the green herb. Some of the grass is not left to come to
ripeness at all, but the mower's scythe removes it, even
as swift-footed death overtakes the careless children of
Adam. "In the morning it flourisheth, and groweth up;
in the evening it is cut down, and withereth. For we are
consumed by thine anger, and by thy wrath are we
troubled." "As for man, his days are as grass: as a flower
of the field, so he flourisheth. For the wind passeth over
it, and it is gone; and the place thereof shall know it no
more." This is very humbling; and we need frequently
to be reminded of it or we dream of immortality beneath
the stars. We ought never to tread upon the grass
without remembering that whereas the green sod covers
our graves, it also reminds us of them, and preaches by
every blade a sermon to us concerning our mortality, of
which the text is, "All flesh is grass, and all the
goodliness thereof is as the flower of the field."

In the second place, grass is frequently used in
Scripture as *an emblem of the wicked.* David tells us

from his own experience that the righteous man is apt to grow envious of the wicked when he sees the prosperity of the ungodly. We have seen them spreading themselves like green bay trees, and apparently fixed and rooted in their places; and when we have smarted under our own troubles, and felt that all the day long we were scourged, and chastened every morning, we have been apt to say, "How can this be consistent with the righteous government of God?" We are reminded by the Psalmist that in a short time we shall pass by the place of the wicked, and lo, he shall not be; we shall diligently consider his place, and lo, it shall not be; for he is soon cut down as the grass, and withereth as the green herb. The grass withereth, the flower thereof fadeth away, and even so shall pass away for ever the glory of those who build upon the estate of time, and dig for lasting comfort in the mines of earth. As the Eastern husbandman gathers up the green herb, and, despite its former beauty, casts it into the furnace, such must be your lot, O vainglorious sinners! Thus will the judge command his angels, "Bind them in bundles to burn." Where now your merriment? Where now your confidence? Where now your pride and your pomp? Where now your boastings and your loud-mouthed blasphemies? They are silent for ever; for, as thorns crackle under a pot, but are speedily consumed, and leave nothing except a handful of ashes, so shall it be with the wicked as to this life; the fire of God's wrath shall devour them.

It is more pleasing to recollect that the grass is used in Scripture as *a picture of the elect of God.* The wicked are comparable to the dragons of the wilderness, but God's own people shall spring up in their place, for it is written, "In the habitation of dragons, where each lay, shalt be grass with reeds and rushes." The elect are compared to grass, because of their number as they shall be in the latter days, and because of the rapidity of their growth. You remember the passage, "There shall be a handful of corn in the earth upon the top of the mountains; the fruit thereof shall shake like Lebanon: and they of the city shall flourish like grass of the earth." O that the long expected day might soon come, when God's people shall no longer be like a lone tuft of grass, but when they shall spring up "as among the grass, as willows by the watercourses." Grass and willows are two of the fastest growing things we know of: so shall a nation be born in a day; so shall crowds be converted at once; for when the Spirit of God shall be mightily at work in the midst of the church, men shall fly unto Christ as doves fly to their dovecotes, so that the astonished church shall exclaim, "These, where had they been?" O that we might live to see the age of gold, the time which prophets have foretold, when the company of God's people shall be innumerable as the blades of grass in the meadows and grace and truth shall flourish.

How like the grass are God's people for this reason, that they are absolutely dependent upon the influences of heaven! Our fields are parched if vernal showers and gentle dews are withheld, and what are our souls without the gracious visitations of the Spirit? Sometimes through severe trials our wounded hearts are like the mown grass and then we have the promise, "He shall come down like rain upon the mown grass as showers that water the earth." Our sharp troubles have taken away our beauty, and lo, the Lord visits us and we revive again. Thank God for that old saying, which is a gracious doctrine as well as a true proverb, "Each blade of grass has its own drop of dew." God is pleased to give his own peculiar mercies to each one of his own servants. "Thy blessing is upon thy people."

Once again, grass is comparable to *the food wherewith the Lord supplies the necessities of his chosen ones.* Take the twenty-third Psalm, and you have the metaphor worked out in the sweetest form of pastoral song: "He maketh me to lie down in green pastures: he leadeth me beside the still waters." Just as the sheep has nourishment according to its nature, and this nourishment is abundantly found for it by its shepherd, so that it not only feeds, but then lies down in the midst of the fodder, satiated with plenty, and perfectly content and at ease; even so are the people of God when Jesus Christ leads them into the pastures of the covenant, and opens up to them the precious truths upon which their souls shall be fed. Beloved, have we not proved that promise true, "In this mountain shall the Lord of hosts make unto all people a feast of fat things, a feast of wines on the lees, of fat things full of marrow, of wines on the lees well refined"? My soul has sometimes fed upon Christ till I have felt as if I could receive no more, and then I have laid me down in the bounty of my God to take my rest, satisfied with favour, and full of the goodness of the Lord.

Thus, you see, the grass itself is not without instruction for those who will incline their ear.

II. In the second place, GOD IS SEEN IN THE GROWING OF THE GRASS. He is seen first as a worker, "He *causeth* the grass to grow." He is seen secondly as a caretaker, "He causeth the grass to grow *for the cattle.*"

1. First, as a *worker,* God is to be seen in every blade of grass, if we have but eyes to discern him. A blind world this, which always talks about "natural laws," and "the effects of natural causes," but forgets that laws cannot operate of themselves, and that natural causes,

so called, are not causes at all unless the First Cause shall set them in motion. The old Romans used to say, *God* thundered; *God* rained. We say, *it* thunders; *it* rains. What "it"? All these expressions are subterfuges to escape from the thought of God. We commonly say, "How wonderful are the works of *nature!*" What is "nature"? Do you know what *nature* is? I remember a lecturer in the street, an infidel, speaking about nature, and he was asked by a Christian man standing by whether he would tell him what nature was. He never gave a reply. The production of grass is not the result of natural law apart from the actual work of God; mere law would be inoperative unless the great Master himself sent a thrill of power through the matter which is regulated by the law—unless, like the steam engine, which puts force into all the spinning-jennies and wheels of a cotton-mill, God himself were the motive power to make every wheel revolve. I find rest on the grass as on a royal couch, now that I know that my God is there at work for his creatures.

Having asked you to see God as a worker, I want you to make use of this—therefore I bid you to see God in *common things*. He makes the grass to grow—grass is a common thing. You see it everywhere, yet God is in it. Dissect it and pull it to pieces: the attributes of God are illustrated in every single flower of the field, and in every green leaf. In like manner see God in your common matters, your daily afflictions, your common joys, your every day mercies. Do not say, "I must see a miracle before I see God." In truth, everything teems with marvel. See God in the bread of your table and the water of your cup. It will be the happiest way of living if you can say in each providential circumstance, "My Father has done all this." See God also in *little things*. The little things of life are the greatest troubles.

A man will hear that his house is burned down more quietly than he will see ill-cooked joint of meat upon his table, when he reckoned upon its being done to a turn. It is the *little* stone in the shoe which makes the pilgrim limp. To see God in little things, to believe that there is as much the presence of God in a limb falling from the elm as in the avalanche which crushes a village; to believe that the guidance of every drop of spray, when the wave breaks on the rock, is as much under the hand of God as the steerage of the mightiest planet in its course: to see God in the little as well as in the great—all this is true wisdom.

Think, too, of God working among *solitary things;* for grass does not merely grow where men take care of it, but up there on the side of the lone Alp, where no traveller has ever passed. Where only the eye of the wild bird has beheld their lonely verdure, moss and grass display their beauty; for God's works are fair to other eyes than those of mortals. And you, solitary child of God, dwelling unknown and obscure, in a remote hamlet; you are not forgotten by the love of heaven. He maketh the grass to grow all alone, and shall he not make you flourish despite your loneliness? He can bring forth your graces and educate you for the skies in solitude and neglect. The grass, you know, is a thing we tread upon, nobody thinks of its being crushed by the foot, and yet God makes it grow. Perhaps you are oppressed and down-trodden, but let not this depress your spirit, for God executeth righteousness for all those that are oppressed: he maketh the grass to grow, and he can make your heart to flourish under all the oppressions and afflictions of life, so that you shall still be happy and holy though all the world marches over you; still living in the immortal life which God himself bestows upon you though hell itself set its heel upon you. Poor and needy one, unknown, unobserved, oppressed and down-trodden, God makes the grass to grow, and he will take care of you.

2. But I said we should see in the text God also as a great *caretaker.* "He causeth the grass to grow *for the cattle."* "Doth God take care for oxen? Or saith he it altogether for our sakes?" "Thou shalt not muzzle the mouth of the ox that treadeth out the corn," shows that God has a care for the beasts of the field; but it shows much more than that, namely, that he would have those who work for him feed as they work. God cares for the beasts, and makes grass to grow for them. Then, my soul, though sometimes thou hast said with David, "So foolish was I, and ignorant: I was as a beast before thee," yet God cares for thee. "He giveth to the beast his food, and to the young ravens which cry"—there you have an instance of his care for birds, and here we have his care for beasts; and though you, my hearer, may seem to yourself to be as black and defiled as a raven, and as far from anything spiritually good as the beasts, yet take comfort from this text; he gives grass to the cattle, and he will give grace to you, though you think yourself to be as a beast before him.

Observe, he cares for these beasts who are *helpless* as to caring for themselves. The cattle could not plant the grass, nor cause it to grow. Though they can do nothing in the matter, yet he does it all for them; he causeth the grass to grow. You who are as helpless as cattle to help yourselves, who can only stand and moan out your misery, but know not what to do, God can prevent you in his lovingkindness, and favour you in his tenderness. Let the bleatings of your prayer go up to heaven, let the moanings of your desires go up to him, and help shall come to you though you cannot help yourselves. Beasts are *dumb, speechless things,* yet God makes the grass grow for them. Will he hear those that cannot speak, and will he not hear those who can? Since our God views with kind consideration the cattle in the field, he will surely have compassion upon his own sons and daughters when they desire to seek his face.

There is this also to be said, God not only cares for cattle, but *the food* which he provides for them is fit food—he causeth *grass* to grow for the cattle, just the sort of food which ruminants require. Even thus the Lord God provides fit sustenance for his people. Depend upon him by faith and wait upon him in prayer and you shall have food convenient for you. You shall find in God's mercy just that which your nature demands, suitable supplies for peculiar wants.

This "convenient" food the Lord takes care to reserve for the cattle, for no one eats the cattle's food but the cattle. There is grass for them, and nobody else cares for it, and thus it is kept for them; even so God has a special food for his own people; "the secret of the Lord is with them that fear him, and he will show them his covenant." Though the grass be free to all who choose to eat it, yet no creature careth for it except the cattle for whom it is prepared; and though the grace of God be free to all men, yet no man careth for it except the elect of God, for whom he prepared it, and whom he prepares to receive it. There is as much reserve of the grass for the cattle as if there were walls around it; and so, though the grace of God be free, and there be no bound set about it, yet it is as much reserved as if it were restricted.

God is seen in the grass as the worker and the caretaker: then *let us see his hand in providence at all times.* Let us see it, not only when we have abundance, but even when we have scant supplies; for the grass is preparing for the cattle even in the depth of winter. And you, ye sons of sorrow, in your trials and troubles, are still cared for by God; he will accomplish his own divinely gracious purposes in you: only be still and see the salvation of God. Every winter's night has a direct connection with the joyous days of mowing and reaping, and each time of grief is linked to future joy.

III. Our third head is most interesting. GOD'S WORKING IN THE GRASS FOR THE CATTLE GIVES US ILLUSTRATIONS CONCERNING GRACE.

I will soliloquize, and say to myself as I read the text, "He causeth the grass to grow for the cattle. In this I perceive a satisfying provision for that form of creature. I am also a creature, but I am a nobler creature than the cattle. I cannot imagine for a moment that God will provide all that the cattle need and not provide for me. But naturally I feel uneasy: I cannot find in this world what I want—if I were to win all its riches I should still be discontented; and when I have all that heart could wish of time's treasures, yet still my heart feels as if it were empty. There must be somewhere or other something that will satisfy me as a man with an immortal soul. God altogether satisfies the ox; he must therefore have something or other that would altogether satisfy me if I could get it. There is the grass, the cattle get it, and when they have eaten their share, they lie down and seem perfectly contented; now, all I have ever found on earth has never satisfied me so that I could lie down and be satisfied; there must, then, be something somewhere that would content me if I could get at it." Is not this good reasoning? I ask both the Christian and the unbeliever to go with me so far; but then let us proceed another step:—The cattle do get what they want—not only is the grass provided, but they get it. Why should not I obtain what I want? I find my soul hungering and thirsting after something more than I can see with my eyes or hear with my ears: there must be something to satisfy my soul, why should I not find it? The cattle pasture upon that which satisfies them: why should not I obtain satisfaction too? Then I begin to pray, "O Lord, satisfy my mouth with good things, and renew my youth."

While I am praying I also meditate and think,—God has provided for cattle that which is consonant to their nature: they are nothing but flesh, and flesh is grass, there is therefore grass for their flesh. I also am flesh, but I am something else besides: I am spirit, and to satisfy me I need spiritual meat. Where is it? When I turn to God's word, I find there that though the grass withereth, the word of the Lord endureth for ever; and the word which Jesus speaks unto us is spirit and life. "Oh! then," I say, "here is spiritual food for my spiritual nature, I will rejoice therein. O may God help me to know what that spiritual meat is, and enable me to lay hold upon it, for I perceive that though God provides the grass for the cattle, *the cattle must eat it themselves.* They are not fed if they refuse to eat. I must imitate the cattle, and receive that which God provides for me! What do I find provided in Scripture? I am told that the Lord Jesus came into this world to suffer, and bleed, and die instead of me, and that if I trust in him I shall be saved; and, being saved, the thoughts of his love will give solace and joy to me and be my strength. What have I to do but to feed on these truths? I do not find the cattle bringing any preparation to the pasture except hunger, but they enter it and partake of their portion. Even so must I by an act of faith live upon Jesus. Lord, give me grace to feed upon

Christ; make me hungry and thirsty after him; give me
the faith by which I may be a receiver of him, that so I
may be satisfied with favour, and full of the goodness
of the Lord.

My text, though it looked small, grows as we meditate
upon it. I want to introduce you to a few more
illustrations of divine grace. *Preventing grace may here
be seen in a symbol.* Grass grew before cattle were made.
We find in the first chapter of Genesis that God provided
the grass before he created the cattle. And what a mercy
that covenant supplies for God's people were prepared
before they were born. God had given his Son Jesus
Christ to be the Saviour of his chosen before Adam fell;
long before sin came into the world the everlasting mercy
of God foresaw the ruin of sin, and provided a refuge
for every elect soul. What a thought it is for me, that,
before I hunger, God has prepared the manna; before I
thirst, God has caused the rock in the wilderness to
send forth crystal streams to satisfy the thirst of my
soul! See what sovereign grace can do! Before the cattle
come to the pasture the grass has grown for them, and
before I feel my need of divine mercy, that mercy is
provided for me. Then I perceive an illustration of free
grace, for *when the ox comes into the field, he brings no
money with him.* So I, a poor needy sinner, having
nothing, come and receive Christ without money and
without price. The Lord maketh the grass to grow for
the cattle, and so doth he provide grace for my needy
soul, though I bare now no money, no virtue, no
excellence of my own.

And why is it, my friends, why is it that God gives
the cattle the grass? The reason is, *because they belong
to him.* Here is a text to prove it. "The silver and the
gold are mine, and the cattle upon a thousand hills."
God provides grass for his own cattle, and grace is

provided for God's people? Of every herd of cattle in the world, God could say, "They are mine. Long before the grazier puts his brand on the bullock God has set his creating mark upon it; so, before the stamp of Adam's fall was set upon our brow, the stamp of electing love was set there: "In thy book all my members were written, which in continuance were fashioned, when as yet there was none of them."

God also feeds cattle because *he has entered into a covenant with them to do so.* "What! a covenant with the cattle!" says somebody. Ay! truly so, for when God spake to his servant Noah, in that day when all the cattle came out of the ark, we find him saying, "I establish my covenant with you, and with your seed after you; and with every living creature that is with you, of the fowl, of *the cattle,* and of every beast of the earth with you." Thus a covenant was made with the cattle, and that covenant was that seed-time and harvest should not fail; therefore the earth brings forth for them, and for them the Lord causeth the grass to grow. Does Jehovah keep his covenant with cattle, and will he not keep his covenant with his own beloved? Ah! it is because his chosen people are his covenanted ones in the person of the Lord Jesus, that he provides for them all things that they shall need in time and in eternity, and satisfies them out of the fulness of his everlasting love.

Once, again, God feeds the cattle, and then *the cattle praise him.* We find David saying, in the hundred and forty-eighth Psalm, "Praise the Lord . . . . ye beasts and all cattle." The Lord feeds his people to the end that their glory may sing praise unto him and not be silent. While other creatures give glory to God, let the redeemed of the Lord especially say so, whom he has redeemed out of the hand of the enemy.

Nor even yet is our text exhausted. Turning one

moment from the cattle, I want you to notice the grass. It is said of the grass, *"He causeth* the grass to grow": here is a doctrinal lesson, for if grass does not grow without God's causing it to grow, how could grace arise in the human heart apart from divine operations? Surely grace is a much more wonderful product of divine wisdom than the grass can be! And if grass does not grow without a divine cause, depend upon it grace does not dwell in us without a divine implantation. If I have so much as one blade of grace growing within me, I must trace it all to God's divine will, and render to him all the glory.

Again, if God thinks it worth his while to make grass, and take care of it, much more will he think it to his honour to cause his grace to grow in our hearts. If the great invisible Spirit, whose thoughts are high and lofty, condescends to look after that humble thing which grows by the hedge, surely he will condescend to watch over his own nature, which he calls "the incorruptible seed, which liveth and abideth for ever!" Mungo Park, in the deserts of Africa, was much comforted when he took up a little piece of moss, and saw the wisdom and power of God in that lonely piece of verdant loveliness. So, when you see the fields ripe and ready for the mower, your hearts should leap for joy to see how God has produced the grass, caring for it all through the rigorous cold of winter, and the chill months or spring, until at last he sent the genial rain and sunshine, and brought the fields to their best condition. And so, my soul, though thou mayest endure many a frost of sorrow and a long winter of trial, yet the Lord will cause thee to grow in grace, and in the knowledge of our Lord and Saviour Jesus Christ: to whom be glory for ever. Amen.

The Joy of Harvest

"They joy before thee according to the joy in harvest."—Isaiah ix. 3.

THE other day I kept the feast with a company who shouted "Harvest Home." I was to see the rich and poor rejoicing together; and when the cheerful meal was ended, I was glad to turn one of the tables into a pulpit, and in the large barn to preach the gospel of the ever-blessed God to an earnest audience. My heart was merry in harmony with the occasion, and I shall now keep in the same key, and talk to you a little upon the joy of harvest. Londoners forget that it is harvest time; living in this great desert of dingy bricks we hardly know what a wheat-ear is like, except as we see it dry and white in the window of a corn-dealer's shop; yet let us all remember that there is such a season as harvest, when by God's goodness the fruits of the earth are gathered in.

WHAT IS THE JOY OF HARVEST which is here taken as the simile of the joy of the saints before God? I am afraid that to the more selfish order of spirits the joy of harvest is simply that of personal gratification at the increase of wealth. Sometimes the farmer only rejoices because *he sees the reward of his toils,* and is so much the richer man. I hope that with many there mingles the second cause of joy; namely, gratitude to God that an abundant harvest will give bread to the poor, and remove complaining from our streets. There is a lawful joy in harvest, no doubt, to the man who is enriched by it; for any man who works hard has a right to rejoice when at last he gains his desire. It would be well if men would always recollect that their last and greatest harvest will be to them according to their labour. He that soweth to the flesh will of the flesh reap corruption, and only the man that soweth to the spirit will of the spirit reap life everlasting. Many a young man commences life by sowing what he calls his wild oats, which he had better never have sown, for they will bring him a terrible harvest. He expects that from these wild oats he will gather a harvest of true pleasure, but it cannot be: the truest pleasures of life spring from the good seed of righteousness, and not from the hemlock of sin. As a man who sows thistles in his furrows must not expect to reap the golden wheatsheaf, so he who follows the ways of vice must not expect happiness. On the contrary, if he sows the wind he will reap the whirlwind. When a sinner feels the pangs of conscience he may well say, "This is what I sowed." When he shall at last receive the punishment of his evil deeds he will blame no one but himself: he sowed tares and he must reap tares. On the other hand, the Christian man, though his salvation is not of works, but of grace, will have a gracious reward given to him by his Master. Sowing in tears, he shall reap in joy. Putting out his talents to interest, he shall enter into his Master's joy, and hear him say, "Well done, good and faithful servant." The joy of harvest in part consists of the reward of labour; may such be our joy in serving the Lord.

The joy of harvest has another element in it, name, that of *gratitude to God for favours bestowed*. We are singularly dependent on God; far more so than most of us imagine. When the children of Israel were in the wilderness they went forth every morning and gathered the manna. Our manna does not come to us every morning, but it comes once a year. It is as much a heavenly supply as if it lay like a hoar-frost round about the camp. If we went out into the field and gathered food which dropped from the clouds we should think it a great miracle; and is it not as great a marvel that our bread should come up from the earth as that it should come down from the sky? The same God who bade the heavens drop with angels' food bids the dull earth in its due season yield corn for mankind. Therefore, whenever we find that harvest comes, let us be grateful to God, and let us not suffer the season to pass over without psalms of thanksgiving. I believe I shall be correct if I say that there is never in the world, as a rule, more than sixteen months' supply of food; that is to say, when the harvest is gathered in, there may be sixteen months' supply; but at the time of harvest there is not usually enough wheat in the whole world to last the population more than four or five months; so that if the harvest did not come we should be on the verge of famine. We live still from hand to mouth. Let us pause and bless God, and let the joy of harvest be the joy of gratitude.

To the Christian it should be great joy, by means

of the harvest, *to receive an assurance of God's faithfulness.* The Lord has promised that seed-time and harvest, summer and winter, shall never cease; and when you see the loaded wain carrying in the crop you may say to yourself, "God is true to his promise. Despite the dreary winter and the damp spring, autumn has come with its golden grain." Depend upon it, that as the Lord keeps this promise he will keep all the rest. All his promises are yea and amen in Christ Jesus: if he keeps his covenant to the earth, much more will he keep his covenant with his own people, whom he hath loved with an everlasting love. Go, Christian, to the mercy-seat with the promise on your lip and plead it. Be assured it is not a dead letter. Let not unbelief cause you to stammer when you mention the promise before the throne, but say it boldly.— "Fulfil this word unto thy servant on which thou hast caused me to hope." Shame upon us that we so little believe our God. The world is full of proofs of his goodness. Every rising sun, every falling shower, every revolving season certifies his faithfulness. Wherefore do we doubt him? If we never doubt him till we have cause for it we shall never know distrust again. Encouraged by the return of harvest, let us resolve in the strength of the Spirit of God that we will not waver, but will believe in the divine word and rejoice in it.

Once more. To the Christian, in the joy of harvest there will always be *the joy of expectation.* As there is a harvest to the husbandman for which he waiteth patiently, so there is a harvest for all faithful waiters who are looking for the coming and the appearing of our Lord and Saviour Jesus Christ. The mature Christian, like the ripe ear of corn, hangs down his head with holy humility. When he was but green in the things of God he stood erect and was somewhat boastful, but now that he has become full of the blessing of the Lord he is humbled thereby, and bows himself down; he is waiting for the sickle, and he dreads it not, for no common reaper shall come to gather Christ's people—he himself shall reap the harvest of the world. The Lord leaves the destroying angel to reap the vintage and to cast it into the wine-vat to be trodden with vengeance; but as for the grain which he himself has sown, he will gather it himself with his own golden sickle. We are looking for this. We are growing amongst the tares, and sometimes we are half afraid lest the tares should be stronger than ourselves and choke the wheat; but we shall be separated by-and-by, and when the corn is well winnowed and stored in the garner, we shall be there. It is this expectation which even now makes our hearts throb with joy. We have gone to the grave with precious sheaves that belonged to our Master, and when we were there we thought we could almost say, "Lord, if they sleep they shall do well. Let us die with them." Our joy of harvest is the hope of being at rest with all the saints, and for ever with the Lord. A view of these shadowy harvests upon earth should make us exceedingly glad, because they are the image and foreshadowing of the eternal harvest above.

So much about the joy of harvest; but I hasten onward. WHAT JOYS ARE THOSE WHICH TO THE BELIEVER ARE AS THE JOY OF HARVEST? It is a common notion that Christians are an unhappy people. It is true that we are tried, but it is false that we are miserable. With all their trials, believers have such a compensation in the love of Christ that they are still a blessed generation, and it may be said of them, "Happy art thou, O Israel."

One of the first seasons in which we knew a joy

equal to the joy of harvest—a season which has
continued with us ever since it commenced—was *when
we found the Saviour,* and so obtained salvation. You
recollect for yourselves, brethren and sisters, the time
of the ploughing of your souls. My heart was fallow,
and covered with weeds; but on a certain day the great
Husbandman came and began to plough my soul. Ten
black horses were his team, and it was a sharp
ploughshare that he used, and the ploughers made
deep furrows. The ten commandments were those
black horses, and the justice of God, like a
ploughshare, tore my spirit. I was condemned, undone,
destroyed, lost, helpless, hopeless,—I thought hell was
before me. Then there came a cross ploughing, for
when I went to hear the gospel it did not comfort me;
it made me wish I had a part in it, but I feared that
such a boon was out of the question. The choicest
promises of God frowned at me, and his threatenings
thundered at me. I prayed but found no answer of
peace. It was long with me thus. After the ploughing
came the sowing. God who ploughed the heart made
it conscious that it needed the gospel, and the gospel
seed was joyfully received. Do you recollect that
auspicious day when at last you began to have some
little hope? It was very little-like a green blade that
peeps up from the soil: you scarce knew whether it
was grass or corn, whether it was presumption or true
faith. It was a little hope, but it grew very pleasantly.
Alas, a frost of doubt came; snow of fear fell; cold winds
of despondency blew on you, and you said, "There can
be no hope for me." But what a glorious day was that
when at last the wheat which God had sown ripened,
and you could say, "I have looked unto him and have
been lightened: I have laid my sins on Jesus, where
God laid them of old, and they are taken away, and I

am saved." I remember well that day, and so no doubt
do many of you. O sirs! no husbandman ever shouted
for joy as our hearts shouted when a precious Christ
was ours, and we could grasp him with full assurance
of salvation in him. Many days have passed since then,
but the joy of it is still fresh with us. And, blessed be
God, it is not the joy of the first day only that we look
back upon; it is the joy of every day since then, more
or less; for our joy no man taketh from us; still we are
walking in Christ, even as we received him. Even now
all our hope on him is stayed, all our help from him
we bring; and our joy and peace continue with us
because they are based upon an immovable
foundation. We rejoice in the Lord, yea, and we will
rejoice.

The joy of harvest generally shows itself by the
farmer giving a feast to his friends and neighbours;
and, usually, those who find Christ express their joy
by telling their friends and their neighbours how great
things the Lord hath done for them. The grace of God
is communicative. A man cannot he saved, and always
hold his tongue about it: as well look for dumb choirs
in heaven as for a silent church on earth. If a man
has been thirsty, and has come to the living stream,
his first impulse will be to cry, "Ho! every one that
thirsteth!" Do you feel the joy of harvest, the joy that
makes you wish that others should share with you? If
so, do not repress the impulse to proclaim your
happiness. Speak of Christ to brothers and sisters, to
friends and kinsfolk; and, if the language be
stammering, the message in itself is so important that
the words in which you couch it will be a secondary
consideration. Tell it, tell it out far and wide—that there
is a Saviour, that you have found him, and that his
blood can wash away transgression. Tell it everywhere;

and so the joy of harvest shall spread o'er land and sea, and God shall be glorified.

We have another joy which is like the joy of harvest. We frequently have it too. It is *the joy of answered prayer.* I hope you know what it is to pray in faith. Some prayer is not worth the words used in presenting it because there is no faith mixed with it. "With all thy sacrifices thou shalt offer salt," and the salt of faith is needful if we would have our sacrifices accepted. Those who are familiar with the mercy-seat know that prayer is a reality, and that the doctrine of divine answers to prayer is no fiction. Sometimes God will delay to answer for wise reasons: then his children must cry, and cry, and cry again. They are in the condition of the husbandman who must wait for the precious fruits of the earth; and when at last the answer to prayer comes, they are then in the husbandman's position when he receives the harvest. Remember Hannah's wail and Hannah's word. In the bitterness of her soul she cried to God, and when her child was given to her she called it "Samuel," meaning, "Asked of God"; for, said she, "For this child I prayed." He was a dear child to her, because he was a child of prayer. Any mercy that comes to you in answer to prayer will be your Samuel mercy, your darling mercy. You will say of it, "For this mercy I prayed," and it will bring the joy of harvest to your spirit. If the Lord desires to surprise his children he has only to answer their prayers; for the most of them would be astonished if an answer came to their petitions. I know how they speak about answers to prayer. They say, "How remarkable! How wonderful!" as if it were anything remarkable that God should be true, and that the Most High should keep his promise. Oh for more faith to rest upon his word! and we should have more of these harvest joys.

We have another joy of harvest in ourselves *when we conquer a temptation.* We know what it is to get under a cloud sometimes: sin within us rises with a darkening force, or an external adversity beclouds us, and we miss the plain path we were accustomed to walk in. A child of God at such times will cry mightily for help; for he is fearful of himself and fearful of his surroundings. Some of God's people have been by the week and month together exposed to the double temptation, from without and from within, and have cried to God in bitter anguish. It has been a very hard struggle: the sinful action has been painted in very fascinating colours, and the siren voice of temptation has almost enchanted them. But when at last they have got through the valley of the shadow of death without having slipped with their feet; when, after all, they have not been destroyed by Apollyon, but have come forth again into the daylight, they feel a joy unspeakable, compared with which the joy of harvest is mere childish merriment. Those know deep joy who have felt bitter sorrow. As the man feels that he is the stronger for the conflict, as he feels that he has gathered experience and stronger faith from having passed through the trial, he lifts up his heart, and rejoices, not in himself, but before his God, with the joy of harvest. Brethren beloved, you know what that means.

Again, there is such a thing as the joy of harvest *when we have been rendered useful.* The master passion of every Christian is to be useful. There should be a burning zeal within us for the glory of God. When the man who desires to be useful has laid his plans and set about his work, he begins to look out for the results; but perhaps it will be weeks, or years, before results will come. The worker is not to be blamed that there are no fruits as yet but he is to be blamed if he is content to be without fruits. A preacher may preach without conversions, and who shall blame him? but if he be happy, who shall excuse him? It is ours to break our own hearts if we cannot by God's grace break other men's hearts; if others will not weep for their sins it should be our constant habit to weep for them. When the heart becomes earnest, warm, zealous, God usually gives a measure of success, some fifty-fold, some a hundred-fold. When the success comes it is the joy of harvest indeed. I cannot help being egotistical enough to mention the joy I felt when first I heard that a soul had found peace through my youthful ministry. I had been preaching in a village some few Sabbaths with an increasing congregation, but I had not heard of a conversion, and I thought, "Perhaps I am not called of God. He does not mean me to preach, for if he did he would give me spiritual children." One Sabbath my good deacon said, "Don't be discouraged. A poor woman was savingly impressed last Sabbath." How long do you suppose it was before I saw that woman! It was just as long as it took me to reach her cottage. I was eager to hear from her own lips whether it was a work of God's grace or not. I always looked upon her with interest, though only a poor labourer's wife, till she was taken away to heaven, after having lived a holy life. Many since then have I rejoiced over in the Lord, but that first seal to my ministry was peculiarly dear to me. It gave me a sip of the joy of harvest. If somebody had left me a fortune it would not have caused me one hundredth part of the delight I had in discovering that a soul had been led to the Saviour. I am sure Christian people who have not this joy have missed one of the choicest delights that a believer can know this side heaven. In fact, when I see souls saved,

I do not envy Gabriel his throne nor the angels their harps. It shall be our heaven to be out of heaven for a season if we can but bring others to know the Saviour and so add fresh jewels to the Redeemer's crown.

I will mention another delight which is as the joy of harvest, and that is, *fellowship with the Lord Jesus Christ.* This is not so much a matter for speech as for experience and delight. If we try to speak of what communion with Christ is, we fail. Solomon, the wisest of men, when inspired to write of the fellowship of the church with her Lord, was compelled to write in allegories and emblems, and though to the spiritual mind the Book of Canticles is always delightful, yet to the carnal mind it seems a mere love song. The natural man discerneth not the things that be of God, for they are spiritual, and can only be spiritually discerned. But, oh, the bliss of knowing that Christ is yours, and of entering into nearness of communion with him. To thrust your hand into his side, and your finger into the print of the nails; these be not everyday joys; but when such near and dear communings come to us on our highdays and holydays, they make our souls like the chariots of Amminadib, or, if you will, they cause us to tread the world beneath our feet and all that earth calls good or great. Our condition matters nothing to us if Christ be with us;—he is our God, our comfort, and our all, and we rejoice before him as with the joy of harvest.

I have no time to enlarge further; for I want to close with one other practical word. Many of us are anxiously desiring a harvest which would bring to us an intense delight. Of late, divers persons have communicated to me in many ways the strong emotion they feel of pity for the souls of men. Others of us have felt a mysterious impulse to pray more than we did, and to be more anxious than ever we were that Christ would save poor perishing sinners. We shall not be satisfied until there is a thorough awakening in this land. We did not raise the feeling in our own minds, and we do not desire to repress it. We do not believe it can be repressed; but others will feel the same heavenly affection, and will sigh and cry to God day and night until the blessing comes. This is the sowing, this is the ploughing, this is the harrowing—may it go on to harvesting. I long to hear my brethren and sisters universally saying, "We are full of anguish, we are in agony till souls be saved." The cry of Rachel, "Give me children, or I die," is the cry of your minister this day, and the longing of thousands more besides. As that desire grows in intensity a revival is approaching. We must have spiritual children born to Christ or our hearts will break for the longing that we have for their salvation. Oh for more of these longings, yearnings, cravings, travailings! If we plead till the harvest of revival comes we shall partake in the joy of it.

Who will have the most joy? Those who have been the most concerned about it. You who do not pray in private, nor come out to prayer-meetings, will not have the joy when the blessing comes, and the church is increased. You had no share in the sowing, therefore you will have little share in the reaping. You who never speak to others about their souls, who take no share in Sunday-school or mission work, but simply eat the fat and drink the sweet—you shall have none of the joy of harvest, for you do not put your hands to the work of the Lord. And who would wish that idlers should be happy? Rather in our zeal and jealousy feel inclined to say, "Curse ye Meroz, curse ye bitterly the inhabitants thereof; because they came not up to the help of the Lord, to the help of the Lord against the mighty." If you come to the help of the Lord by his own divine Spirit, you shall share the joy of harvest. Perhaps none will have more of that joy than those who shall have the privilege of seeing their own dear ones brought to God. Some of you have children who are a trial to you whenever you think of them; let them be such a trial to you that they drive you to incessant prayer for them, and, if the blessing comes, why should it not drop on them? If a revival comes, why should not your daughter yet be converted, and that wild boy of yours be brought in, or even your grey-headed father, who has been sceptical and unbelieving—why should not the grace of God come to him? And, oh, what a joy of harvest you will have then! What bliss will thrill through your spirit when you see those who are united to you in ties of blood united to Christ your Lord! Pray much for them with earnest faith, and you shall yet have the joy of harvest in your own house, a shout of harvest home in your own family.

Possibly, my hearer, you have not much to do with such joy, for you are yourself unsaved. Yet it is a grand thing for an unconverted person to be under a ministry that God blesses, and with a people that pray for conversions. It is a happy thing for you, young man, to have a Christian mother. It is a great boon for you, O unconverted woman, that you have a godly sister. These make us hopeful for you. Whilst your relations are prayerful, we are hopeful for *you*. May the Lord Jesus be yours yet. But, ah! if you remain unbelieving, however rich a blessing comes to others, it will leave *you* none the better for it. "If ye be willing and obedient, ye shall eat the good of the land"; but there are some who may cry in piteous accents, "The harvest is past, the summer is ended, and we are not saved." It has been remarked that those who pass through a season of revival and remain unconverted are more hardened and unimpressed than before. I believe it to be so, and I therefore pray the divine Spirit to come with such energy that none of you may escape his power. May you be led to pray,

> "Pass me not O mighty Spirit!
>   Thou canst make the blind to see;
> Witnesser of Jesus' merit,
>   Speak the word of power to me,
>   Even me.

> "Have I long in sin been sleeping,
>   Long been slighting, grieving thee?
> Has the world my heart been keeping?
>   Oh forgive and rescue me,
>   Even me."

Oh for earnest, importunate prayer from all believers throughout the world! If our churches could be stirred up to incessant, vehement crying to God, so as to give him no rest till he make Zion a praise in the earth, we might expect to see God's kingdom come, and the power of Satan fall. As many of you as love Christ I charge you by his dear name to be much in prayer; as many of you as love the Church of God, and desire her prosperity, I beseech you keep not back in this time of supplication. The Lord grant that you may be led to plead till the harvest joy is granted. Do you remember one Sabbath my saying, "The Lord deal so with you as you deal with his work during this next month." I feel as if it will be so with many of you— that the Lord will deal so with you as you shall deal with his Church. If you scatter little you shall have little, if you pray little you shall have little favour; but if you have zeal and faith, and plead much and work much for the Lord, good measure, pressed down and running over, shall the Lord return into your own bosoms. If you water others with drops you shall receive drops in return; but if the Spirit helps you to pour out rivers of living water from your own soul, then floods of heavenly grace shall flow into your spirit. God bring in the unconverted, and lead them to a simple trust in Jesus; then shall they also know the joy of harvest. We ask it for his name's sake. Amen.

Spiritual Gleaning

"Let her glean even among the sheaves, and reproach her not."—Ruth ii. 15.

COUNTRY friends need no explanation of what is meant by gleaning. I hope the custom will never be banished from the land, but that the poor will always be allowed their little share of the harvest. I am afraid that many who see gleaning every year in the fields of their own parish are not yet wise enough to understand the heavenly art of spiritual gleaning. That is the subject which I have chosen on this occasion, and my text is taken from the charming story of Ruth, which is known to every one of you. I shall use the story as setting forth our own case, in a homely but instructive way. In the first place, we shall observe that there is a *great Husbandman:* it was Boaz in Ruth's case, it is our heavenly Father who is the Husbandman in our case. Secondly, we shall notice *a humble gleaner:* the gleaner was Ruth in this instance, but she may be looked upon as the representative of every believer. And, in the third place, here is *a gracious permission given* to Ruth: "Let her glean even among the sheaves, and reproach her not," and the same permission is spiritually given to us.

I. In the first place, the God of the whole earth is A GREAT HUSBANDMAN. This is true in *natural* things. As a matter of fact all farm operations are carried on by his power and prudence. Man may plough the soil, and sow the seed; but as Jesus said, "My Father is the husbandman." He appoints the clouds and allots the sunshine; he directs the winds and distributes the dew and the rain; he also gives the frost and the heat, and so by various processes of nature he brings forth food for man and beast. All the farming, however, which God does, is for the benefit of others, and never for himself. He has no need of any of our works of husbandry. If he were hungry, he would not tell us. "The cattle on a thousand hills," says he, "are mine." The purest kindness and benevolence are those which dwell in the heart of God. Though all things are God's, his works in creation and in providence are not for himself, but for his creatures. This should greatly encourage us in trusting to him.

In *spiritual* matters God is a great husbandman; and there, too, all his works are done for his children, that they may be fed upon the finest of the wheat. Permit me to speak of the wide gospel fields which our heavenly Father farms for the good of his children. There is a great variety of these fields, and they are all fruitful for "the fountain of Jacob shall be upon a land of corn and wine; also his heavens shall drop down dew." Deut. xxxiii. 28. Every field which our heavenly Father tills yields a plentiful harvest, for there are no failures or famines with him.

1. One part of his farm is called *Doctrine field.* What full sheaves of finest wheat are to be found there! He who is permitted to glean in it will gather bread enough and to spare, for the land brings forth by handfuls. Look at that goodly sheaf of election; full, indeed, of heavy ears of corn, such as Pharaoh saw in his first dream—ears full and strong. There is the great sheaf of final perseverance, where each ear is a promise that the work which God has begun he will assuredly complete. If we have not faith enough to partake of either of these sheaves, we may glean around the choice sheaves of redemption by the blood of Christ. Many a poor soul who could not feed on electing love, nor realise his perseverance in Christ, can yet feed on the atonement and rejoice in the sublime doctrine of substitution. Many and rich are the sheaves which stand thick together in Doctrine-field; these, when threshed by meditation and ground in the mill of thought, furnish royal food for the Lord's family.

I wonder why it is that some of our Master's stewards are so prone to lock the gate of this field, as if they thought it dangerous ground. For my part, I wish my people not only to glean here, but to carry home the sheaves by the waggon-load for they cannot be too well fed when truth is the food. Are my fellow-labourers afraid that Jeshurun will wax fat and kick, if he has too much food? I fear there is more likelihood of his dying of starvation if the bread of sound doctrine is withheld. If we have a love to the precepts and warnings of the word, we need not be afraid of the doctrines; on the contrary, we should search them out and feed upon them with joy. The doctrines of distinguishing grace are to be set forth in due

proportions to the rest of the word, and those are poor
pulpits from which these grand truths are excluded.
We must not keep the Lord's people out of this field. I
say, swing the gate open, and come in, all of you who
are children of God! I am sure that in my Master's
field nothing grows which will harm you. Gospel
doctrine is always safe doctrine. You may feast upon
it till you are full, and no harm will come of it. Be
afraid of no revealed truth. Be afraid of spiritual
ignorance, but not of holy knowledge. Grow in grace
and in the knowledge of your Lord and Saviour Jesus
Christ. Everything taught in the word of God is meant
to be the subject of a Christian's study, therefore
neglect nothing. Visit the doctrine-field daily, and glean
in it with the utmost diligence.

2. The great Husbandman has another field called
Promise field; of that I shall not need to speak, for I
hope you often enter it and glean from it. Just let us
take an ear or two out of one of the sheaves, and show
them to you that you may be induced to stay there
the live-long day, and carry home a rich load at night.
Here is an ear: "The mountains shall depart, and the
hills be removed; but my kindness shall not depart
from thee, neither shall the covenant of my peace be
removed." Here is another: "When thou passest
through the waters, I will be with thee; and through
the rivers, they shall not overflow thee; when thou
walkest through the fire, thou shalt not be burned;
neither shall the flame kindle upon thee." Here is
another; it has a short stalk, but a heavy ear; "My
strength is sufficient for thee." Another is long in the
straw, but very rich in corn: "Let not your heart be
troubled: ye believe in God, believe also in me. In my
Father's house are many mansions: if it were not so I
would have told you. I go to prepare a place for you;

and if I go and prepare a place for you I will come again and receive you unto myself; that where I am, there ye may be also." What a word is that!—"I will come again." Yes, beloved, we can say of the Promise field what cannot be said of a single acre in all England; namely, that it is so rich a field that it could not be richer, and that it has so many ears of corn in it that you could not insert another. As the poet sings:

"What more can he say, than to you he hath said,—
You who unto Jesus for refuge have fled?"

Glean in that field, O ye poor and needy ones, and never think that you are intruding. The whole field is your own, every ear of it; you may draw out from the sheaves themselves, and the more you take the more you may.

3. Then there is *Ordinance field;* a great deal of good wheat grows in this field. The field of Baptism has been exceedingly fruitful to some of us, for it has set forth to us our death, burial, and resurrection in Christ, and thus we have been cheered and instructed. It has been good for us to declare ourselves on the Lord's side, and we have found that in keeping our Lord's commandments there is great reward. But I will not detain you long in this field, for some of our friends think it has a damp soil: I wish them more light and more grace. However, we will pass on to the field of the Supper, where grows the very best of our Lord's corn. What rich things have we fed upon in this choice spot! Have we not there tasted the sweetest and most sustaining of all spiritual food? In all the estate no field is to be found to rival this centre and crown of all the domain: this is the King's Acre. Gospel gleaner, abide in that field; glean it on the first day of every week, and expect to see your Lord there; for it is

written, "He was known of them in the breaking of bread."

4. The heavenly Husbandman has one field upon a hill, which equals the best of the others, even if it does not excel them. You cannot really and truly go into any of the other fields unless you pass into this; for the road to the other fields lies through this hill farm; it is called *Fellowship and Communion with Christ.* This is the field for the Lord's choicest ones to glean in. Some of you have only run through it, you have not stopped long enough in it; but he who knows how to stay here, yea, to live here, shall spend his hours most profitably and pleasantly. It is only in proportion as we hold fellowship with Christ, and communion with him, that either ordinances, or doctrines, or promises can profit us. All other things are dry and barren unless we are enjoying the love of Christ, unless we bear his likeness, unless we dwell continually with him, and rejoice in his love. I am sorry to say that few Christians think much of this field; it is enough for them to be sound in doctrine, and tolerably correct in practice; they care far less than they should about intimate intercourse with Christ Jesus, their Lord, by the Holy Ghost. I am sure that if we gleaned in this field we should not have half so many naughty tempers, nor a tenth as much pride, nor a hundredth part so much sloth. This is a field hedged and sheltered, and in it you will find better food than that which angels feed upon: yea, you will find Jesus himself as the bread which came down from heaven. Blessed, blessed field; may we visit it every day. The Master leaves the gate wide open for every believer; let us enter in and gather the golden ears till we can carry no more. Thus we have seen the great Husbandman in his fields; let us rejoice that we have

such a great Husbandman near, and such fields to glean in.

II. And now, in the second place, we have A HUMBLE GLEANER. Ruth was a gleaner, and may serve as an illustration of what every believer should be in the fields of God.

1. The believer is a favoured gleaner, for he *may take home a whole sheaf, if he likes:* he may bear away all that he can possibly carry, for all things are freely given him of the Lord. I use the figure of a gleaner, because I believe that few Christians ever go much beyond it, and yet they are free to do so if they are able. Some may say, why does not the believer reap all the field, and take all the corn home with him? I answer that he is welcome to do so if he can: for no good thing will the Lord withhold from them that walk uprightly. If your faith is like a great waggon, and you can carry the whole field of corn, you have full permission to take it. Alas, our faith is so little that we rather glean than reap; we are straitened in ourselves, not in our God. May you all outgrow the metaphor, and come home, bringing your sheaves with you.

2. Again, we may remark, that the gleaner, in her business *has to endure much toil and fatigue.* She rises early in the morning, and she trudges off to a field; if that be closed, she hastens to another; and if that be shut up, or gleaned already, she hurries further still; and all day long, while the sun is shining upon her, she seldom sits down to refresh herself, but still she goes on, stoop, stoop, stoop, gathering the ears one by one. She returns not to her home till nightfall; for she desires, if the field is good, to do much business that day, and she will not go home until she is loaded

down. Beloved, so let each one of us do when we seek spiritual food. Let us not be afraid of a little fatigue in the Master's fields: if the gleaning is good, we must not soon weary in gathering the precious spoil, for the gains will richly reward our pains. I know a friend who walks five miles every Sunday to hear the gospel, and has the same distance to return. Another thinks little of a ten miles' journey; and these are wise, for to hear the pure word of God no labour is extravagant. To stand in the aisle till ready to drop, listening all the while with strained attention, is a toil which meets a full reward if the gospel be heard and the Spirit of God bless it to the soul. A gleaner does not expect that the ears will come to her of themselves; she knows that gleaning is hard work. We must not expect to find the best field next to our own house, we may have to journey to the far end of the parish, but what of that? Gleaners must not be choosers, and where the Lord sends the gospel, there he calls us to be present.

3. We remark, next, that *every ear the gleaner gets she has to stoop for.* Why is it that proud people seldom profit under the word? Why is it that certain "intellectual" folk cannot get any good out of our soundest ministers? Why, because they must needs have the corn lifted up for them; and if the wheat is held so high over their heads that they can hardly see it, they are pleased, and cry, "Here is something wonderful." They admire the extraordinary ability of the man who can hold up the truth so high that nobody can reach it but truly that is a sorry feat. The preacher's business is to place truth within the reach of all, children as well as adults; he is to let fall handfuls on purpose for poor gleaners, and these will never mind stooping to collect the ears. If we preach to the educated people only, the wise ones can

understand, but the illiterate cannot; but when we preach in all simplicity to the poor, other classes can understand it if they like, and if they do not like, they had better go somewhere else. Those who cannot stoop to pick up plain truth had better give up gleaning. For my part, I would be taught by a child if I could thereby know and understand the gospel better: the gleaning in our Lord's field is so rich that it is worth the hardest labour to be able to carry home a portion of it. Hungry souls know this, and are not to be hindered in seeking their heavenly food. We will go down on our knees in prayer; and stoop by self-humiliation, and confession of ignorance, and so gather with the hand of faith the daily bread of our hungering souls.

4. Note, in the next place, that what a gleaner gets *she wins ear by ear;* occasionally she picks up a handful at once, but as a rule it is straw by straw. In the case of Ruth, handfuls were let fall on purpose for her; but she was highly favoured. The gleaner stoops, and gets one ear, and then she stoops again for another. Now, beloved, where there are handfuls to be got at once, there is the place to go and glean; but if you cannot meet with such abundance, be glad to gather ear by ear. I have heard of certain persons who have been in the habit of hearing a favourite minister, and when they go to another place, they say, "I cannot hear anybody after my own minister; I shall stay at home and read a sermon." Please remember the passage, "Not forsaking the assembling of yourselves together, as the manner of some is." Let me also entreat you not to be so foolishly partial as to deprive your soul of its food. If you cannot get a handful at one stoop, do not refuse to gather an ear at a time. If you are not content to learn here a little and there a

little, you will soon be half starved, and then you will be glad to get back again to the despised minister and pick up what his field will yield you. That is a sorry ministry which yields nothing. Go and glean where the Lord has opened the gate for you. Why the text alone is worth the journey; do not miss it.

5. Note, next, that *what the gleaner picks up she keeps in her hand;* she does not drop the corn as fast as she gathers it. There is a good thought at the beginning of the sermon, but the hearers are so eager to hear another, that the first one slips away. Towards the end of the sermon a large handful falls in their way, and they forget all that went before in their eagerness to retain this last and richest portion. The sermon is over, and, alas, it is nearly all gone from the memory, for many are about as wise as a gleaner would be if she should pick up one ear, and drop it; pick up another, and drop it, and so on all day. The net result of such a day's work in a stubble is a bad backache; and I fear that all our hearers will get by their hearing will be a headache. Be attentive but be retentive too. Gather the grain and tie it up in bundles for carrying away with you, and mind you do not lose it on the road home. Many a person when he has got a fair hold of the sermon, loses it on the way to his house by idle talk with vain companions. I have heard of a Christian man who was seen hurrying home one Sunday with all his might. A friend asked him why he was in such haste. "Oh!" said he, "two or three Sundays ago, our minister gave us a most blessed discourse, and I greatly enjoyed it; but when I got outside there were two deacons discussing, and one pulled the sermon one way, and the other the other, till they pulled it all to pieces, and I lost all the savour of it." Those must have been very bad deacons; let us

not imitate them; and if we know of any who are of their school, let us walk home alone in dogged silence sooner than lose all our gleanings by their controversies. After a good sermon go home with your ears and your mouth shut. Act like the miser, who not only gets all he can, but keeps all he can. Do not lose by trifling talk that which may make you rich to all eternity.

6. Then, again, the gleaner *takes the wheat home and threshes it.* It is a wise thing to thresh a sermon whoever may have been the preacher, for it is certain that there is a portion of straw and chaff about it. Many thresh the preacher by finding needless fault; but that is not half so good as threshing the sermon to get out of it the pure truth. Take a sermon, beloved, when you get one which is worth having, and lay it down on the floor of meditation, and beat it out with the flail of prayer, and you will get bread-corn from it. This threshing by prayer and meditation must never be neglected. If a gleaner should stow away her corn in her room, and leave it there, the mice would get at it; but she would have no food from it if she did not thresh out the grain. Some get a sermon, and carry it home, and allow Satan and sin, and the world, to eat it all up, and it becomes unfruitful and worthless, to them. But he who knows how to flail a sermon well, so as to clear out all the wheat from the straw, he is it that makes a good hearer and feeds his soul on what he hears.

7. And then, in the last place, the good woman, after threshing the corn, no doubt *winnowed it.* Ruth did all this in the field; but you can scarcely do so. You must do some of the work at home. And observe, she did not take the chaff home; she left that behind her in the field. It is a prudent thing to winnow all the

discourses you hear so as to separate the precious from the vile; but pray do not fall into the silly habit of taking home all the chaff, and leaving the corn behind. I think I hear you say, "I shall recollect that queer expression; I shall make an anecdote out of that odd remark." Listen, then, for I have a word for you,— if you hear a man retail nothing about a minister except his oddities, just stop him, and say, "We have all our faults, and perhaps those who are most ready to speak of those of others are not quite perfect themselves: cannot you tell us what the preacher said that was worth hearing?" In many cases the virtual answer will be, "Oh, I don't recollect that." They have sifted the corn, thrown away the good grain, and brought home the chaff. Ought they not to be put in an asylum? Follow the opposite rule; drop the straw, and retain the good corn. Separate between the precious and the vile, and let the worthless material go where it may; you have no use for it, and the sooner you are rid of it the better. Judge with care; reject false teaching with decision, and retain true doctrine with earnestness, so shall you practise the enriching art of heavenly gleaning. May the Lord teach us wisdom, so that we may become "rich to all the intents of bliss;" so shall our mouth be satisfied with good things, and our youth shall be renewed like the eagles.

III. And now, in the last place, here is A GRACIOUS PERMISSION GIVEN: "Let her glean among the sheaves, and reproach her not." Ruth had no right to go among the sheaves till Boaz gave her permission by saying, "Let her do it." For her to be allowed to go amongst the sheaves, in that part of the field where the wheat was newly cut, and none of it carted, was a great favour: but Boaz whispered that handfuls were to be dropped on purpose for her, and that was a greater favour still. Boaz had a secret love for the maiden and even so, beloved, it is because of our Lord's eternal love to us that he allows us to enter his best fields and glean among the sheaves. His grace permits us to lay hold upon doctrinal blessings, promise blessings, and experience blessings: the Lord has a favour towards us, and hence these singular kindnesses. We have no right to any heavenly blessings of ourselves; our portion is due to free and sovereign grace.

I tell you the reasons that moved Boaz's heart to let Ruth go among the sheaves. The master motive was *because he loved her.* He would have her go there, because he had conceived an affection for her, which he afterwards displayed in grander way. So the Lord lets his people come and glean among the sheaves, because he loves them. Didst thou have a soul-enriching season amongst the sheaves the other Sabbath? Didst thou carry home thy sack, filled like those of Joseph's brothers, when they returned from Egypt? Didst thou have an abundance? Wast thou satisfied? Mark; that was thy Master's goodness. It was because he loved thee. Look, I beseech thee, on all thy spiritual enjoyments as proof of his eternal love. Look on all heavenly blessings as being tokens of heavenly grace. It will make thy corn grind all the better, and eat all the sweeter, if thou wilt reflect that eternal love gave it thee. Thy sweet seasons, thy high enjoyments, thy unspeakable ravishments of spirit are all proofs of divine affection, therefore be doubly glad of them.

There was another reason why Boaz allows Ruth to glean among the sheaves; it was because he was her *relative.* This is why our Lord gives us choice

favours at times and takes us into his banqueting
house in so gracious a manner. He is our next of kin,
bone of our bone, and flesh of our flesh. Our Redeemer,
our kinsman, is the Lord Jesus and he will never be
strange to his own flesh. It is a high and charming
mystery that our Lord Jesus is the Husband of his
church; and sure he may well let his spouse glean
among the sheaves; for all that he possesses is hers
already. Her interests and his interests are one, and
so he may well say, "Beloved, take all thou pleasest; I
am none the poorer because thou dost partake of my
fulness, for thou art mine. Thou art my partner, and
my choice, and all that I have is thine." What then,
shall I say to yon who are my Lord's beloved? How
shall I speak with a tenderness and generosity equal
to his desires, for he would have me speak right
lovingly in his name. Enrich yourselves out of that
which is your Lord's. Go a spiritual gleaning as often
as ever you can. Never lose an opportunity of picking
up a golden blessing. Glean at the mercy-seat; glean
in private meditation; glean in reading pious books;
glean in associating with godly men; glean everywhere;
and if you can get only a little handful it will be better
than none. You who are so much in business, and so
much penned up by cares; if you can only spend five
minutes in the Lord's field gleaning a little, be sure to
do so. If you cannot bear away a sheaf, carry an ear,
and if you cannot find an ear, pick up even a grain of
wheat. Take care to get a little, if you cannot get much:
but gather as much as ever you can.

Just one other remark. O child of God, never be
afraid to glean. Have faith in God, and take the
promises home to yourself. Jesus will rejoice to see
you making free with his good things. His voice is "Eat
abundantly; drink, yea, drink abundantly, O beloved."

Therefore, if you find a rich promise, live upon it. Draw the honey out of the comb of Scripture, and live on its sweetness. If you meet with a most extraordinary sheaf, carry it away rejoicing. You cannot believe too much concerning your Lord; let not Satan cheat you into contentment with a meagre portion of grace when all the granaries of heaven are open to you. Glean on with humble industry and hopeful confidence, and know that he who owns both fields and sheaves is looking upon you with eyes of love, and will one day espouse you to himself in glory everlasting. Happy gleaner who finds eternal love and eternal life in the fields in which he gleans!

Mealtime in the Cornfields

"And Boaz said unto her, At mealtime come thou hither, and eat of the bread and dip thy morsel in the vinegar. And she sat beside the reapers: and he reached her parched corn, and she did eat, and was sufficed, and left."—Ruth ii. 14.

WE are going to the cornfields, not so much to glean, as to rest with the reapers and the gleaners, when under some wide-spreading oak they sit down to take refreshment. We hope some timid gleaner will accept our invitation to come and eat with us, and will have confidence enough to dip *her* morsel in the vinegar. May all of us have courage to feast to the full on our own account, and kindness enough to carry home a portion to our needy friends at home.

I. Our first point of remark is this—THAT GOD'S REAPERS HAVE THEIR MEALTIMES.

Those who work for God will find him a good master. He cares for oxen, and he has commanded

255

Israel, "Thou shalt not muzzle the ox when he treadeth out the corn." Much more doth he care for his servants who serve him. "He hath given meat unto them that fear him: he will ever be mindful of his covenant." The reapers in Jesus' fields shall not only receive a blessed reward at the last, but they shall have plenteous comforts by the way. He is pleased to pay his servants twice: first in the labour itself, and a second time in the labour's sweet results. He gives them such joy and consolation in the service of their Master that it is a sweet employ, and they cry, "We delight to do thy will, O Lord." Heaven is made up of serving God day and night, and a foretaste of heaven is enjoyed in serving God on earth with earnest perseverance.

God has ordained certain mealtimes for his reapers; and he has appointed that one of these shall be *when they come together to listen to the Word preached.* If God be with ministers they act as the disciples did of old, for they received the loaves and the fishes from the Lord Jesus, and then they handed them to the people. *We,* of ourselves, cannot feed one soul, much less thousands; but when the Lord is with us we can keep as good a table as Solomon himself, with all his fine flour, and fat oxen, and roebucks, and fallow-deer. When the Lord blesses the provisions of his House, no matter how many thousands there may be, all his poor shall be filled with bread. I hope, beloved, you know what it is to sit under the shadow of the Word with great delight, and find the fruit thereof sweet unto your taste. Where the doctrines of grace are boldly and plainly delivered to you in connection with the other truths of revelation; where Jesus Christ upon his cross is always lifted up; where the work of the Spirit is not forgotten; where the glorious purpose of the Father is never despised, there is sure to be rich provision for the children of God.

Often, too, our gracious Lord appoints us mealtimes *in our private readings and meditations.* Here it is that his "paths drop fatness." Nothing can be more fattening to the soul of the believer than feeding upon the Word and digesting it by frequent meditation. No wonder that men grow so slowly when they meditate so little. Cattle must chew the cud; it is not that which they crop with their teeth, but that which is masticated, and digested by rumination that nourishes them. We must take the truth, and turn it over and over again in the inward parts of our spirit; and so shall we extract suitable nourishment therefrom. My brethren, is not meditation the land of Goshen to you? If men once said, "There is corn in Egypt," may they not always say that the finest of the wheat is to be found in secret prayer? Private devotion is a land which floweth with milk and honey; a paradise yielding all manner of fruits; a banqueting house of choice wines. Ahasuerus might make a great feast, but all his hundred and twenty provinces could not furnish such dainties as meditation offers to the spiritual mind. Where can we feed and lie down in green pastures in so sweet a sense as we do in our musings on the Word? Meditation distils the quintessence of joy from the Scriptures, and gladdens our mouth with a sweetness which excels the virgin honey. Your retired periods and occasions of prayer should be to you refreshing seasons, in which, like the reapers at noonday, you sit with the Master and enjoy his generous provisions. The Shepherd of Salisbury Plain was wont to say that where he was lonely, and his wallet was empty, his Bible was to him meat, and drink, and company too: he is not the only man who has found a fulness in the Word when all else has been empty. During the battle of Waterloo a godly soldier, mortally wounded, was carried by his comrade into the rear, and being placed with his back propped up against a tree, he besought his friend to open his knapsack and take out the Bible which he had carried in it. "Read to me," he said, "one verse before I close my eyes in death." His comrade read him that verse: "Peace I leave with you, my peace I give unto you: not as the world giveth, give I unto you;" and there, fresh from the whistling of the bullets, and the roll of the drum, and the tempest of human conflict, that believing spirit enjoyed such holy calm that ere he fell asleep in the arms of Jesus he said, "Yes, I have a peace with God which passeth all understanding, which keeps my heart and mind through Jesus Christ." Saints most surely enjoy delightful mealtimes when they are alone in meditation.

Let us not forget that there is one specially ordained mealtime which ought to occur at least once in the week—I mean *the Supper of the Lord.* There you have literally, as well as spiritually, a meal. The table is richly spread, it has upon it both bread and wine; and looking at what these symbolize, we have before us a table richer than that which kings could furnish. There we have the flesh and the blood of our Lord Jesus Christ, whereof if a man eat he shall never hunger and never thirst, for that bread shall be unto him everlasting life. Oh! the sweet seasons we have known at the Lord's Supper. If some of you knew the enjoyment of feeding upon Christ in that ordinance you would chide yourselves for not having united with the Church in fellowship. In keeping the Master's commandments there is "great reward," and consequently in neglecting them there is great loss of reward. Christ is not so tied to the sacramental table as to be always found of those who partake thereat, but still it is "in the way" that we may expect the Lord to meet with us. "If ye love me, keep my commandments," is a sentence of touching power. Sitting at this table, our soul has mounted up from the emblem to the reality; we have eaten bread in the kingdom of God, and have leaned our head upon Jesus' bosom. "He brought me to the banqueting-house, and his banner over me was love."

Besides these regular mealtimes, there are others which God gives us, *at seasons when, perhaps, we little expect them.* You have been walking the street, and suddenly you have felt a holy flowing out of your soul toward God; or in the middle of business your heart has been melted with love and made to dance for joy, even as the brooks which have been bound with winter's ice, leap to feel the touch of spring. You have been groaning, dull, and earthbound; but the sweet love of Jesus has enwrapped your heart when you scarce thought of it, and your spirit, all free, and all on fire, has rejoiced before the Lord with timbrel and dance, like Miriam of old. I have had times occasionally in preaching when I would fain have kept on far beyond the appointed hour, for my overflowing soul has been like a vessel wanting vent. Seasons, too, we have had on our sick beds, when we would have been content to be sick always if we could have had our bed so well made by tender love, and our head so softly pillowed on condescending grace.

Our blessed Redeemer comes to us in the morning, and wakes us up by dropping sweet thoughts upon our souls; we know not how they came, but it is as if, when the dew was visiting the flowers, a few drops had taken pity upon us. In the cool eventide, too, as we have gone to our beds, our meditation of him has been sweet; and, in the night watches, when we tossed to and fro, and could not sleep, he has been pleased to become our song in the night.

God's reapers find it hard work to reap; but they gain a blessed solace when in one way or another they sit down and eat of their Master's rich provisions; then, with renewed strength, they rise with sharpened sickle, to reap again in the noontide heat.

Let me observe that, while these mealtimes come we know not exactly when, there are *certain seasons when we may expect them.* The Eastern reapers generally sit down under the shelter of a tree, or a booth, to take refreshment during the heat of the day. And certain I am, that when trouble, affliction, persecution, and bereavement, become the most painful to us, it is then that the Lord hands out to us the sweetest comforts. We must work till the hot sun forces the sweat from our faces, and then we may look for repose; we must bear the burden and heat of the day before we can expect to be invited to those choice meals which the Lord prepares for true labourers. When thy day of trouble is hottest, then the love of Jesus shall be sweetest.

Again, these mealtimes frequently occur *before* a trial. Elijah must be entertained beneath a juniper tree, for he is to go a forty-days' journey in the strength of that meat. You may suspect some danger nigh when your delights are overflowing. If you see a ship taking in great quantities of provision it is probably bound for a distant port and when God gives you extraordinary seasons of communion with Jesus, you may look for long leagues of tempestuous sea. Sweet cordials prepare for stern conflicts.

Times of refreshing also occur *after* trouble or arduous service. Christ was tempted of the devil, and *afterwards* angels came and ministered unto him.

Jacob wrestled with God, and afterwards, at Mahanaim, hosts of angels met him. Abraham fought with the kings, and returned from their slaughter, and then it was that Melchisedec refreshed him with bread and wine. After conflict, content; after battle, banquet. When thou hast waited on thy Lord, then thou shalt sit down, and thy Master will gird himself and wait upon thee.

Let worldlings say what they will about the hardness of religion, we do not find it so. We own that reaping for Christ has its difficulties and troubles; but still the bread which we eat is of heavenly sweetness, and the wine which we drink is crushed from celestial clusters—

> "I would not change my bless'd estate
> For all the world calls good or great;
> And while my faith can keep her hold,
> I envy not the sinner's gold."

II. Follow me while we turn to a second point. To THESE MEALS THE GLEANER IS AFFECTIONATELY INVITED. That is to say, the poor, trembling stranger who has not strength enough to reap, who has no right to be in the field except the right of charity—the poor, trembling sinner, conscious of his own demerit, and feeling but little hope and little joy, is invited to the feast of love.

In the text *the gleaner is invited to come.* "At mealtime, *come* thou hither." We trust none of you will be kept away from the place of holy feasting by any shame on account of your dress, or your personal character, or your poverty; nay nor even on account of your physical infirmities. "At mealtime come thou hither." I knew a deaf woman who could never hear a sound, and yet she was always in the House of God, and when asked why, her reply was that a friend found her the text, and then God was pleased to give her many a sweet thought upon it while she sat with his people; besides, she felt that as a believer she ought to honour God by her *presence* in his courts, and by confessing her union with his people; and, better still, she always liked to be in the best of company, and as the presence of God was there, and the holy angels, and the saints of the Most High, whether she could hear or no, she would go. If *such* persons find pleasure in coming, we who *can* hear should never stay away. Though we feel our unworthiness, we ought to be desirous to be laid in the House of God, as the sick were at the pool of Bethesda, hoping that the waters may be stirred, and that we may step in and be healed. Trembling soul, never let the temptations of the devil keep thee from the assembly of worshippers; "at mealtime come thou hither."

Moreover *she was bidden not only to come but to eat.* Whatever there is sweet and comfortable in the Word of God, ye that are of a broken and contrite spirit are invited to partake of it. "Jesus Christ came into the world to save *sinners*"—sinners such as you are. "In due time Christ died for the *ungodly*"—such ungodly ones as you feel yourselves to be. You desire to be Christ's. You *may* be Christ's. You are saying in your heart, "O that I could eat the children's bread!" You *may* eat it. You say, "I have no right." But the Lord gives you the invitation! Come without any other right than the right of his invitation.

> "Let not conscience make you linger,
>   Nor of fitness fondly dream."

But since he bids you "come," take him at his word; and if there be a promise, believe it; if there be an encouraging word, accept it, and let the sweetness of it be yours.

Note further, that she was not only invited to eat the bread, but to *dip her morsel in the vinegar.* We must not look upon this as being some sour stuff. No doubt there are crabbed souls in the church, who always dip their morsel in the sourest imaginable vinegar, and with a grim liberality invite others to share their misery with them; but the vinegar in my text is altogether another thing. This was either a compound of various juices expressed from fruits, or else it was that weak kind of wine mingled with water which is still commonly used in the harvest-fields of Italy and the warmer parts of the world—a drink not exceedingly strong, but good enough to impart a relish to the food. It was, to use the only word which will give the meaning, a *sauce,* which the Orientals used with their bread. As we use butter, or as they on other occasions used oil, so in the harvest-field, believing it to have cooling properties, they used what is here called "vinegar." Beloved, the Lord's reapers have sauce with their bread; they have not merely doctrines, but the holy unction which is the essence of doctrines; they have not merely truths, but a hallowed delight accompanies the truths. Take, for instance, the doctrine of election, which is like the bread; there is a sauce to dip it in. When I can say, "He loved *me* before the foundations of the world," the personal enjoyment of my interest in the truth becomes a sauce into which I dip my morsel. And you, poor gleaner, are invited to dip your morsel in it too. I used to hear people sing that hymn of Toplady's, which begins—

> "A debtor to mercy alone,
>   Of covenant mercy I sing;

Nor fear, with thy righteousness on,
My person and offering to bring."

The hymn rises to its climax in the lines—

"Yes, I to the end shall endure,
As sure as the earnest is given;
More happy, but not more secure,
The glorified spirits in heaven."

I used to think I should never be able to sing that hymn. It was the sauce, you know. I might manage to eat some of the plain bread, but I could not dip it in that sauce. It was too high doctrine, too sweet, too consoling. But I thank God I have since ventured to dip my morsel in it, and now I hardly like my bread without it. I would have every trembling sinner partake of the *comfortable* parts of God's Word, even those which cavillers call "HIGH DOCTRINE." Let him believe the simpler truth first, and then dip it in the sweet doctrine and be happy in the Lord.

I think I see the gleaner half prepared to come, for she is very hungry, and she has nothing with her; but she begins to say, "I have no right to come, for I am not a reaper; I do nothing for Christ; I am only a *selfish gleaner;* I am not a reaper." Ah! but thou art invited to come. Make no questions about it. Boaz bids thee; take thou his invitation, and approach at once. "But," you say, "I am such a *poor* gleaner; though my labour is all for myself, yet it is little I win by it; I get a few thoughts while the sermon is being preached, but I lose them before I reach home." I know you do, poor weak-handed woman, But still, Jesus invites thee. Come! Take thou the sweet promise as he presents it to thee, and let no bashfulness of thine send thee home hungry. "But," you say, "I am *a stranger;* you do not know my sins, my sinfulness, and the waywardness of my heart." But Jesus does, and yet he invites you. He knows you are but a Moabitess, a stranger from the commonwealth of Israel; but he bids you come. Is not that enough? "But," you say, "I owe so much to him already; it is so good of him to spare my forfeited life, and so tender of him to let me hear the gospel preached at all; I cannot have the presumption to be an intruder, and sit with the reapers." Oh! but he *bids* you. There is more presumption in your doubting than there could be in your believing. HE bids you. Will you refuse Boaz? Shall Jesus' lips give the invitation, and will you say him nay? Come, now, come. Remember that the little which Ruth could eat did not make Boaz any the poorer; and all that thou wantest will make Christ none the less glorious or full of grace. Are thy necessities large? His supplies are larger. Dost thou require great mercy? He is a great Saviour. I tell thee that his mercy is no more to be exhausted than the sea is to be drained. Come at once. There is enough for thee, and Boaz will not be impoverished by thy feasting to the full. Moreover, let me tell thee a secret—Jesus *loves* thee; therefore is it that he would have thee feed at his table. If thou art now a longing, trembling sinner, willing to be saved, but conscious that thou deservest it not, Jesus loves thee, and he will take more delight in seeing thee eat than thou wilt take in the eating. Let the sweet love he feels in his soul toward thee draw thee to him. And what is more—but this is a great secret, and must only be whispered in your ear—*he intends to be married to you;* and when you are married to him, why, the fields will be yours; for, of course, if you are his spouse, you are joint proprietor with him. Is it not so? Doth not the wife share with the husband? All those promises which are "yea and amen in Christ" shall be yours; nay, they all *are* yours now, for "the man is next of kin unto you," and ere long he will take you unto himself for ever, espousing you in faithfulness, and truth, and righteousness. Will you not eat of your own? " Oh! but," says one, "how can it be? I am a stranger." Yes, a stranger; but Jesus Christ loves the stranger. "A publican, a sinner;" but he is "the friend of publicans and sinners." "An outcast;" but he "gathereth together the outcasts of Israel." "A stray sheep;" but the shepherd "leaves the ninety and nine" to seek it. "A lost piece of money;" but he "sweeps the house" to find thee. "A prodigal son;" but he sets the bells a-ringing when he knows that thou wilt return. Come, Ruth! Come, trembling gleaner! Jesus invites thee: accept the invitation. "At mealtime come thou hither, and eat of the bread, and dip thy morsel in the vinegar."

III. Now, thirdly—and here is a very sweet point in the narrative—Boaz REACHED HER THE PARCHED CORN. She did "come and eat." Where did she sit? Note well that she "sat beside the reapers." She did not feel that she was one of them, but she "sat beside" them. Just like some of you who do not come to the Lord's Supper, but sit and look on. You are sitting "beside the reapers." You fear that you are not the people of God; still you love them, and therefore sit beside them. If there is a good thing to be had, and you cannot get it, you will sit as near as you can to those who *do* get it. "She sat beside the reapers."

And while she was sitting there, what happened? Did she stretch forth her hand and take the food herself? No, it is written, "HE reached her the parched corn." Ah! that is it. None but the Lord of the harvest can hand out the choicest refreshments of spiritual minds. I give the invitation in my Master's name, and

I hope I give it earnestly, affectionately, sincerely; but I know very well that at my poor bidding none will come till the Spirit draws. No trembling heart will accept divine refreshing at my hand; unless the King himself comes near, and reaches the parched corn to each chosen guest, none will receive it. How does he do this? By his gracious Spirit, he first of all *inspires your faith.* You are afraid to think that it can be true that such a sinner as you are can ever be "accepted in the Beloved"; he breathes upon you, and your faint hope becomes an expectancy, and that expectation buds and blossoms into an appropriating faith, which says, "Yes, my beloved is *mine,* and his desire is toward *me."*

Having done this, the Saviour does more; *he sheds abroad the love of God in your heart.* The love of Christ is like sweet perfume in a box. Now, he who put the perfume in the box is the only person that knows how to take off the lid. He, with his own skilful hand, opens the secret blessing, and sheds abroad the love of God in the soul.

But Jesus does more than this: he reaches the parched corn with his own hand, when *he gives us close communion with himself.* Do not think that this is a dream; I tell you there is such a thing as speaking with Christ to-day. As certainly as I can talk with my dearest friend, or find solace in the company of my beloved wife, so surely may I speak with Jesus, and find intense delight in the company of Immanuel. It is not a fiction. We do not worship a far-off Saviour; he is a God nigh at hand. His word is in our mouth and in our heart and we do to-day walk with him as the elect did of old, and commune with him as his apostles did on earth; not after the flesh, it is true, but after a real and spiritual fashion.

Yet once more let me add, the Lord Jesus is pleased to reach the parched corn, in the best sense, when *the Spirit gives us the infallible witness within, that we are "born of God."* A man may know that he is a Christian beyond all question. Philip de Morny, who lived in the time of Prince Henry of Navarre, was wont to say that the Holy Spirit had made his own salvation to him as clear a point as a problem demonstrated in Euclid. You know with what mathematical precision the scholar of geometry solves a problem or proves a proposition, and with as absolute a precision, as certainly as twice two are four, we may "know that we have passed from death unto life." The sun in the heavens is not more clear to the eye than his present salvation to an assured believer; such a man could as soon doubt his own existence as suspect his possession of eternal life.

Now let the prayer be breathed by poor Ruth, who is trembling yonder. Lord, reach me the parched corn! "Show me a token for good." "Deal with thy servant." "Draw me, we will run after thee." Lord, send thy love into my heart!

> "Come, Holy Spirit, heavenly Dove,
>   With all thy quickening powers,
>   Come, shed abroad a Saviour's love,
>   And that shall kindle ours."

There is no getting at Christ except by Christ revealing himself to us.

IV. And now the last point. After Boaz had reached the parched corn, we are told that "SHE DID EAT, AND WAS SUFFICED, AND LEFT." So shall it be with every Ruth. Sooner or later every penitent shall become a believer, every mourner a singer. There may be a space of deep conviction, and a period of much hesitation; but there shall come a season when the soul decides for the Lord, and cries, "If I perish, I perish. I will go as I am to Jesus. I will not play the fool any longer with my *buts* and *ifs,* but since he bids me believe that he died for me, I *will* believe it, and will trust his cross for my salvation." Whenever you shall be privileged to do this, you shall be *"satisfied."* "She did eat, and was sufficed." Your *head* shall be satisfied with the precious truth which Christ reveals; your *heart* shall be content with Jesus, as the altogether lovely object of affection; your *hope* shall be filled, for whom have you in heaven but Christ? Your *desire* shall be satiated, for what can even your desire hunger for more than "to know Christ and to be found in him."? You shall find Jesus charm your *conscience,* till it is at perfect peace; he shall content your *judgment,* till you know the certainty of his teachings; he shall supply your *memory* with recollections of what he did, and gratify your *imagination* with the prospects of what he is yet to do.

"She was sufficed, and left." Some of us have had deep draughts of love; we have thought that we could take in all of Christ, but when we have done our best, we have had to leave a vast remainder. We have sat down with a ravenous appetite at the table of the Lord's love, and said, "Nothing but the infinite can ever satisfy me," and that infinite has been granted us. I have felt that I am such a great sinner that nothing short of an infinite atonement could wash my sin away, and no doubt you have felt the same; but we have had our sin removed, and found merit enough and to spare in Jesus; we have had our hunger relieved, and found a redundance remaining for others who are in a similar case. There are certain sweet things in the word of God which you and I have not enjoyed yet, and which we cannot enjoy yet; and these we are obliged to leave for a while, till we are better prepared to receive them. Did not our Lord say, "I have yet many things to say unto you, but ye cannot bear them now"? There is a special knowledge to which we have not attained, a place of intimate fellowship with Christ which we have not yet occupied. There are heights of communion which as yet our feet have not climbed—virgin snows of the mountain of God untrodden by the foot of man. There is yet a beyond, and there will be for ever.

A verse or two further on we are told what Ruth did with her leavings. It is very wrong, I believe, at feasts to carry anything home with you; but *she* was not under any such regulation, for that which was left she took home and gave to Naomi. So it shall be even with you, poor tremblers, who think you have no right to a morsel for yourselves; you shall be allowed to eat, and when you are quite sufficed, you shall have courage to bear away a portion to others who are hungering at home. I am always pleased to find the young believer beginning to pocket something for others. When you hear a sermon you think, "My poor mother cannot get out to-day; how I wish she could have been here, for that sentence would have comforted *her*. If I forget everything else, I will tell her that." Cultivate an unselfish spirit. Seek to love as you have been loved. Remember that "the law and the prophets" are fulfilled in this, to love the Lord your God with all your heart, and your neighbour as yourself. How can you love your neighbour as yourself if you do not love his soul? You *have* loved your own soul; through grace you have been led to lay hold on Jesus; love your neighbour's soul, and never be satisfied till you see him in the enjoyment of those things which are the charm of your life and the joy of your spirit. Take home your gleanings for those you love who cannot glean for themselves.

I do not know how to give you an invitation to Christ more pleasantly, but I would with my whole heart cry, "Come and welcome to Jesus." I pray my Lord and Master to reach a handful of parched corn of comfort to you if you are a trembling sinner, and I also beg him to make you eat till you are fully sufficed.

The Loaded Waggon

"Behold, I am pressed under you, as a cart is pressed that is full of sheaves."—Amos ii. 13.

WE have been into the corn-fields to glean with Boaz and Ruth; and I trust that the timid and faint-hearted have been encouraged to partake of the handfuls which are let fall on purpose for them by the order of our generous Lord. We go to-day to the gate of the harvest-field with another object—to see the waggon piled up aloft with many sheaves come creaking forth, making ruts along the field. We come with gratitude to God, thanking him for the harvest, blessing him for favourable weather, and praying him to continue the same till the last shock of corn shall be brought in, and the husbandmen everywhere shall shout the "Harvest Home."

What a picture is a waggon loaded with corn of you and of me, as loaded with God's mercies! From our cradle up till now, every day has added a sheaf of blessing. What could the Lord do for us more than he has done? He has daily loaded us with benefits. Let us adore his goodness, and yield him our cheerful gratitude.

Alas! that such a sign should be capable of another reading. Alas! that while God loadeth us with mercy, we should load him with sin. While he continually heapeth on sheaf after sheaf of favour we also add iniquity unto iniquity, till the weight of our sin becomes intolerable to the Most High, and he cries out by reason of the burden, saying, "I am pressed under you, as a cart is pressed that is full of sheaves."

Our text begins with a *"Behold!"* and well it may. "Beholds" are put in the Bible as signs are hung out from houses of business, to attract attention. There is something new, important, deeply impressive, or worthy of attention wherever we see a "Behold" in sacred Scripture. I see this "Behold!" standing, as it were, like a maiden upon the steps of the house of wisdom, crying, "Turn in hither, O ye that are wise-hearted, and listen to the voice of God." Let us open our eyes that we may "behold," and may the Spirit make a way through our eyes and ears to our hearts, that repentance and self-abhorrence may take hold upon us, because of our evil conduct towards our gracious God.

It is to be understood before we proceed farther, that our text is only a figure, since God cannot actually be oppressed by man; all the sin that man may commit can never disturb the serenity of the divine perfection, nor cause so much as a wave upon his everlasting calm. He doth but speak to us after the manner of man, and bring down the sublimities and mysteries of heaven to the feebleness and ignorance of earth.

He speaketh to us as a great father may talk to his little child. Just as a cart has the axles bent, and as the wheels creak under the excessive load, so the Lord says that under the load of human guilt he is pressed down, until he crieth out, because he can bear no longer the iniquity of those that offend against him. We shall now turn to our first point; may the Holy Ghost make it pointed to our consciences!

The first and most apparent truth in the text is, that SIN IS VERY GRIEVOUS AND BURDENSOME TO GOD.

Be astonished, O heavens, and be amazed, O earth, that God should speak of being pressed and weighed down! I do not read anywhere so much as half a suggestion that the whole burden of *creation* is any weight to the Most High. "He taketh up the isles as a very little thing." Neither sun, nor moon, nor stars, nor all the ponderous orbs which his omnipotence has created, cost him any labour in their sustenance. The heathen picture Atlas as stooping beneath the globe; but the eternal God, who beareth up the pillars of the universe, "fainteth not neither is weary." Nor do I find even the most distant approach to a suggestion that *providence* fatigues its Lord. He watches both by night and day; his power goeth forth every moment. 'Tis he who bringeth forth Mazzaroth in his season and guideth Arcturus with his sons. He beareth up the foundations of the earth! and holdeth the corner-stone thereof. He causeth the dayspring to know its place, and setteth a bound to darkness and the shadow of death. All things are supported by the power of his hand, and there is nothing without him. Just as a moment's foam subsides into the wave that bears it and is lost for ever, so would the universe depart if the eternal God did not daily sustain it. This incessant working has not diminished his strength, nor is there any failing or thought of failing with him. He worketh all things, and when they are wrought they are as nothing in his sight. But strange, most passing strange, miraculous among miracles, *sin* burdens God, though the world cannot; and iniquity presses the Most High, though the whole weight of providence is as the small dust of the balance. Ah, ye careless sons of Adam, ye think sin a trifle; and as for you, ye sons of Belial, ye count it sport, and say, "He regardeth not; he seeth not; how doth God know? and if he knoweth he careth not for our sins." Learn ye from the Book of God, that so far from this being the truth, your sins are a grief to him, a burden and a load to him, till, like a cart that is overloaded with sheaves, so is he weighed down with human guilt.

This will be very clear if we meditate for a moment upon what sin is, and what sin does. *Sin is the great spoiler of all God's works.* Sin turned an archangel into an arch-fiend, and angels of light into spirits of evil. Sin looked on Eden and withered all its flowers. Ere sin had come the Creator said of the new-made earth, "It is very good"; but when sin had entered, it grieved God at his very heart that he had made such a creature as man. Nothing tarnishes beauty so much as sin, for it mars God's image and erases his superscription.

Moreover, *sin makes God's creatures unhappy,* and shall not the Lord, therefore, abhor it? God never designed that any creature of his hand should be miserable. He made the creatures on purpose that they should be glad; he gave the birds their song, the flowers their perfume, the air its balm; he gave today the smiling sun and tonight its coronet of stars; for he intended that smiles should be his perpetual worship, and joy the incense of his praise. But sin has made God's favourite creature a wretch, and brought down God's offspring, made in his own image, to become naked, and poor, and miserable; and therefore God hateth sin, and is pressed down under it, because it maketh the objects of his love unhappy at their heart.

Moreover, remember that *sin attacks God in all his attributes,* assails him on his throne, and stabs at his existence. What is sin? Is it not an insult to God's wisdom? O sinner, God biddeth thee do his will; when thou doest the contrary it is because thou dost as much as say, "I know what is good for me, and God does not know." You do in effect declare that infinite wisdom is in error, and that you, the creature of a day, are the best judge of happiness. Sin impugns God's *goodness;* for by sin you declare that God has denied you that which would make you happy, and this is not the part of a good, tender, and loving Father. Sin cuts at the Lord's wisdom with one hand, and at his goodness with the other.

Sin also abuses the *mercy* of God. When you, as many of you have done, sin with the higher hand because of his longsuffering towards you; when, because you have no sickness, no losses, no crosses, therefore you spend your time in revelry and obstinate rebellion,—what is this but taking the mercy which was meant for your good and turning it into mischief? It is no small grief to the loving father to see his substance spent with harlots in riotous living; he cannot endure it that his child should be so degraded as to turn even the mercy which would woo him to repentance into a reason why he should sin the more against him. Besides, let me remind the careless and impenitent that every sin is a defiance of divine *power.* In effect it is lifting your puny fists against the majesty of heaven, and defying God to destroy you. Every time you sin, you defy the Lord to prove whether he can maintain his law or no. Is this a slight thing, that a worm, the creature of a day, should defy the Lord of ages, the God that filleth and upholdeth all things by the word of his power? Well may he be weary, when he has to bear with such provocations and insults as these! Mention what attribute you will, and sin has blotted it; speak of God in any relationship you choose, and sin has cast a slur upon him. It is evil, only evil, and that continually: in every view of it it must be offensive to the Most High. Sinner, dost thou know that every act of disobedience to God's law is virtually an act of *high treason?* What dost thou do but seek to be God thyself, thine own master, thine own lord? Every time thou swervest from his will, it is to put thy will into his place; it is to make thyself a god, and to undeify the Most High. And is this a little offence, to snatch from his brow the crown, and from his hand the sceptre? I tell thee it is such an act that heaven itself could not stand unless it were resented: if this crime were suffered to go unpunished, the wheels of heaven's commonwealth would be taken from their axles, and the whole frame of moral government would be unhinged. Such a treason against God shall certainly be visited with punishment.

To crown all, *sin is an onslaught upon God himself,* for sin is atheism of heart. Let his religious profession be what it may, the sinner hath said in his head, "No God." He wishes that there were no law and no Supreme Ruler. Is this a trifle? To be a Deicide! To desire to put God out of his own world! Is this a thing to be winked at? Can the Most High hear it and not be pressed down beneath its weight? I pray you do not think that I would make a needless outcry against sin and disobedience. It is not in the power of human imagination to exaggerate the evil of sin, nor will it ever be possible for mortal lips, though they should be touched like those of Esaias with a live coal from off the altar, to thunder out the ten-thousandth part of the enormity of the least sin against God. Think, dear friends! We are his creatures, and yet we will not do his will. We are fed by him, the breath in our nostrils he gives us, and yet we spend that breath in murmuring and rebellion.

Once more, we are always in the sight of our omniscient God, and yet the presence of God is not enough to compel us to obedience. Surely if a man should insult law in the very presence of the lawgiver, that were not to be borne with; but this is your case and mine. We must confess, "Against thee, thee only, have I sinned, and done this evil in thy sight." We must remember also, that we offend, knowing that we are offending. We do not sin as the Hottentot, or the cannibal. We in England sin against extraordinary light and sevenfold knowledge; and is this a light thing? Can you expect that God shall pass by wilful and deliberate offences? Oh, that these lips had language, that this heart could burn for once! for if I could declare the horrible infamy of sin it would make the blood chill in even a haughty Pharaoh's veins, and proud Nebuchadnezzar would bow his head in fear. It is indeed a terrible thing to have rebelled against the Most High. The Lord have mercy upon his servants and forgive them.

This is our first point, but *I* cannot teach you it, God himself must teach it by his Spirit. Oh, that the Holy Ghost may make you feel that sin is exceedingly sinful, so that it is grievous and burdensome to God!

Secondly, SOME SINS ARE MORE ESPECIALLY GRIEVOUS TO GOD. The connection of our text will help you to see the force of this observation.

There is no such thing as a little sin, but still there are degrees of guilt, and it were folly to say that a sinful thought hath in it the same extent of evil as a sinful act. A filthy imagination is sinful—wholly sinful and greatly sinful, but still a filthy act has attained a higher degree of provocation. There are sins which especially provoke God. In the connection of the text we read that *licentiousness* does this. The Jewish people in the days of Amos seem to have gone to a very high degree of fornication and lechery. This sin is not uncommon in our day; let our midnight streets and our divorce courts be the witness. I say no more. Let each one keep his body pure; for want of chastity is a grievous evil before the Lord.

Oppression, too, according to the prophet, is another great provocation to God. The prophet speaks of selling the poor for a pair of shoes; and some would grind the widow and the orphan, and make the labourer toil for nought. How many businessmen have no "bowels of compassion." Men form themselves into societies, and then exact an outrageous usury upon loans from the unhappy beings who fall into their hands. Cunning legal quibbles and crafty evasions of just debts often amount to heavy oppression, and are sure to bring down the anger of the Most High.

Then, again, it seems that *idolatry* and *blasphemy* are highly offensive to God, and have a high degree of heinousness. He says that the people drank the wine of false gods. If any man sets up his belly, or his gold, or his wealth as his god, and if he lives to these instead of living to the Most High, he hath offended by idolatry. Woe to such, and equal woe to those who adore crosses, sacraments, or images.

Specially is *blasphemy* a God-provoking sin. For blasphemy there is no excuse. As George Herbert says, "Lust and wine plead a pleasure;" there is gain to be pleaded for avarice, "but the cheap swearer from his open sluice lets his soul run for nought." There is nothing gained by profane talk; there can be no pleasure in cursing; this is offending for offending's sake, and hence it is a high and crying sin, which makes the Lord grow weary of men. There may be some among you to whom these words may be personal accusations. Do I address the lecherous, or the oppressive, or the profane? Ah, soul, what a mercy God hath borne with thee so long; the time will come, however, when he will say, "Ah, I will ease me of mine adversaries," and how easily will he cast you off and appoint you an awful destruction.

Again, whilst some sins are thus grievous to God for their peculiar heinousness, many men are especially obnoxious to God because of the *length* of their sin. That grey-headed man, how many times has he provoked the Most High! Why, those who are but lads have cause to count their years and apply their hearts unto wisdom because of the length of time they have lived in rebellion; but what shall I say of you who have been half a century in open war against God— and some of you sixty, seventy, what if I said near upon eighty years? Ah, you have had eighty years of mercies, and returned eighty years of neglect: for eighty years of patience you have rendered eighty years of ingratitude. O God, well mayest thou be wearied by the length and number of man's sins!

Furthermore, God taketh special note and feeleth an especial weariness of sin that is mixed with *obstinacy*. Oh how obstinate some men are! They will be damned; there is no helping them; they seem as if they would leap the Alps to reach perdition, and swim through seas of fire that they may destroy their souls. I might tell you cases of men that have been sore sick of fever, ague, and cholera, and they have only recovered their health to return to their sins. Some of them have had troubles in business thick, and threefold: they were once in respectable circumstances, but they spent their living riotously, and they became poor; yet they still struggle on in sin. They are growing poorer every day, most of their clothes have gone to the pawnshop; but they will not turn from the tavern and the brothel. Another child is dead! The wife is sick, and starvation stares the family in the face; but they go on still with a high hand and an outstretched arm. This is obstinacy, indeed. Sinner! God will let thee have thine own way one of these days, and that way will be thine everlasting ruin. God is weary of those who set themselves to do mischief, and, against warnings, and invitations, and entreaties, are determined to go on in sin.

The context seems to tell us that *ingratitude* is intensely burdensome to God. He tells the people how he brought them out of Egypt; how he cast out the Amorites; how he raised up their sons for prophets, and their young men for Nazarites; and yet they rebelled against him! This was one of the things that pricked my heart when I first came to God as a guilty sinner, not so much the peculiar heinousness of my outward life, as the peculiar mercies that I had enjoyed. How generous God has been to some of us,— some of us who never had a want! God has never cast us into poverty, nor left us to infamy, nor given us up to evil example, but he has kept us moral, and made us love his house even when we did not love *him,* and all this he has done year after year: and what poor returns we have made! To us, his people, what joy he has given, what deliverances, what love, what comfort, what bliss—and yet we have sinned to his face! Well may he be as a cart that is pressed down, that is full of sheaves.

Let me observe, before I leave this point, that it seems from our text, that the Lord is so pressed, that *he even crieth out.* Just as the cart when laden with the sheaves, groaneth under the weight, so the Lord crieth out under the load of sin. Have you never heard those accents? "Hear, O heavens, and give ear, O earth: for the Lord hath spoken, I have nourished and brought up children, and they have rebelled against me!" Hear again: "Turn ye, turn ye from your evil ways; for why will ye die, O house of Israel?" Better still, hear the lament from the lip of Jesus, soft and gentle as the dew,—"Jerusalem, Jerusalem, thou that killest the prophets, and stonest them which are sent unto thee, how often would I have gathered thy children together, even as a hen gathereth her chickens under her wings, and ye would not!" Sinner, God is cut to the head by thy sin; thy Creator grieves over that which thou laughest at; thy Saviour crieth out in his spirit concerning that which thou thinkest to be a trifle,— "O do not this abominable thing which I hate!" For God's sake do it not! We often say "for God's sake," without knowing what we mean; but here see what it means, for the sake of God, that ye grieve not your Creator, that ye cause not the Eternal One himself to cry out by reason of weariness of you. Cease ye, cease ye, from your evil ways; for why will ye die, O house of Israel? I now leave those two points to pass on very briefly to the next.

While it is true that sin is grievous to the Lord, it magnifies his mercy when we see that HE BEARS THE LOAD. As the cart is not said to break, but is pressed only, so is he pressed, and yet he bears. If you and I were in God's place, should we have borne it? Nay, within a week we should have burned the universe with fire, or trodden it to powder beneath our feet. If the law of heaven were as swift to punish as the law of man, where were we? How easily could he avenge his honour! How many servants wait around him ready to do his bidding! As the Roman consul went out, attended by his lictors carrying the axe, so God is ever attended by his executioners, who are ready to fulfil his sentence. A stone, a tile from a roof, a thunderbolt, a puff of wind, a grain of dust, a whiff of gas, a broken blood-vessel, and all is over, and you are dead, and in the hands of an angry God. Indeed, the Lord has to restrain the servants of his anger, for the heavens cry, "Why should we cover that wretch's head?" Earth asks, "Why should I yield a harvest to the sinner's plough?" The lightnings thunder, and say, "Let us smite the rebel," and the seas roar upon the sinner, desiring him as their prey. There is no greater proof of the omnipotence of God than his longsuffering; for it shows the greatest possible power for God to be able to control himself. Sinner, yet Jehovah bears with thee. The angels have been astonished at it; they thought he would strike, but yet he bears with you. Have you ever seen a patient man insulted? He has been met in the street by a villain, who insults him before a mob of boys. He bears it. The fellow spits in his face. He bears it still. The offender strikes him. He endures it quietly. "Give him in charge," says one. "No," says he, "I forgive him all." The fellow knocks him down, and rolls him in the kennel, but he bears it still; yes, and when he rises all covered with mire, he says, "If there be anything that I can do to befriend you, I will do it now." Just at that moment the wretch is arrested by a sheriff's officer for debt; the man who has been insulted takes out his purse and pays the debt, and says, "You may go free." See, the wretch spits in his face after that! "Now," you say, "let the law have its way with him." Is there any room for patience now? So would it have been with man; it has not been so with God. Though like the cart he is pressed under the load of sheaves, yet like the cart the axle does not break. He bears the load. He bears with impenitent sinners still.

And this brings me to the fourth head, on which I would have your deepest attention. Some of you, I fear, have never seen sin in the light of grieving God, or else you would not wish to grieve him any more. On the other hand some of you feel how bitter a thing evil is, and you wish to be rid of it. This is our fourth head. Not only doth God still bear with sin, but God, IN THE PERSON OF HIS SON, DID BEAR AND TAKE AWAY SIN.

These words would have deep meaning if put into the lips of Jesus—"I am pressed under you, as a cart is pressed that is full of sheaves." Here stood the great problem. God must punish sin, and yet he desired to have mercy. How could it be? Lo! Jesus comes to be the substitute for all who trust him. The load of guilt is laid upon his shoulders. See how they pile on him the sheaves of human sin!

> "My soul looks back to see
>   The burdens thou didst bear,
> When hanging on the cursed tree,
>   And hopes her guilt was there."

"The Lord hath laid on him the iniquity of us all."

There they lie, sheaf on sheaf, till he is pressed down like the wain that groaneth as it moves along. "He is despised and rejected of men; a man of sorrows, and acquainted with grief." See him, he did "sweat as it were great drops of blood falling to the ground." Herod mocks him. Pilate jeers him. They have smitten the Prince of Judah upon the cheek. "I gave my back to the smiters, and my cheeks to them that plucked off the hair: I hid not my face from shame and spitting." They have tied him to the pillar; they are beating him with rods, not this time forty stripes *save one,* for there is no "save one" with him. "The chastisement of our peace was upon him; and with his stripes we are healed." See him; like a cart pressed down with sheaves traversing the streets of Jerusalem. Well may ye weep, ye daughters of Jerusalem, though he bids ye dry your tears! Abjects hoot at him as he walks along bowed beneath the load of his own cross, which was the emblem of our sin. They bring him to Golgotha. They throw him on his back, they stretch out his hands and his feet. The accursed iron penetrates the tenderest part of his body, where most the nerves do congregate. They lift up the cross. O bleeding Saviour, thy time of woe is come! They dash it into the socket with cruel force, the nails are tearing through his hands and feet. He hangeth in extremity, for God hath forsaken him; his enemies persecute and take him, for there is none to deliver him. They mock his nakedness; they point at his agonies. They look and stare upon him. With ribald jests they insult his griefs. They make puns upon his prayers. He is now indeed a worm, and no man, crushed till you can scarcely think that divinity dwells within him. Fever parches him; his tongue is dried up like a potsherd, and he cries, "I thirst!" Vinegar is all they yield him. The sun refuses to shine, and the dense midnight of that awful mid-day is a fitting emblem of the tenfold darkness of his soul. Out of that all-encompassing horror he crieth, "My God, my God, why hast thou forsaken me?" Then, indeed, was he pressed down! There was never sorrow like unto his sorrow. All mortal griefs found a reservoir in his heart, and the punishment of human guilt spent itself upon his body and his soul. Shall sin ever be a trifle to me? Shall I laugh at that which made my Saviour groan? Shall I toy and dally with that which stabbed him to the heart? Sinner, wilt thou not give up thy sins for the sake of him who suffered for sin? "Yes," sayest thou, "yes, if I could believe that he suffered for my sake." Wilt thou trust thy soul in his hands at once? Dost thou do so? Then he died *for thee* and took *thy* guilt, and carried all *thy* sorrows, and thou mayest go free, for God is satisfied, and thou art absolved. Christ was burdened that thou mightest be lightened; he was pressed that thou mightest be free. I would I could talk of my precious Master as John would speak, who saw him and bare witness, for he could tell in plaintive tones of the sorrows of Calvary. Such as I have I give you; oh that God would give you with it the power, the grace to believe on Jesus at once.

For if not, and here is our last point, God will only bear the load of our provocation for a little while; and if we are not in Christ when the end shall come THAT SAME LOAD WILL CRUSH FOR EVER.

My text is translated by many learned men in a different way from the version before us. According to them it should be read, "I will press you as a cart that is full of sheaves presseth your place." That is, just as a heavy loaded waggon pressed into the soft eastern roads and left deep furrows, so will I crush you, saith

Farm Sermons

God, beneath the load of your sin. This is to be your doom, my hearer, if you are out of Christ: your own deeds are to press upon you. Need we enlarge upon this terror? I think not. It only needs that you should make a personal application of the threatening! Divide yourselves now. Divide yourselves, I say! Answer each one for himself,—Dost thou believe on the Lord Jesus Christ? then the threatening is not thine. But if thou believest not I conjure thee listen to me now as if thou wert the only person here. A Christless soul will ere long be a castaway; he that believeth not in Christ is condemned already, because he believeth not. How wilt thou escape if thou wilt neglect so great salvation? Thus saith the Lord unto thee, "Consider thy ways." By time, by eternity, by life, by death, by heaven, by hell, I do conjure thee believe in him who is able to save unto the uttermost them that come unto him; but if thou believest not in Christ thou shalt die in thy sins.

After death the judgment! Oh the judgment, the thundering trumpet, the multitude, the books, the great white throne, the "Come, ye blessed," the "Depart, ye cursed!"

After judgment, to a soul that is out of Christ, Hell! Who among us? who *among us* shall abide with the devouring flame? Who among US? Who among US shall dwell with everlasting burnings? I pray that none of us may. But we *must* unless we fly to Christ. I beseech thee, my dear hearer, fly to Jesus! I may never see thy face again; thine eyes may never look into mine again; but I shake my skirts of thy blood if thou believest not in Christ. My tears entreat thee; my lips persuade thee. God has had patience with thee; let his longsuffering lead thee to repentance. He willeth not the death of any, but that they should turn unto him and live: and this turning lies mainly in trusting Jesus with your soul. Wilt thou believe in Christ? Nay, I know thou wilt not unless the Spirit of God shall constrain thee; but if thou wilt not it shall not be for want of pleading and entreating. Come, 'tis mercy's welcome hour. I pray thee, come. Jesus with pierced hands invites thee, though thou hast long rejected him. He knocks again. His unconquerable love defies thy wickedness. He begs thee to be saved. Sinner, wilt thou have him or no! "Whosoever will, let him come and take of the water of life freely." God help you to come, for the glorious Redeemer's sake. Amen.

Threshing

"For the fitches are not threshed with a threshing instrument, neither a cart wheel turned about upon the cummin; but the fitches are beaten out with a staff, and the cummin with a rod. Bread corn is bruised; because he will not ever be threshing it, nor break it with the wheel of his cart, nor bruise it with his horsemen."-Isaiah xxviii. 27,28.

HE art of husbandry was taught to man by God. He would have starved while he was discovering it, and so the Lord, when he sent him out of the Garden of Eden, gave him a measure of elementary instruction in agriculture, even as the prophet puts it,— "His God doth instruct him to discretion, and doth teach him." God has taught man to plough, to break the clods, to sow the different kinds of grain, and to thresh out the different orders of seeds.

The Eastern husbandman could not thresh by machinery as we do; but still he was ingenious and discreet in that operation. Sometimes a heavy instrument was dragged over the corn to tear out the grain. This is what is intended in the first clause by the "threshing instrument," as also in that passage, "I have made thee a sharp threshing instrument having teeth." When the corn-drag was not used, they often turned the heavy solid wheel of a country cart over the straw. This is alluded to in the next sentence: "Neither is a cart wheel turned about upon the cummin." They had also flails not very unlike our own, and then for still smaller seeds, such as dill and cummin, they used a simple staff or a slender switch. "The fitches are beaten out with a staff, and the cummin with a rod."

This is not the time or place to give a dissertation upon threshing. We find every information upon that subject in proper books; but the meaning of the illustration is this—that as God has taught husbandmen to distinguish between different kinds of grain in the threshing, so does he in his infinite wisdom deal discreetly with different sorts of men. He does not try us all alike, seeing we are differently constituted. He does not pass us all through the same agony of conviction: we are not all to the same extent threshed with terrors. He does not give us all to endure the same family or bodily affliction; one escapes with only being beaten with a rod, while another feels, as it were, the feet of horses in his heavy tribulations.

Our subject is just this. *Threshing:* all kinds of seeds need it, *all sorts of men need it.* Secondly, the *threshing is done with discretion,* and, thirdly, *the threshing will not last for ever;* for so the second verse of the text says: "Bread corn is bruised; because he will not ever be threshing it, nor break it with the wheel of his cart, nor bruise it with his horsemen."

I. First, then, WE ALL NEED THRESHING. Some have a foolish conceit of themselves that they have no sin; but they deceive themselves, and the truth is not in them. The best of men are men at the best; and being men, they are not perfect, but are still compassed about with infirmity. What is the object of threshing the grain? Is it not to separate it from the straw and the chaff?

About the best of men there is still a measure of chaff. All is not grain that lies upon the threshing-floor. All is not grain even in those golden sheaves which have been brought into our garner so joyfully. Even the wheat is joined to the straw, which was necessary to it at one time. About the kernel of the wheat the husk is wrapped, and this still clings to it even when it lies upon the threshing-floor. About the holiest of men there is something superfluous, something which must be removed. We either sin by omission or by trespass. Either in spirit, or motive, or lack of zeal, or want of discretion, we are faulty. If we escape one error, we usually glide into its opposite. If before an action we are right, we err in the doing of it, or, if not, we become proud after it is over. If sin be shut out at the front door, it tries the back gate, or climbs in at the window, or comes down the chimney. Those who cannot perceive it in themselves are frequently blinded by its smoke. They are so thoroughly in the water that they do not know that it rains. So far as my own observation goes I have found out no man whom the old divines would have called perfectly perfect; the absolutely all-round man is a being whom I expect to see in heaven, but not in this poor fallen world. We all need such cleansing and purging as the threshing-floor is intended to work for us.

Now, *threshing is useful in loosening the connection between the good corn and the husk.* Of course, if it would slip out easily from its husk, the corn would only need to be shaken. There would be no necessity for a staff or a rod, much less for the feet of horses, or the wheel of a cart to separate it. But there's the rub: our soul not only lieth in the dust, but "cleaveth" to it. There is a fearful intimacy between fallen human nature and the evil which is in the world; and this compact is not soon broken. In our hearts we hate every false way, and yet we sorrowfully confess, "When I would do good, evil is present with me." Sometimes when our spirit cries out most ardently after God, a holy will is present with us, but how to perform that which is good we find not. Flesh and blood have tendencies and weaknesses which, if not sinful in themselves, yet tend in that direction. Appetites need but slight excitement to germinate into lusts. It is not easy for us to forget our own kindred and our father's house even when the king doth most greatly desire our beauty. Our alien nature remembers Egypt and the flesh-pots while yet the manna is in our mouths. We were all born in the house of evil, and some of us were nursed upon the lap of iniquity, so that our first companionships were among the heirs of wrath. That which was bred in the bone is hard to get out of the flesh. Threshing is used to loosen our hold of earthly things and break us away from evil. This needs a divine hand, and nothing but the grace of God can make the threshing effectual. Something is done by threshing when the soul ceases to be bound up with its sin, and sin is no longer pleasurable or satisfactory. Still, as the work of threshing is never done till the corn is separated altogether from the husk, so chastening and discipline have never accomplished their design till

God's people give up every form of evil, and abhor all iniquity. When we shake right out of the straw, and have nothing further to do with sin, then the flail will lie quiet. It has taken a good deal of threshing to bring some of us anywhere near that mark, and I am afraid many more heavy blows will be struck before we shall reach the total separation. From a certain sort of sins we are very easily separated by the grace of God early in our spiritual life; but when those are gone, another layer of evils comes into sight, and the work has to be repeated. The complete removal of our connection with sin is a work demanding the divine skill and power of the Holy Ghost, and by him only will it be accomplished.

Threshing becomes needful for the sake of our usefulness; for the wheat must come out of the husk to be of service. We can only honour God and bless men by being holy, harmless, undefiled, and separate from sinners. O corn of the Lord's threshing-floor, thou must be beaten and bruised, or perish as a worthless heap! Eminent usefulness usually necessitates eminent affliction.

Unless thus severed from sin, we cannot be gathered into the garner. God's pure wheat must not be defiled bv an admixture of chaff. There shall in no wise enter into heaven anything that defileth, therefore every sort of imperfection must come away from us by some means or other ere we can enter into the state of eternal blessedness and perfection. Yea, even here we cannot have true fellowship with the Father unless we are daily delivered from sin.

Peradventure some of us today are lying up on the threshing-floor, suffering from the blows of chastisement. What then? Why, let us rejoice therein; for *this testifies to our value in the sight of God.* If the wheat were to cry out and say, "The great drag has gone over me, therefore the husbandman has no care for me," we should instantly reply,—The husbandman does not pass the corn-drag over the darnel or the nettles; it is only over the precious wheat that he turns the wheel of his cart, or the feet of his oxen. Because he esteems the wheat, therefore he deals sternly with it and spares it not. Judge not, O believer, that God hates you because he afflicts you; but interpret truly and see that he honours you by every stroke which he lays upon you. Thus saith the Lord, "You only have I known of all the nations of the earth, therefore I will punish you for all your iniquities." Because a full atonement has been made by the Lord Jesus for all his people's sins, therefore he will not punish us as a judge; but because we are his dear children, therefore he will chastise us as a father. In love he corrects his own children that he may perfect them in his own image, and make them partakers of his holiness. Is it not written, "I will bring them under the rod of the covenant"? Has he not said, "I have refined thee, but not with silver, I have chosen thee in the furnace of affliction"? Therefore do not judge according to the sight of the eyes or the feeling of the flesh, but judge according to faith, and understand that, as threshing is a testimony to the value of the wheat, so affliction is a token of God's delight in his people.

Remember, however, that as threshing is a sign of the impurity of the wheat, so is *affliction an indication of the present imperfection of the Christian.* If you were no more connected with evil, you would be no more corrected with sorrow. The sound of a flail is never heard in heaven, for it is not the threshing-floor of the imperfect but the garner of the completely sanctified. The threshing instrument is therefore a humbling token, and so long as we feel it we should humble ourselves under the hand of God, for it is clear that we are not yet free from the straw and the chaff of fallen nature.

On the other hand, the threshing instrument is *a prophecy of our future perfection.* We are undergoing from the hand of God a discipline which will not fail: we shall by his prudence and wisdom be clean delivered from the husk of sin. We are feeling the blows of the staff, but we are being effectually separated from the evil which has so long surrounded us, and for certain we shall one day be pure and perfect. Every tendency to sin shall be beaten off. "Foolishness is bound in the heart of a child; but the rod of correction shall drive it far from him." If, we being evil, yet succeed with our children by our poor, imperfect chastening, how much more shall the Father of spirits cause us to live unto himself by his holy discipline? If the corn could know the necessary uses of the flail, it would invite the thresher to his work; and since we know whereunto tribulation tendeth, let us glory in it, and yield ourselves with cheerfulness to its processes. We need threshing, the threshing proves our value in God's sight, and while it marks our imperfection, it secures our ultimate cleansing.

II. Secondly, I would remark that GOD'S THRESHING IS DONE WITH GREAT DISCRETION; "for the fitches are not threshed with a threshing instrument." The poor little fitches, a kind of small seed used for flavouring cakes, were not crushed out with a heavy drag, for by such rough usage they would have been broken up and spoiled. "Neither is a cart-wheel turned about upon the cummin": this little seed, perhaps the carraway, would have been ground by so great a weight: it would

have been preposterous to treat it in that rough
manner. The fitches were soon removed from the stalks
by being "beaten out with a staff," and the cummin
needed nothing but a touch of a rod. For tender seeds
the farmer uses gentle means, and for the hardier
grains he reserves the sterner processes. Let us think
of this, as it conveys a valuable spiritual lesson.

Reflect my brother, that your threshing and mine
are in God's hands. Our chastening is not left to
servants, much less to enemies; "we are chastened of
the Lord!" The Great Husbandman himself personally
bids the labourers do this and that for they know not
the time or the way except as divine wisdom shall
direct: they would turn the wheel upon the cummin,
or attempt to thresh wheat with a staff. I have seen
God's servants trying both these follies; they have
crushed the weak and tender, and they have dealt with
partiality and softness with those who needed to be
sternly rebuked. How roughly some ministers, some
elders, some good men and women will go to work
with timid, tender souls; yet we need not fear that they
will destroy the true-hearted, for, however much they
may vex them, the Lord will not leave his chosen in
their hands, but will overrule their mistaken severity,
and preserve his own from being destroyed thereby.
How glad I am of this; for there are many nowadays
who would grind the tender ones to powder if they
could!

As the Lord has not left us in the power of man, so
also he has not left us in the power of the devil. Satan
may sift us as wheat, but he shall not thresh us as
fitches. He may blow away the chaff from us even with
his foul breath, but he shall not have the management
of the Lord's corn: "the Lord preserveth the righteous."
Not a stroke in providence is left to chance; the Lord

ordains it, and arranges the time, the force, and the place of it. The divine decree leaves nothing uncertain; the jurisdiction of supreme love occupies itself with the smallest events of our daily lives. Whether we bear the teeth of the corn-drag, or men do ride over our heads, or we endure the gentler touches of the divine hand, everything is by appointment and the appointment is fixed by infallible wisdom, Let this be a mine of comfort to the afflicted.

Next, remark that *the instruments used for our threshing are chosen also by the Great Husbandman.* The Eastern farmer, according to the text, has several instruments, and so has our God. No form of threshing is pleasant to the seed which bears it; indeed, each one seems to the sufferer to be peculiarly objectionable. We say, "I think I could bear anything but this sad trouble." We cry, "It was not an enemy, then I could have borne it," and so on. Perhaps the tender cummin foolishly fancies that the horse-hoofs would be a less terrible ordeal than the rod, and the fitches might even prefer the wheel to the staff; but happily the matter is left to the choice of One who judges unerringly. What dost thou know about it, poor sufferer? How canst thou judge of what is good for thee? "Ah!" cries a mother, "I would not mind poverty; but to lose my darling child is too terrible!" Another laments, "I could have parted with all my wealth, but to be slandered cuts me to the quick." There is no pleasing us in the matter of chastisement. When I was at school, with my uncle for master, it often happened that he would send me out to find a cane for him. It was not a very pleasant task, and I noticed that I never once succeeded in selecting a stick which was liked by the boy who had to feel it. Either it was too thin, or too stout; and in consequence I was threatened by the sufferers with condign punishment if I did not do better next time. I learned from that experience never to expect God's children to like the particular rod with which they are chastened. You smile at my simile, but you may smile also at yourself when you find yourself crying, "Any trouble but this, Lord. Any affliction but this." How idle it is to expect a pleasant trial; for it would then be no trial at all. Almost every really useful medicine is unpleasant: almost all effectual surgery is painful: no trial for the present seemeth to be joyous, but grievous, yet it is the right trial, and none the less right because it is bitter.

Notice, too, that God not only selects the instruments, but *he chooses the place.* Farmers in the East have large threshing-floors upon which they throw the sheaves of corn or barley, and upon these they turn horses and drags; but near the house door I have often noticed in Italy a much smaller circle of hardened clay or cement, and here I have seen the peasants beating out their garden seeds in a more careful manner than would naturally be used towards the greater heaps upon the larger area. Some saints are not afflicted in the common affairs of life, but they have peculiar sorrow in their innermost spirits: they are beaten on the smaller and more private threshing-floor; but the process is none the less effectual. How foolish are we when we rebel against our Lord's appointment, and speak as if we had a right to choose our own afflictions! "Should it be according to thy mind?" Should a child select the rod? Should the grain appoint its own thresher? Are not these things to be left to a higher wisdom? Some complain of the time of their trial; it is hard to be crippled in youth, or to be poor in age, or to be widowed when your children are young. Yet in all this there is wisdom. A part of the skill of the physician may lie, not only in writing a prescription, but in arranging the hours at which the medicine shall be taken. One draught may be most useful in the morning, and another may be more beneficial in the evening; and so the Lord knows when it is best for us to drink of the cup which he has prepared for us. I know a dear child of God who is enduring a severe trial in his old age, and I would fain screen him from it because of his feebleness, but our heavenly Father knows best and there we must leave it. The instrument of the threshing, the place, the measure, the time, the end, are all appointed by infallible love.

It is interesting to notice in the test the limit of this threshing. The husbandman is zealous to beat out the seed, but he is careful not to break it in pieces by too severe a process. His wheel is not to grind, but to thresh; the horses' feet are not to break, but to separate. He intends to get the cummin out of its husk, but he will not turn a heavy drag upon it utterly to smash it up and destroy it. In the same way the Lord has a measure in all his chastening. Courage, tried friend, you shall be afflicted as you need, but not as you deserve: tribulation shall come as you are able to bear it. As is the strength such shall the affliction be: the wheat may feel the wheel, but the fitches shall bear nothing heavier than a staff. No saint shall be tempted beyond the proper measure, and the limit is fixed by a tenderness which never deals a needless stroke.

It is very easy to talk like this in cool blood, and quite another thing to remember it when the flail is hammering you; yet have I personally realised this truth upon the bed of pain, and in the furnace of mental distress. I thank God at every remembrance of my afflictions; I did not doubt his wisdom then, nor have I had any reason to question it since. Our Great Husbandman understands how to divide us from the husk, and he goes about his work in a way for which he deserves to be adored for ever.

It is a pleasant thought that God's limit is one beyond which trials never go—

> "If trials six be fix'd for men
>   They shall not suffer seven.
> If God appoint afflictions ten
>   They ne'er can be eleven."

The old law ordained forty stripes save one, and in all our scourgings there always comes in that "save one." When the Lord multiplies our sorrows up to a hundred, it is because ninety-and-nine failed to effect his purpose; but all the powers of earth and hell cannot give us one blow above the settled number. We shall never endure a superfluity of threshing. The Lord never sports with the feelings of his saints. "He does not afflict willingly," and so we may be sure he never gives an unnecessary blow.

The wisdom of the husbandman in limiting his threshing is far exceeded in the wisdom of God by which he sets a limit to our griefs. Some escape with little trouble, and perhaps it is because they are frail and sensitive. The little garden seeds must not be beaten too heavily lest they be injured; those saints who bear about with them a delicate body must not be roughly handled, nor shall they be. Possibly they have a feeble mind also, and that which others would laugh at would be death to them; they shall be kept as the apple of the eye.

If you are free from tribulation never ask for it; that would be a great folly. I did meet with a brother a little while ago who said that he was much perplexed because he had no trouble. I said, "Do not worry about that; but be happy while you may." Only a queer child would beg to be flogged. Certain sweet and shining saints are of such a gentle spirit that the Lord does not expose them to the same treatment as he metes out to others: they do not need it, and they could not bear it; why should they wish for it?

Others, again, are very heavily pressed; but what of that if they are a superior grain, a seed of larger usefulness, intended for higher purposes? Let not such regret that they have to endure a heavier threshing since their use is greater. It is the bread corn that must go under the feet of the horseman and must feel the wheel of the cart; and so the most useful have to pass through the sternest processes. There is not one amongst us but what would say; "I could wish that I were Martin Luther, or that I could play as noble a part as he did?" Yes; but in addition to the outward perils of his life, the inward experiences of that remarkable man were such as none of us would wish to feel. He was frequently tormented with Satanic temptations, and driven to the verge of despair. At one hour he rode the whirlwind and the storm, master of all the world, and then after days of fighting with the pope and the devil he would go home to his bed and lie there broken down and trembling. You see God's heroes only in the pulpit or in other public places, you know not what they are before God in secret. You do not know their inner life: else you might discover that the bread corn is bruised, and that those who are most useful in comforting others have to endure frequent sorrow themselves. Envy no man; for you do not know how he may have to be threshed to make him right and keep him so.

Brethren, we see that our God uses discretion in the chastisement of his people; let us use a loving prudence when we have to deal with others in that way. Be gentle as well as firm with your children; and if you have to rebuke your brother do it very tenderly. Do not drive your horses over the tender seed. Recollect that the cummin is beaten out with a staff and not crushed out with a wheel. Take a very light rod. Perhaps it would be as well if you had no rod at all, but left that work to wiser hands. Go you and sow, and leave your elders to thresh.

Next, let us firmly believe in God's discretion, and be sure that he is doing the right thing by us. Let us not be anxious to be screened from affliction. When we ask that the cup may pass from us let it be with a "nevertheless not as I will." Best of all, let us freely part with our chaff. The likeliest way to escape the flail is to separate from the husk as quickly as possible. "Come ye out from among them." Separate yourselves from sin and sinners, from the world and worldliness, and the process of threshing will all the sooner be completed. God make us wise in this matter!

III. A word or two is all we can afford upon the third head, which is that THE THRESHING WILL NOT LAST FOR EVER.

The threshing will not last all our days even here: "Bread corn is bruised, but he will not always be threshing it." Oh, no. "For a small moment have I forsaken thee, but with great mercies will I gather thee." "He will not always chide, neither will he keep his anger for ever." "Weeping may endure for a night, but joy cometh in the morning." Rejoice, ye daughters of sorrow! Be comforted, ye sons of grief! Have hope in God, for you shall yet praise him who is the health of your countenance. The rain does not always fall, nor will the clouds always return. Sorrow and sighing shall flee away. Threshing is not an operation which the corn requires all the year round; for the most part the flail is idle. Bless the Lord, O my soul! The Lord will yet bring home his banished ones. Above all, tribulation will not last for ever, for we shall soon be gone to another and better world. We shall soon be carried to the land where there are neither threshing-floors nor corn-drags. I sometimes think I hear the herald calling me. His trumpet sounds: "Up and away! Boot and saddle! Up and away! Leave the camp and the battle, and return in triumph." The night is far spent with some of you, but the morning cometh. The daylight breaks above yon hills. The day is coming— the day that shall go no more down for ever. Come, eat your bread with joy, and march onward with a merry heart; for the land which floweth with milk and honey is but a little way before you. Until the day break and the shadows flee away, abide the Great Husbandman's will, and may the Lord glorify himself in you. Amen.

Wheat in the Barn

"Gather the wheat into my barn."—Matthew xiii. 30.

"GATHER the wheat into my barn." Then the purpose of the Son of man will be accomplished. He sowed good seed, and he shall have his barn filled with it at the last. Be not dispirited, Christ will not be disappointed. "He shall see of the travail of his soul, and shall be satisfied." He went forth weeping, bearing precious seed, but he shall come again rejoicing, bringing his sheaves with him.

"Gather the wheat into my barn": then Satan's policy will be unsuccessful. The enemy came and sowed tares among the wheat, hopeful that the false wheat would destroy or materially injure the true; but he failed in the end, for the wheat ripened and was ready to be gathered. Christ's garner shall be filled; the tares shall not choke the wheat. The evil one will be put to shame.

In gathering in the wheat, good angels will be employed: "the angels are the reapers." This casts special scorn upon the great evil angel. He sows the tares, and tries to destroy the harvest; and therefore the good angels are brought in to celebrate his defeat, and to rejoice together with their Lord in the success of the divine husbandry. Satan will make a poor profit out of his meddling; he shall be baulked in all his efforts, and so the threat shall be fulfilled, "Upon thy belly shalt thou go, and dust shalt thou eat."

By giving the angels work to do, all intelligent creatures, of whose existence we have information, are made to take an interest in the work of grace: whether for malice or for adoration, redemption excites them all. To all, the wonderful works of God are made manifest: for these things were not done in a corner.

We too much forget the angels. Let us not overlook their tender sympathy with us; they behold the Lord rejoicing over our repentance, and they rejoice with him; they are our watchers and the Lord's messengers of mercy; they bear us up in their hands lest we dash our foot against a stone; and when we come to die, they carry us to the bosom of our Lord. It is one of our joys that we have come to an innumerable company of angels; let us think of them with affection.

At this time I will keep to my text, and preach from it almost word by word. It begins with "but" and that is A WORD OF SEPARATION.

Here note that the tares and the wheat will grow together until the time of harvest shall come. It is a great sorrow of heart to some of the wheat to be growing side by side with tares. The ungodly are as thorns and briars to those who fear the Lord. How frequently is the sigh forced forth from the godly heart: "Woe is me, that I sojourn in Mesech, that I dwell in the tents of Kedar!" A man's foes are often found within his own household; those who should have been his best helpers are often his worst hinderers: their conversation vexes and torments him. It is of little use to try to escape from them, for the tares are permitted in God's providence to grow with the wheat, and they will do so until the end. Good men have emigrated to distant lands to found communities in which there should be none but saints, and, alas! sinners have sprung up in their own families. The attempt to weed the ungodly and heretical out of the settlement has led to persecution and other evils, and the whole plan has proved a failure. Others have shut themselves away in hermitages to avoid the temptations of the world, and so have hoped to win the victory by running away: this is not the way of wisdom. The word for this present is,—"Let both grow together"; *but* there will come a time when a final separation will be made. Then, dear Christian woman, your husband will never persecute you again. Godly sister, your brother will heap no more ridicule upon you. Pious workman, there will be no more jesting and taunting from the ungodly. That "but" will be an iron gate between the god-fearing and the godless; then will the tares be cast into the fire, *but* the Lord of the harvest will say, "Gather the wheat into my barn."

This separation must be made; for the growing of the wheat and the tares together on earth has caused much pain and injury, and therefore it will not be continued in a happier world. We can very well suppose that godly men and women might be willing that their unconverted children should dwell with them in heaven; but it cannot be, for God will not have his cleansed ones defiled nor his glorified ones tried by the presence of the unbelieving. The tares must be taken away in order to the perfectness and usefulness of the wheat. Would you have the tares and the wheat heaped up together in the granary in one mass? That would be ill husbandry with a vengeance. They can neither of them be put to appropriate use till thoroughly separated. Even so, mark you, the saved and the unsaved may live together here, but they must not live together in another world. The command is absolute,—"Gather the tares, and bind them in bundles to burn them: *but* gather the wheat into my barn." Sinner, can you hope to enter heaven? You never loved your mother's God, and is he to endure

you in his heavenly courts? You never trusted your
father's Saviour, and yet are you to behold his glory
for ever? Are you to go swaggering down the streets of
heaven, letting fall an oath, or singing a loose song?
Why, you know, you get tired of the worship of God
on the Lord's day; do you think that the Lord will
endure unwilling worshippers in the temple above?
The Sabbath is a wearisome day to you; how can you
hope to enter into the Sabbath of God? You have no
taste for heavenly pursuits, and these things would
be profaned if you were permitted to partake in them;
therefore that word "but" must come in, and you must
part from the Lord's people never to meet again. Can
you bear to think of being divided from godly friends
for ever and ever?

That separation involves an awful difference of
destiny. "Gather the tares in bundles to burn them." I
do not dare to draw the picture; but when the bundle
is bound up there is no place for it except the fire.
God grant that you may never know all the anguish
which burning must mean; but may you escape from
it at once. It is no trifle which the Lord of love compares
to being consumed with fire. I am quite certain that
no words of mine can ever set forth its terror. They
say that we speak dreadful things about the wrath to
come; but I am sure that we understate the case. What
must the tender, loving, gracious Jesus have meant
by the words, "Gather the tares, and bind them in
bundles to burn them"? See what a wide distinction
between the lot of the Lord's people and Satan's people.
Burn the wheat! Oh, no; "Gather the wheat into my
barn." There let them be happily, safely housed for
ever. Oh, the infinite distance between heaven and
hell!—the harps and the angels, and the wailing and
gnashing of teeth! Who can ever measure the width of

that gulf which divides the glorified saint, white-robed and crowned with immortality, from the soul which is driven for ever away from the presence of God, and from the glory of his power? It is a dreadful "but"— that "but" of separation. I pray you, remember that it will interpose between brother and brother,—between mother and child,—between husband and wife. "One shall be taken and the other left." And when that sword shall descend to divide, there shall never be any after union. The separation is eternal. There is no hope or possibility of change in the world to come.

But says one, "That dreadful *'but'!* Why must there be such a difference?" The answer is, Because there always was a difference. The wheat was sown by the Son of man: the false wheat was sown by the enemy. There was always a difference in character the wheat was good, the tares were evil. This difference did not appear at first, but it became more and more apparent as the wheat ripened, and as the tares ripened too. They were totally different plants; and so a regenerate person and an unregenerate person are altogether different beings. I have heard an unregenerate man say that he is quite as good as the godly man; but in so boasting he betrayed his pride. Surely there is as great a difference in God's sight between the unsaved and the believer as between darkness and light, or between the dead and the living. There is in the one a life which there is not in the other, and the difference is vital and radical. Oh, that you may never trifle with this essential matter, but be really the wheat of the Lord! It is vain to have the name of wheat, we must have the nature of wheat. God will not be mocked: he will not be pleased by our calling ourselves Christians while we are not so. Be not satisfied with church membership; but seek after membership with Christ.

Do not talk about faith, but exercise it. Do not boast of experience, but possess it. Be not *like* the wheat, but be the wheat. No shams and imitations will stand in the last great day: that terrible "but" will roll as a sea of fire between the true and the false. Oh Holy Spirit! let each of us be found transformed by thy power.

II. The second word of our text is "gather,"—that is A WORD OF CONGREGATION. What a blessed thing this gathering is! I feel it a great pleasure to gather multitudes together to hear the gospel; and is it not a joy to see a house full of people, on week-days and Sabbath-days, who are willing to leave their homes and to come considerable distances to listen to the gospel? It is a great thing to gather people together for that; but the gathering of the wheat into the barn is a far more wonderful business. Gathering is in itself better than scattering, and I pray that the Lord Jesus may ever exercise his attracting power in this place; for he is no Divider, but "unto him shall the gathering of the people be." Has he not said, "I, if I be lifted up from the earth, will draw all men unto me"?

Observe, that the congregation mentioned in our text is selected and assembled by skilled gatherers: "The angels are the reapers." Ministers could not do it, for they do not know all the Lord's wheat, and they are apt to make mistakes—some by too great leniency and others by excessive severity. Our poor judgments occasionally shut out saints, and often shut in sinners The angels will know their Master's property. They know each saint, for they were present at his birthday. Angels know when sinners repent, and they never forget the persons of the penitents They have witnessed the lives of those who have believed, and have helped them in their spiritual battles, and so they know them. Yes, angels by a holy instinct discern the Father's children, and are not to be deceived. They will not fail to gather all the wheat and to leave out every tare.

But they are gathered under a very stringent regulation; for, first of all, according to the parable, the tares, the false wheat, have been taken out and then the angelic reapers gather nothing but the wheat. The seed of the serpent, fathered by Satan, is thus separated from the seed of the kingdom, owned by Jesus, the promised deliverer. This is the one distinction; and no other is taken into consideration. If the most amiable unconverted persons could stand in the ranks with the saints, the angels would not bear them to heaven for the mandate is, "Gather the wheat." Could the most honest man be found standing in the centre of the church, with all the members round about him, and with all the ministers entreating that he might be spared, yet if he were not a believer he could not he carried into the divine garner. There is no help for it. The angels have no choice in the matter: the peremptory command is, "Gather *the wheat,*" and they must gather none else.

It will be a gathering from very great distances. Some of the wheat ripens in the South Sea Islands, in China, and in Japan. Some flourishes in France, broad acres grow in the United States: there is scarce a land without a portion of the good grain. Where all God's wheat grows I cannot tell. There is a remnant, according to the election of grace, among every nation and people; but the angels will gather all the good grain to the same garner.

"Gather the wheat." The saints will be found in all ranks of society. The angels will bring in a few ears from palaces, and great armfuls from cottages! Many will be collected from the lowly cottages of our villages and hamlets, and others will be upraised from the back slums of our great cities to the metropolis of God. From the darkest places angels will bring those children of sweetness and light who seldom beheld the sun, and yet were pure in heart and saw their God. The hidden and obscure shall be brought into the light; for the Lord knoweth them that are his, and his harvest men will not miss them.

To me it is a charming thought that they will come from all the ages. Let us hope that our first father Adam will be there, and mother Eve, following in the footsteps of their dear son Abel, and trusting in the same sacrifice. We shall meet Abraham and Isaac, and Jacob, and Moses, and David, and Daniel, and all the saints made perfect. What a joy to see the apostles, martyrs, and reformers! I long to see Luther and Calvin, and Bunyan and Whitefield. I like the rhyme of good old father Ryland:

> "They all shall be there, the great and the small,
> Poor I shall shake hands with the blessed St. Paul."

I do not know how that will be, but I have not much doubt that we shall have fellowship with all the saints of every age in the general assembly and church of the firstborn, whose names are written in heaven.

No matter when or where the wheat grew, it shall be gathered into the one barn; gathered never to be scattered; gathered out of all divisions of the visible church, never to be divided again. They grew in different fields. Some flourished on the hillside where Episcopalians grow in all their glory, and others in the lowlier soil, where Baptists multiply, and Methodists flourish; but once the wheat is in the barn none can tell in which field the ears grew. Then, indeed, shall the Master's prayer have a glorious answer—"that they all may be one." All our errors removed and our mistakes corrected and forgiven, the one Lord, the one faith, and the one baptism will be known of us all, and there will be no more vexings and envyings. What a blessed gathering it will be! What a meeting! The elect of God, the *élite* of all the centuries, of whom the world was not worthy. I should not like to be away. If there were no hell, it would be hell enough to me to be shut out of such heavenly society. If there were no weeping and wailing and gnashing of teeth, it would be dreadful enough to miss the presence of the Lord, and the joy of praising him for ever, and the bliss of meeting with all the noblest beings that ever lived. Amid the needful controversies of the age, I, who have been doomed to seem a man of strife, sigh for the blessed rest wherein all spiritual minds shall blend in eternal accord before the throne of God and of the Lamb. Oh that we were all right, that we might be all happily united in one spirit!

In the text there is next A WORD OF DESIGNATION. I have already trespassed upon that domain. "Gather *the wheat.*" Nothing but "the wheat" must be placed in the Lord's homestead. Lend me your hearts while I urge you to a searching examination for a minute or two. The wheat was sown of the Lord. Are you sown of the Lord? Friend, if you have any religion, how did you get it? Was it self-sown? If so, it is good for nothing. The true wheat was sown by the Son of man. Are you sown of the Lord? Did the Spirit of God drop eternal life into your bosom? Did it come from that dear hand which was nailed to the cross? Is Jesus your life? Does you life begin and end with him? If so it is well.

The wheat sown of the Lord is also the object of

the Lord's care. Wheat needs a deal of attention. The farmer would get nothing from it if he did not watch it carefully. Are you under the Lord's care? Does he keep you? Is that word true to your soul,—"I the Lord do keep it; I will water it every moment: lest any hurt it, I will keep it night and day"? Do you experience such keeping? Make an honest answer, as you love your soul.

Next, wheat is a useful thing, a gift from God for the life of men. The false wheat was of no good to anybody: it could only be eaten of swine, and then it made them stagger like drunken men. Are you one of those who are wholesome in society,—who are like bread to the world, so that if men receive you and your example and your teaching they will be blessed thereby? Judge yourselves whether ye are good or evil in life and influence.

"Gather the wheat." You know that God must put the goodness, the grace, the solidity, and the usefulness into you, or else you will never be wheat fit for angelic gathering. One thing is true of the wheat—that it is the most dependent of all plants. I have never heard of a field of wheat which sprang up, and grew, and ripened without a husbandman's care. Some ears may appear after a harvest when the corn has shaled out; but I have never heard of plains in America or elsewhere covered with unsown wheat. No, no. There is no wheat where there is no man, and there is no grace where there is no Christ. We owe our very existence to the Father, who is the husbandman.

Yet dependent as it is, wheat stands in the front rank of honour and esteem; and so do the godly in the judgment of all who are of understanding heart. We are nothing without Christ; but with him we are full of honour. Oh, to be among those by whom the world is preserved, the excellent of the earth in whom the saints delight; God forbid we should be among the base and worthless tares!

Our last head, upon which also I will speak briefly, is A WORD OF DESTINATION. "Gather the wheat *into my barn.*" The process of gathering in the wheat will be completed at the day of judgment but it is going on every day. From hour to hour saints are gathered; they are going heavenward even now. I am so glad to hear as a regular thing that the departed ones from my own dear church have such joy in being harvested. Glory be to God, our people die well. The best thing is to live well, but we are greatly gladdened to hear that the brethren die well; for, full often, that is the most telling witness for vital godliness. Men of the world feel the power of triumphant deaths.

Every hour the saints are being gathered into the barn. That is where they want to be. We feel no pain at the news of ingathering, for we wish to be safely stored up by our Lord. If the wheat that is in the field could speak, every ear would say, "The ultimatum for which we are living and growing is the barn, the granary." For this the frosty night; for this the sunny day; for this the dew and the rain; and for this everything. Every process with the wheat is tending towards the granary. So is it with us; everything is working towards heaven—towards the gathering place—towards the congregation of the righteous—towards the vision of our Redeemer's face. Our death will cause no jar in our life-music; it will involve no pause or even discord; it is part of a programme, the crowning of our whole history.

To the wheat the barn is the place of security. It dreads no mildew there; it fears no frost, no heat, no drought, no wet when once in the barn. All its growth-perils are past. It has reached its perfection. It has rewarded the labour of the husbandman, and it is housed. Oh, long-expected day, begin! Oh, brethren, what a blessing it will be when you and I shall have come to our maturity, and Christ shall see in us the travail of his soul!

I delight to think of heaven as *his* barn; *his* barn, what must that be? It is but the poverty of language that such an expression has to be used at all concerning the home of our Father, the dwelling of Jesus. Heaven is the palace of the King, but so far, to us a barn, because it is the place of security, the place of rest for ever. It is the homestead of Christ to which we shall be carried, and for this we are ripening. It is to be thought of with ecstatic joy; for the gathering into the barn involves a harvest home, and I have never heard of men sitting down to cry over an earthly harvest home, nor of their following the sheaves with tears. Nay, they clap their hands, they dance for joy, and shout right lustily. Let us do something like that concerning those who are already housed. With grave, sweet melodies let us sing around their tombs. Let us feel that, surely, the bitterness of death is passed. When we remember their glory, we may rejoice like the travailing woman when her child is born, who "remembereth no more the anguish, for joy that a man is born into the world." Another soul begins to sing in heaven: why do you weep, O heirs of immortality? Is the eternal happiness of the righteous the birth which comes of their death-pangs? Then happy are they who die. Is glory the end and outcome of that which fills our home with mourning? If so, thank God for bereavements: thank God for saddest severings. He has promoted our dear ones to the skies! He has blessed them beyond all that we could ask or even think: he has taken them out of this weary world to lie in his own bosom for ever. Blessed be his name if it were for nothing else but this. Would you keep your old father here, full of pain, and broken down with feebleness? Would you shut him out of glory? Would you detain your dear wife here with all her suffering? Would you hold back your husband from the crown immortal? Could you wish your child to descend to earth again from the bliss which now surrounds her? No, no. We wish to be going home ourselves to the heavenly Father's house and its many mansions; but concerning the departed we rejoice before the Lord as with the joy of harvest. "Wherefore comfort one another with these words."